THE TWILIGHT OF
THE U-BOATS

THE TWILIGHT OF THE U-BOATS

by

BERNARD EDWARDS

LEO COOPER

First published in Great Britain in 2004 by
LEO COOPER
an imprint of Pen & Sword Books
47 Church Street,
Barnsley,
South Yorkshire,
S70 2AS

ISBN 1 84415 035 6

A catalogue record for this book
is available from the British Library

Typeset in 11/13pt Sabon by
Phoenix Typesetting, Auldgirth, Dumfriesshire

Printed in England by CPI UK

For Hamburg – and some old memories.

For I've a husband out at sea
Afloat on feeble planks of wood;
He does not know what fear may be;
I would have told him if I could.

Christina Rossetti

Contents

Prologue

At the seaward end of Kiel harbour a tall monument to war dominates the eastern foreshore at Möltenort. Built of red Weser sandstone, topped by a bronze eagle, wings outstretched, the U-boat memorial contains a record, flotilla by flotilla, boat by boat, man by man, of the price paid for Germany's bid to win control of the sea lanes.

The flowers that honour the dead in the shaded cloisters of the memorial are always fresh, and the pages of the Book of Remembrance are still turned each day, but the heady scent of glory is no longer in the air. Now, in winter, when the fog rolls in from the Kattegat, the ghosts of those whose bones lie in the deep waters listen to the mournful wail of sirens as ships pass by unmolested offshore. In summer, day trippers, most too young to remember war, sunbathe and play on the beach below, unaware that they are in the shadow of momentous history.

They are old men now, those of Grand Admiral Dönitz's submariners who survived, reliving the war days at reunions and paying homage at Möltenort when their ageing bodies allow. But they have a pride, for misguided though they may have been, they fought a good fight. Theirs was a cruel trade but, with a few exceptions, they played by the rules. The toll they exacted of Allied merchant shipping was unprecedented; 2,828 ships totalling 14,687,231 tons gross were sent to the bottom, taking with them many millions of tons of cargo. But this staggering achievement was not without grievous cost; 739 U-boats were lost, and 28,728 men died with them. It was a heavy sacrifice that was so very nearly justified, for in 1943 the U-boats almost succeeded in breaking the Allied supply lines. Had they done so, they would have changed the course of history forever.

Chapter One

Atlantic Shooting Gallery

For those who struggled to keep open the sea lanes between Britain and the Americas, the winter of 1942-43 in the North Atlantic was a nightmare of unrelieved horror. For those intent on opposing them, it was no less.

It was one of those winters when this consistently hostile ocean was at its worst, swept by an unending procession of vigorous depressions, each one following so close on the heels of the other as to give no let-up in the ferocity of the weather. Hurricane-force winds, mountainous seas, accompanied by scudding clouds at mast-top height and driving rain – sleet or snow if the latitude was high – were all that the ocean seemed to know. For those obliged to challenge this unrelenting maelstrom, whether shipping green seas in a geriatric tramp, roller-coasting from crest to trough in a tiny escort corvette, or lashed in the conning tower of a half submerged U-boat, the days were nerve-racking, the nights full of dark fears. How they longed for the warm kiss of the tropic breeze and the gentle push of a storm-free swell. But, for all of them, there was a battle to be fought, a war to be won.

In November 1942, the Battle of the Atlantic appeared to be going only one way – and that was in favour of Admiral Dönitz's wolf packs. Up to 100 U-boats were operating in the North Atlantic, searching out, shadowing, and ambushing Allied ships as they fought their way to and fro across the ocean. British and American troops had landed on the North African coast early in the month with a subsequent huge increase of the number of ships ferrying supplies, arms and ammunition on the west to east route. In spite of the appalling weather, which served to hide some of the convoys from view, they were Iron Cross days for the U-boats.

In November, no fewer than 117 merchantmen, totalling 718,000 gross register tons, most of them deep-loaded for North Africa, fell to German torpedoes. As the year drew to a close, so the situation worsened, the final count for 1942 being 7.8 million tons of Allied shipping lost. And this was at a time when, even with the prodigious output of the American yards, the Allies built only 7.2 million tons in replacement. Unless the run of the tide was checked, the outcome of the war was in the balance.

As the year 1942 drew to a close, further south, in the sun-drenched Caribbean, and as far from the sound of the drums of war as anyone could wish to be, a convoy was about to leave Port of Spain, Trinidad. The convoy, designated TM 1, Trinidad – Mediterranean, was the first of its kind. It consisted of nine oil tankers, the *British Dominion*, 6,983 tons, the *British Vigilance*, 8,093 tons, the *Empire Lytton*, 9,807 tons and the *Oltenia II*, 6,394 tons, all sailing under the Red Ensign, the Norwegian-registered *Albert. L. Ellsworth*, 8,309 tons, *Cliona*, 9,000 tons, *Minister Wedel*, 6,833 tons, and *Vanja*, 9,807 tons, and the American-owned, Panama-flag *Norvik*, 10,034 tons. These were all well-found, well-manned ships, carrying between them in excess of 30 million gallons of aviation spirit and diesel oil for Allied forces in North Africa. Given the nature of this cargo, and its vital importance to the Allied cause, it would have been expected that TM 1 would be under heavy escort for its Atlantic crossing. This was not so.

Northern convoys apart, the British and US navies were stretched to the limit in this theatre of the war, a great number of ships being required to cover the beachheads of Operation *Torch* in North Africa. All that could be spared for TM 1 was a small force of the Royal Navy's B 5 Escort Group, namely the Havant-class destroyer *Havelock*, supported by the Flower-class corvettes *Pimpernel* and *Saxifrage* and *Godetia*, the latter being Belgian-manned. Under the command of an experienced Senior Officer Escort (S.O.E.) Commander Richard Boyle, RN in HMS *Havelock*, this was a tough, battle-hardened quartet, but they were hardly adequate for the job in hand. It can only be surmised that, with large numbers of U-boats known to be then engaged further north with the slow westbound convoy ONS 154, the Admiralty considered TM 1 would be safe enough on the crossing until covered by destroyers and aircraft from Gibraltar. The B 5 Group ships arrived in Port of Spain late on 27 December after a rough passage from New York, relieved to be in quieter waters, but urgently in need of refuelling, provisioning and repairs. Apart from other minor faults, *Havelock*'s HF/DF, essential for tracking U-boats, was only working intermittently, and *Godetia* had one boiler out of commission. There would be little rest that night for Commander Boyle's men.

The convoy was scheduled to sail before noon next day, 28 December, but having worked through the night to bring his escorts into a state of readiness, Commander Boyle was dismayed to find the tankers were dragging their heels. It was not until half-way through the afternoon that TM 1 pulled out of Port of Spain, and then it had to leave three of the tankers, *Cliona*, *Empire Lytton* and *Vanja*, behind, all with engine problems. Reluctantly, Boyle detailed *Godetia* to stay with them, while he pressed on with the other six, now very thinly escorted. The *Cliona* caught up with them at dusk, but within the hour her engines were playing up again and she began to fall behind. It was not an auspicious start to the voyage.

In consolation, and as might be expected in 10 degrees north latitude in December, the weather on sailing was excellent, and expected to remain so for much of the crossing to the Straits of Gibraltar. The six loaded tankers, with air cover provided by Catalinas of the US Navy, and *Havelock*, *Pimpernel* and *Saxifrage* in close attendance, made good progress to the northeast. Meanwhile, it was reported that the other ships, *Empire Lytton* and *Vanja*, escorted by HMS *Godetia*, had left Port of Spain, and were making their best speed to catch up.

The first indication that TM 1 was under observation by the enemy came late that night, when *Godetia* obtained a contact with her Asdic off Tobago. The contact was classified *submarine* and the corvette immediately attacked with depth charges. The contact was lost soon afterwards, but at 02.25 on the 29th, with the moon well up in a cloudless sky and visibility unlimited, one of the convoy's escorting Catalinas sighted a U-boat on the surface. It is debateable which was the most surprised, the Catalina or the U-boat, but when the aircraft attacked with depth bombs, the U-boat dived quickly enough. *Godetia*, then about seven miles from the spot, was sent in to search the area, but her efforts went unrewarded. The enemy, having given the men of TM 1 a sleepless night, had shown its pursuers a clean pair of heels.

Unknown to Commander Boyle, thanks to the US Navy and HMS *Godetia*, his convoy had escaped the attentions of a very dangerous enemy. The U-boat put to flight was *U-124*, commanded by one of Dönitz's top aces, *Kapitänleutnant* Johann Mohr. Twenty-six-year-old Mohr already had a score of nearly 100,000 tons of Allied shipping, and only that morning had sunk the 4,692-ton British steamer *Treworlas* within sight of the island of Tobago.

A little before dawn that morning, the missing tankers *Empire Lytton* and *Vanja*, shepherded by *Godetia*, joined, and the convoy, with *Cliona* back in the ranks, formed up into five columns abreast. *Oltenia II* was appointed Commodore ship, and while *Havelock* scouted ahead, the three corvettes covered the flanks and rear of the convoy. By now, the ships were feeling the full force of the prevailing trade winds, blowing fresh from the north-east and bringing squally rain. It was a head wind, and the convoy speed was soon down to 8¼ knots, comfortable, but a lot less than was needed for a quick passage. In the course of the next three days, *Godetia* completed repairs to her second boiler, and was fully operational, but some of the tankers were again experiencing engine trouble, and Boyle had great difficulty in keeping them together. It was evident that more than one of them had leaking cargo tanks, and were leaving a long trail of oil on the water astern of the convoy. For the U-boats, this was like a finger pointing the way, but there was nothing Boyle could do but pray that the sea would become rough enough to wipe out the slick.

With so much activity going on in the approaches to the Straits of Gibraltar and beyond, Dönitz had moved his wolf packs close to the Spanish and Portuguese coasts, and much of TM 1's route should have been free of the enemy. But the age-old Murphy's Law was at work. On the morning of 3 January 1943, *U-514*, having been operating in and around the Caribbean since early September, was on her way home, her fuel tanks running low, and with only a few torpedoes left. By pure chance, her path crossed TM 1's oil slick, and her commander, *Kapitänleutnant*

Hans-Jurgen Auffermann decided to follow the trail. By late afternoon, he had the smoke of the convoy in sight. He reported his sighting by radio, and then settled down to shadow the tankers on the surface, taking care to keep out of range of the escorts' radars. In the event, he need not have bothered; the corvettes' radars were not fully functional, and *Havelock* was well ahead of the convoy, and unlikely to pick up the trimmed-down U-boat on her screen.

Unfortunately for Hans Auffermann, the Allies were at that time reading the German naval codes with ease, and his transmission, brief though it may have been, was picked up by a shore station and decoded within minutes. An urgent warning was then flashed to Boyle in *Havelock*, advising a change of course after dark. TM 1 was forewarned.

The warning came too late. The sun went down over the convoy at 17.30, and with the suddenness peculiar to the low latitudes, it was completely dark half an hour later. Boyle then ordered a bold alteration of course, hoping to throw off any shadower, but Auffermann had already got round ahead of the convoy. As the tankers were in the process of their turn, the *British Vigilance*, lead ship of the centre column, burst into flames.

Chief Officer Alfred Baughn, Officer of the Watch in the *Empire Lytton*, which was following close in the wake of the *British Vigilance*, immediately ordered the helm hard to starboard to swing his ship clear of the burning tanker. Seconds later, he was joined on the bridge by Captain John Andrews, whose evening meal had been rudely interrupted.

Shortly after Andrews reached the bridge, *U-514* was seen on the surface in the light of the flames consuming the *British Vigilance*. The U-boat was just forward of the *Empire Lytton*'s port beam, and Andrews, forgetting in the heat of the moment that he was standing on top of 13,000 tons of high octane aviation spirit, put the helm hard to port, rang for emergency full speed, and charged at the enemy.

It was fortunate for Hans Auffermann that the *Empire Lytton* was hard pressed to make 12 knots, even when pushed, and that *U-514*'s diesels gave her a speed of 17 knots. She managed to slip across the avenging tanker's bow with twenty yards to spare, but then, when Aufferman thought he had escaped, he ran into a hail of fire. The *Empire Lytton*'s bridge Oerlikons opened up, raking the U-boat's conning tower with 20-mm HE and armour-piercing, and at the same time the US Navy gunners manning the *Norvik*'s 4-inch began to lob shells at *U-514* with dangerous accuracy. Other ships of the convoy joined in the mêleé and, very wisely, Auffermann ran for the shadows and dived deep.

Led by HMS *Havelock*, the escorts now came tearing in, firing snowflakes to illuminate the scene and hurling depth charges in all directions, but *U-514* was already beyond their reach. The corvette *Saxifrage* was given the unenviable task of pulling the oil-covered survivors of the *British Vigilance* from the water. Of her crew of fifty-four, twenty-eight had lost their lives in the fire that consumed her.

The convoy, with a sense of vulnerability spreading through the remaining ships, now regrouped and resumed course to the north-east. Commander Boyle was well aware that, following *U-514*'s successful attack, TM 1 would soon be the prime target for every other U-boat in the area, and beyond. However, for the time being, there was a more pressing need. All the escorts were running short of fuel, but they would be unable to top up their tanks from the *Cliona*, which was equipped for refuelling at sea, until calmer waters were reached. Another forty-eight hours passed before the wind dropped sufficiently for the operation, during which time *U-514* was the convoy's persistent shadow, Aufferman reporting its position to *Befehlshaber der Unterseeboote* (Commander-in-Chief Submarines) every four hours. Dönitz lost no time in forming a wolf pack. The seven boats of the *Delphin* pack, then stationed in the western approaches to the Straits of Gibraltar, and four other U-boats patrolling independently off the Portuguese coast, were ordered to make for TM 1 at all possible speed.

Meanwhile, the convoy, unaware that it was being shadowed, and uncertain what dangers might be lurking over the horizon, sailed on. For five more days, as the weather steadily improved, and the patent logs trailing astern ticked off the miles, hopes of a passage without further attack began to rise. Then, on the evening of 8 January, with 1,300 miles still to go to Gibraltar, the ambush was sprung.

The night was dark, the moon not yet up, and the black velvet sky twinkling with myriad bright stars. There was a light easterly breeze blowing that barely disturbed the surface of the sea, and the visibility was excellent. It was one of those nights which in more peaceful times would have called for yarning on the hatch-tops to the accompaniment of the wavering tones of a mouth organ. A night for nostalgia. Then, just after seven thirty, the spell was broken. HMS *Havelock*, stationed some two and a half miles ahead and to port of the leading ships, obtained a firm radar contact at 3,200 yards directly astern, between her and the nearest tanker. The destroyer buried her port rails as Boyle heaved her round onto a reciprocal course under full helm. When she had settled on the radar bearing, her lookouts reported a submarine right ahead at about 2,000 yards. Boyle rang for full speed, with the intention of ramming, but as *Havelock* raced towards it the U-boat crash-dived and disappeared from sight. Cursing in frustration, Boyle dropped a five-charge pattern of depth charges as they ploughed through the disturbed water left by the submerging U-boat.

Havelock's actions were largely futile, for the convoy was surrounded by U-boats. The *Delphin* wolf pack, now numbering eleven boats, including Johann Mohr's *U-124* and Hans-Jurgen Auffermann's *U-514*, was in position. Some boats were on the surface, others at periscope depth, all manoeuvring to bring the slow-moving tankers into their sights. As *Godetia* and *Pimpernel* were again experiencing problems with their radars, the presence of the enemy in force was largely undetected.

Günther Seibicke, in *U-436*, was on the surface, but trimmed right down so that only the conning tower was above water, was to port of the convoy. His fan of three torpedoes was fired simultaneously with the crash of *Havelock*'s depth charges as she went after *U-514*, their target the lead ship of the port column, the *Albert L. Ellsworth*. One torpedo hit the Norwegian tanker squarely amidships, and she immediately burst into flame, bathing the convoy in an eerie, flickering light as she drifted quickly astern.

Seibicke's two remaining torpedoes passed ahead of the burning *Albert L. Ellsworth* to plough into the leading ship of the next column, TM 1's commodore ship *Oltenia II*. The combined effect of two torpedoes blasting open her hull was sufficient to break *Oltenia II*'s back, and she went to the bottom in two minutes. Captain Ladle and sixteen of his crew went with her.

The sudden ferocity of the attack caused momentary panic in the convoy, with Boyle's escorts racing to and fro, firing starshell and hurling depth charges at real and imaginary foes. At one point, the Norwegian tanker *Vanja*, while manoeuvring to avoid the drifting *Albert L. Ellsworth*, opened fire on HMS *Pimpernel*, believing the corvette to be an attacking U-boat. *Havelock*, meanwhile, had a strong radar contact at 1,000 yards, and as she altered towards it, a U-boat in the act of submerging was sighted in the light of the starshell. As Boyle raced towards it, the U-boat disappeared below the surface, but was picked up a few moments later by the destroyer's Asdic. Boyle saturated the area with depth charges without visible result. The Asdic contact was lost, and Boyle began a painstaking cat and mouse game, searching in widening circles, until, twenty-three minutes later, the Asdic beam returned a loud echo. Again, *Havelock* went in with depth charges, and again the contact was lost. However, an underwater explosion heard a few minutes later indicated that the U-boat might have been hit. Boyle cast around, but no wreckage or oil slick was seen on the surface, and all Asdic contact was lost.

Mindful that his convoy was protected by only three corvettes, Boyle abandoned the search and returned to stand by the torpedoed *Albert L. Ellsworth*. With *Saxifrage* covering him, he then went about the grim task of picking up survivors, some of whom were horribly burnt. While *Havelock* was thus engaged, *Pimpernel*, guarding the starboard quarter of the convoy, reported an Asdic contact. A few minutes later, the corvette sighted a surfaced U-boat 2,200 yards to starboard. *Pimpernel* fired starshell to raise the alarm, then charged at the enemy, firing with her single 4-inch gun as she went in. The U-boat easily eluded her by diving.

This was only the opening act of a very long night for TM 1. Abandoning the *Albert L. Ellsworth* to her fate, *Havelock* and *Saxifrage* rejoined the convoy, which now consisted of six ships, at around 02.00 on the morning of the 9th. The *British Dominion* was appointed commodore ship in place of *Oltenia II*, and the tankers were closed up in a tight formation. The U-boats tried again, but could only probe at the boundaries of the convoy, for Commander Boyle's escorts, few though they might be, seemed to be in all places at all times. Then, unexpectedly, the wolf pack withdrew and the night was quiet again. TM 1 was now 600 miles due west of the Canary Islands, but with more than 1,000 miles hard steaming still to go before it came under the protection of the guns of the Gibraltar force. There was no sleep in the ships, for there was not a man who believed the U-boats would not be back.

Surprisingly, the respite was longer than expected. More than an hour passed and peace reigned while the steaming cocoa and corned beef sandwiches were handed round and the guns reloaded in merchantman and warship alike. And all the time the sun climbed nearer to the eastern horizon, and there were those who dared to hope the coming of dawn might save them. It was not to be. The U-boats were only regrouping. Herbert Schneider, in *U-522*, made the first move. He had carefully manoeuvred into a favourable position ahead and to port of the convoy, and taking careful aim, fired a fan of three torpedoes from his bow tubes, two of which slammed into the side of the 6,833-ton Norwegian *Minister Wedel*, ripping her open to the sea. The tanker, listing heavily to starboard, caught fire and dropped astern.

Schneider's third torpedo passed astern of the *Minister Wedel*, and found its mark in the hull of the convoy's largest ship, the 10,034-ton Panama-flag *Norvik* in the next column. She did not catch fire, but she fell astern with a list that was so obviously fatal.

The sudden shock of the new attack brought an instant reaction from the other ships of the convoy. As before, the burning tanker, the *Minister Wedel*, acted as a torch to reveal the attacking U-boat. Schneider was attempting to escape on the surface, running down the starboard side of the convoy, his diesels belching black smoke. The *British Dominion*, the *Cliona* and the *Vanja*, their guns' crews spoiling for a fight, opened up with their 4-inch guns, and anything else that could be brought to bear. At the same time, the escorts came racing in. *Saxifrage*, steering for the centre of the convoy, spotted *U-522* crossing astern of the port column, and switched on her searchlight. Caught in the briliant beam, Schneider dived only seconds before *Saxifrage*'s depth charges came raining down on him.

9

This might certainly have been a kill for B 5 Group, had not Commander Boyle decided to intervene. *Saxifrage*'s Asdic had a strong contact at 100 yards – obviously the escaping *U-522* – and was about to drop another five-charge pattern, when *Havelock* swept across her bows. The corvette was forced to alter hard to port to avoid a certain collision, and in the confusion that followed, she lost contact with her target. Masked by the frothing wakes of the two warships, *U-522* made good her escape. For the next hour, the four escorts searched in and around the convoy with their Asdics pinging, but without success. However, their frenzied activity did deter the *Delphin* boats, some of whom were desperately trying to penetrate the screen before the dawn came.

They were waiting for the dawn aboard the *Empire Lytton*, too. At 04.25, when much of the furore had died down, Captain Andrews decided it was safe for him to leave the bridge for a quick wash. He handed over to Chief Officer Baughn, and went below, completely unaware that Hans-Joachim Hesse's *U-442* was lurking beneath the waves on the tanker's starboard bow. Andrews had not been below for more than two minutes, when he heard a muffled explosion and felt the shock as Hesse's torpedo slammed into the *Empire Lytton*'s forward bunker tank.

Regaining the bridge, Andrews quickly ascertained the extent of the damage, which was not as bad as he had feared. Hesse's torpedo had been badly aimed, for the thick fuel oil in the forward tank had absorbed much of the explosion. Had it hit a few feet further aft, in one of the cargo tanks, the *Empire Lytton* and all on board would have been vapourized as the aviation spirit went up.

Andrews' main concern now was for his crew, many of whom were in a state of near-panic and attempting to lower the lifeboats before the way was off the ship. A thick coating of fuel oil, blown aft from the ruptured tank, covered the boat deck, which made a bad situation even worse. One boat had already capsized, throwing its frightened occupants into the sea, and another was upended as it was being lowered. Andrews decided to use the two remaining lifeboats to evacuate the ship, planning to lie off until dawn, and then, assuming the *Empire Lytton* to be still afloat, to reboard in the hope of getting the ship under way again.

The tanker was still there two hours later at first light, down by the bow, but still very much afloat. Andrews took his boats back, and as they neared the ship they came across twelve survivors in the oil-covered water, among them Chief Officer Alfred Baughn. When the survivors had been picked up, a head count was made, which showed that fifteen of the *Empire Lytton*'s men were missing. When they were back aboard the tanker, it was found that Baughn was not breathing, and despite strenuous efforts to revive him by artificial respiration, Andrews had the sad duty of pronouncing his chief officer dead.

Captain Andrews, accompanied by Chief Engineer Fletcher Canning, now went forward to assess the state of the ship. The two men found that, although the foredeck was littered with wreckage, and Hesse's torpedo had blown a hole 10 feet by 4 feet in each side of the bow on the waterline, the ship was in no real danger of sinking. Canning then went below, and was able to report no major damage to the main engine, that he would be able to get under way within two hours, but could not guarantee to give revolutions for more than 6 knots. Andrews reported the findings by lamp to HMS *Saxifrage* which had pulled alongside, who in turn passed the report to Commander Boyle in *Havelock*.

Boyle had some hard decisions to make. Earlier that morning, he had received a signal from the Admiralty warning that six or seven U-boats had been confirmed as still in the vicinity of the convoy – a danger of which he needed no reminding. The *Empire Lytton*'s cargo of aviation spirit was desperately needed in North Africa, and steaming at 6 knots she was capable of reaching Gibraltar. On the other hand, the three remaining tankers must go ahead at all speed, so one of the corvettes would have to be detached to look after the *Empire Lytton*. This would leave only his destroyer and two corvettes to guard the undamaged tankers; one for one, perhaps, but hardly adequate when so many U-boats were around. He could easily end up losing the lot. In the end, Boyle was forced to reach a compromise. Working on the basis that the *Empire Lytton*'s cargo of aviation spirit would be of no practical use to the U-boats, he decided to leave the damaged tanker to drift, in the hope that she could be salvaged later. Captain Andrews and the surviving members of his crew were taken off, and their ship was left to her fate. All that was left of Convoy TM 1, the *British Dominion*, the *Cliona* and the *Vanja*,

11

closely attended by their four escorts, pressed on towards Gibraltar.

Boyle's hopes for the *Empire Lytton* were dashed when, soon after the abandoned tanker dropped out of sight, a huge pall of black smoke was seen on the horizon astern. Hans-Joachim Hesse had completed the job he had begun in the early hours of the morning. Of the three other abandoned tankers, the *Minister Wedel* and *Norvik* had already been disposed of by Herbert Schneider, in *U-522*, while Günther Seibecke finished off the *Albert L. Ellsworth* at his leisure before the night closed in.

With the tankers zig-zagging at 10 knots, and their escorts sweeping the seas around them, TM 1 steamed on. The U-boats were still with them, constantly probing the escort screen throughout the night. Apart from keeping in the shadows, they made no attempt to hide their presence, making free of their radios to chatter amongst themselves. Their confidence was such that they ignored the danger that *Havelock* and shore stations might be listening in, and plotting their positions with HF/DF, which, of course, they were. Only when full daylight came on the 10th did they withdraw.

The day that followed was a quiet one for TM 1. The weather was fine and clear, allowing the exhausted crews of the tankers and their escorts to snatch a few hours' rest. But the U-boats were back again as soon as the sun went down, Heinz Stein, in *U-620* creeping in to fire a fan of torpedoes into the midst of the convoy. Stein claimed two hits on overlapping tankers, but was mistaken. His torpedoes missed their target, detonating at the end of their run, and alerting the escorts to the attack. *Saxifrage* obtained an Asdic contact at 2,500 yards, and raced in to drop a ten-charge pattern, but she too achieved no visible result.

After dark, the convoy made a 45 degree alteration of course to the south in an attempt to throw off its pursuers. The ships were then 130 miles to the north-west of the Canaries, with Gibraltar only three days steaming away. It was another exceptionally fine night, the wind southerly and light, the sea flat calm, the sky cloudless. With the moon already down, the darkness was complete, and Boyle hoped the convoy would lose itself in the vastness of the empty ocean. At 21.30, reluctant to divert any further to the south, and reasonably confident that they had shaken off the U-boats, he brought the ships back on course for Gibraltar.

Boyle's confidence was misplaced, for four of the *Delphin* pack were still in contact. Ten minutes after the resumption of course to the north-east, Herbert Schneider, who had stealthily infiltrated *U-522* into the middle of the convoy without being discovered, lined up his sights on the *British Dominion* and fired a fan of three torpedoes. All three ran true, and the tanker, another high-octane carrier, was blown apart in one massive explosion.

The ball of fire that shot skywards from the *British Dominion* turned the dark night into brilliant day, and lit up the other ships, silhouetting them starkly against the horizon. What had been a peaceful scene, with the three tankers and their escorts steaming in company through a tranquil sea, was suddenly and brutally transformed into a madhouse. Caught in the glow of the fire consuming the *British Dominion*, the convoy scattered in all directions, *Havelock* and the corvettes turning inwards and, somewhat unnecessarily, firing starshell. The Norwegian tanker *Vanja* took the most effective action. Sighting a U-boat, most probably *U-522*, on the surface no more than 300 yards off her port side, she went hard to port to bring her stern-mounted 4-inch to bear. With the U-boat 400 yards astern, the *Vanja*'s gunners opened fire, a heavy machine gun joining in from her bridge. Of the three rounds fired by the 4-inch, one was claimed as a hit, and the U-boat's conning tower was sprayed by the machine gun before she made a hurried crash-dive.

Three other U-boats were spotted on the surface and attacked by gunfire from the escorts before they submerged. Extensive depth charging continued throughout the rest of the night, holding the U-boats at bay until the sun came up on the 11th. And with the sun came succour for the battered convoy, B 5 Group being reinforced by the destroyers HMS *Pathfinder*, HMS *Penn* and HMAS *Quiberon*. Not surprisingly, the U-boats of the *Delphin* pack made a discreet exit. The convoy reached Gibraltar on 14 January.

Convoy TM 1 had turned into an unmitigated disaster for the Allies. Seven valuable tankers, 56,453 gross tons of shipping, carrying nearly 22 million gallons of fuel, much of it high-octane aviation spirit, had gone down. With them more than 100 merchant seamen had died, trained men who could ill be spared at this stage of the war. This was a major blow, the highest percentage loss suffered by any convoy at the hands of the U-boats. It is debatable where the blame for this unprecedented defeat lay. The Admiralty's conclusions were:

> This disaster was in large measure due to the fact that the U-boats got the upper hand on the evening of 8th February. The escorts failed to detect the U-boats in the initial stages of the attack and, once casualties started, the number of the escort was too small to enable effective offensive action to be taken.

Commander Boyle was critical of another aspect:

> Visibility was extreme and both convoy and escorts were easily visible at great distances silhouetted against a very clear horizon. During the last refit of B 5 Group, the Western Approaches camouflage had been painted over with grey. This was done at the request of the Commander, Eastern Sea Frontier, New York, who wished to have all his escorts the same colour, and was approved by British Admiralty Maintenance Representative. The absence of protective colouring is considered materially to have assisted the enemy to sight and avoid the escorts.

Undeniably, for a convoy of such importance, TM 1 was woefully under escorted. If Commander Boyle had been blessed with another destroyer or so, he might well have given the *Delphin* pack a bloody nose. Almost certainly, some, or all, of the four tankers left drifting astern could have been protected until salvage tugs arrived to tow them to safety. As it was, they were picked off as and when convenient to the *Delphin* boats; helpless victims used as target practice.

After completing their near destruction of TM 1, the *Delphin* pack moved north to set up an ambush line south of the Azores in the hope of catching more Mediterranean-bound convoys. Like all of Admiral Karl Dönitz's protégés, they were riding the crest of the wave.

Chapter Two

First Time Out

News of a victory travels on swift wings, and word of the *Delphin* pack's annihilation of Convoy TM 1 in the Atlantic had already reached Kiel when, shortly before sunrise on 12 January 1943, as the remnants of the convoy limped towards Gibraltar, *U-223* sailed on her first war patrol.

As he carefully eased the U-boat away from the Tirpitz Pier, her home for some five and a half weeks past following her initial work-up in the Baltic, twenty-six-year-old *Oberleutnant* Karl-Jürgen Wächter had good cause to be satisfied with his lot. He had under his command the best of German underwater technology, built in one of Germany's finest shipyards, Krupp's Germania in Kiel. *U-223* was a brand new Type VIIC boat, 66.5 metres long, 6.2 metres in the beam, and displacing 769 tons. Her twin-Mann diesels, developing 2,800 horse power, gave her a maximum speed on the surface of 17.7 knots, and an extreme range of 7,900 miles at 10 knots. Below the surface, two electric motors, with a combined output of 750 horse power, gave her a speed of 7.6 knots, and a maximum range submerged of eighty miles at 4 knots. Her main attack capability lay in fourteen torpedoes, launched through four bow tubes and one stern tube. On deck, as in 1943 the greatest threat to a U-boat was expected to come from the air, she carried, in place of the standard 88-mm gun, a quadruple 20-mm gun on the lower gun platform, and a twin 20-mm on the upper platform. She was also equipped with a Metox receiver capable of detecting radar impulses at ranges exceeding 100 kilometres.

It was a grey, drizzly morning, with a cold easterly wind blowing in off the Kattegat as *U-223* backed astern into the harbour. The naval band on the quay played a rousing march with less than enthusiasm, and the small crowd gathered to see the boat off was already dispersing, hurrying towards staff cars, the naval barracks, or the nearest cafe to revive their frozen extremities with hot coffee and schnapps. There were those among them who muttered it was all very well for the U-boat types, off into the Atlantic, where the war was going their way, and there was glory to be had, medals to be won. For those left behind, the reality was that Germany's dream of world conquest was fast turning into a nightmare.

While the year 1943 had opened with over 300 U-boats at sea, 164 of them in the Atlantic and sweeping all before them, on land and in the air Germany's fortunes were moving in another direction. On the Russian front, Hitler's once-invincible armies, ill-prepared and ill-equipped for the severity of the Russian winter, were retreating steadily before the hammer blows of an enemy bent on exacting a terrible revenge. In North Africa, two months after Allied forces had stormed ashore in Morocco, German forces were fighting a rearguard action on two fronts, caught between the landings and Montgomery's victorious Eighth Army advancing east from Libya. In the air, payment in kind was being made by the RAF for the Luftwaffe's blitz on British cities in 1940 and 1941. Up to 1,000 Wellingtons and Lancasters were crossing the North Sea nightly to rain down bombs on the Ruhr and other German industrial areas. They were soon to be joined by Flying Fortresses and Liberators of the US Army Air Force. Nor was Germany's new ally, Japan, faring any better. Her troops were being slowly ousted from island after island in the Pacific as vastly superior American naval, air and land forces bulldozed their way towards Tokyo. For Germany, and for the Axis, there was the stench of defeat in the air.

Karl Wächter was in no mood to entertain such dismal thoughts, as with the strains of martial music fading astern, he conned his new command through the Holteneau Roads, past the lines of grey-painted warships, and headed out into Kiel Bay. The wind was bone-chilling, penetrating even his heavy leather watch coat, the drizzle fogged his binoculars, and flurries of icy spray lashed at his face as the U-boat gathered speed. But nothing could dampen the sheer joy of being in command for the first time, the

16

pinnacle of achievement for any man that ever went to sea. His boat, *U-223*, was fully stored for two months, fresh vegetables, bread, eggs, smoked hams, tins and boxes crammed into every available space, her fuel tanks were full, batteries charged, ammunition lockers stocked, and her crew of fifty trained to perfection. She was off on a great adventure.

It was only when, at the mouth of the harbour, engines idling while a salt-caked tug dragged aside the heavy boom-defence nets, that Wächter felt a tiny shiver of apprehension. Briefly, the drizzle parted to starboard to show a glimpse of the red sandstone U-boat memorial at Möltenort, a grim reminder of the 4,744 German submariners lost in another war. For a moment, while he watched the black smoke rolling back from the funnel of the straining tug, Wächter found his thoughts going back to his native Thüringer Wald, another world away to the east. There would be snow there now, pristine, sparkling. No war. The tug's siren whooped, signalling the channel was clear, and the Atlantic beckoned.

An hour later, *U-223* slipped past the red-painted light vessel, and left it astern, its powerful beam still struggling to pierce the gloom of the rain-swept horizon. A few miles further on, Wächter focused his glasses on the low silhouette of the first of the five other U-boats he was to join company with for the passage out into the North Atlantic. Then, one by one, the long, low shapes closed on him and identified themselves by signal lamp, *U-187* (*Oberleutnant* Ralph Münnich), *U-267* (*Kapitänleutnant* Otto Tinschert), *U-358* (*Kapitänleutnant* Rolf Manke), *U-466* (*Oberleutnant* Gerhard Thäter) and U707 (*Oberleutnant* Günter Gretschel). Tinschert, Manke and Gretschel, Karl Wächter knew well, having spent five months in their company practising the arts of attack and survival in the Bay of Danzig with the 8th Training Flotilla under the command of the tough *Korvettenkapitän* Hans Eckermann. They had trained hard together and, whenever the opportunity arose, played equally hard ashore. Münnich and Thäter were not known to Wächter but, like himself and the others, they were all young men taking their first commands to sea, bound for the killing field of the North Atlantic.

After the initial exchange of signals, the small flotilla formed up into line abreast, huddling close together in the poor visibility, and moved out into the deeper waters of Kiel Bay. Once clear of the land, the wind freshened, drawing aside the dismal curtain of drizzle, lifting the visibility to ten miles. Late in the afternoon, with the early winter dusk closing in, the U-boats were joined by two minesweepers, their escort through the restricted waters of the Kattegat and Skagerrak, and so to Kristiansand, on the southern tip of Norway.

The passage north was uneventful, and the U-boats reached Kristiansand in the early hours of the morning of the 14th. Their stay there was brief. Four hours after entering the port, they were on their way around the coast to Egersund for refuelling. The snow was falling heavily when they reached Egersund late that afternoon, and with the wind having shifted to the north-west, the temperature fell sharply. The night passed behind the break-waters of the Norwegian fishing port, sheltered from the icy wind, was a welcome break for the U-boat crews, hardened though they thought they were to the rigours of winter in the high northern latitudes.

Fully fuelled and with their provisions topped up, the six boats and their escorting minesweepers sailed from Egersund at 10.00 on the 15th and moved up the Norwegian coast under a heavily overcast sky and visibility that could be classed as no more than moderate. Mercifully, the wind had dropped, but the thermometer, already near freezing, was continuing to fall. This presented no hardship for those below in the warm fug of the U-boats' hulls, but for the unfortunate watchkeepers in the open conning towers, with barely room to stamp their frozen feet or swing their arms, every watch was a long drawn out torture session. But there must be no relaxing of vigilance. These were dangerous waters, regularly patrolled by British Coastal Command aircraft based in Scotland, only 200 miles to the west. The war was coming closer.

Four hours out of Egersund, the escorting minesweepers flashed their goodbyes and turned for home. The U-boats then split up to proceed independently. *U-187* and *U-267* were to join the *Landsnecht* pack, then assembling to the west of Ireland, while Wächter and the others had orders to join the *Haudegen* pack to the south of Cape Race. Both packs were to create what havoc they could amongst convoys using the northern route between New York and Halifax, Nova Scotia and the UK.

Within the hour, all six boats had lost sight of each other. Wächter, suddenly alone on a wide and very hostile ocean, eased away from the Norwegian coast and adjusted speed to an economical 10 knots. *U-223* had a long and dangerous road to travel, more than 2,000 miles, first reaching north, almost into the Arctic Circle, then through the Faeroes Channel, running the gauntlet of Allied warships and aircraft operating out of Scotland and Iceland, before breaking out into the open ocean.

Wächter was not unduly surprised when, moving away from the coast, the weather began to take on an ugly look. The wind had gone round to the south-east, heaping up small, angry waves that slammed spitefully at the casing on the quarter and, to add to the discomfort of the watch occasionally sent an icy deluge into the conning tower. And there was worse to come. During the night, the barometer fell with every mile of northing gained, bringing passing squalls of rain and sleet, which reduced the visibility to a mere 500 metres at times. As Wächter altered on to a more westerly course, and the sea came around on the beam, the boat took on a short, erratic roll that made life above and below deck sheer hell. The temptation was to submerge, to drop down into the calmer water below the waves, to give his men a few hours relief from the sickening motion, but this would only prolong *U-223*'s exposure to danger. Wächter's immediate priority was to get through the Faeroes Channel as quickly as possible.

At around noon on the 18th, *U-223* reached the furthest point north in her passage, being then 130 miles north of the Faeroe Islands, and within a little over 100 miles of the Arctic Circle. Now Wächter altered onto a south-westerly course to run through the 240-mile-wide channel, an innocent enough looking stretch of water, with no land visible in any direction, but there was a hidden danger here. So many boats had met an untimely end in the Faeroes Channel, lulled into a false sense of security by the emptiness, and caught unawares by a four-engined Liberator roaring out of the horizon with bomb doors open. This was the ultimate test for *U-223*, but the rough beam sea that made life so uncomfortable on board, and increasingly frequent sleet and snow squalls provided perfect cover for the trimmed-down submarine. She was almost invisible in the welter of spray and the squalls that swept across her.

A dramatic illustration of the danger of being caught in the Faeroes Channel occurred on the morning of the 19th. The wind had backed to the north-east and eased, with the result that the sea went down, the visibility improved and there were breaks in the cloud cover. The change for the better was welcomed, but it left *U-223* uncomfortably exposed. Wächter opted to stay on the surface, but increased speed and posted extra lookouts. His caution was well founded, for the morning was not many hours old when a low-flying aircraft appeared on the horizon. Without waiting to identify the plane, Wächter sought cover below the waves.

Wächter decided to stay below until dark, and for the next six and a half hours *U-223* crept slowly south-westwards away from the danger area. She surfaced after sunset to recharge her batteries and air the boat through. During the night, a message was received from BdU ordering Wächter to proceed to a position south-east of Cape Farewell, the southernmost point of Greenland. Working on dead reckoning, for there had been no opportunity for sun or star sights since leaving Norway, course was altered accordingly.

Over the next forty-eight hours, the weather took a turn for the worse again, the wind reaching gale force from the east, with a very rough quarterly sea. Soon, the boat was running before a huge following sea big enough to poop an ocean liner. *U-223*'s after casing was permanently submerged, and with green seas breaking against the after end of the conning tower, the oil-skinned watchkeepers were engaged in a constant battle to avoid being washed overboard. On the following morning, 22 January, it all changed again. The wind suddenly veered to the south-south-west, and *U-223* was a bucking bronco, smashing her bows into a head sea. The North Atlantic was on its mettle.

Far on the other side of this troubled ocean, some 2,500 miles to the south-west, the city of New York was also in the grip of winter. Here the wind was muted, and the snow was falling in great, thick flakes that covered the rail tracks and softened the hard outlines of the warehouses on Staten Island's Stapleton Pier.

A long convoy of Army trucks rolled along the pier, leaving their herringbone tyre imprints in the virgin snow. The trucks ground to a halt alongside a tall-masted steamer, whose high promenade deck and elegant counter stern set her apart from the rust-streaked tramps leaning against the other berths. She had the air of a crack passenger liner of another era, now painted a drab wartime grey like all her sisters.

The 5,649-ton *Dorchester* had once been amongst the elite of her trade. Built in Newport News in 1926 for the Merchants & Miners Transportation Company of Baltimore, she had served her owners well between the two world wars. The Merchants & Miners was founded when the great gold rush to the mines of California was at its height. Overland transport in North America was still a hazardous and uncomfortable undertaking, and would-be miners and merchants with hardware to sell were desperate to take passage from the East Coast to the West by Cape Horn. Initially, Merchants & Miners ran a service from the New England ports to Baltimore, the setting off point for the long sea voyage to California. Later, the service was extended south-ward to Norfolk, Savannah, Jacksonville and Miami, and the company's ships established a reputation for solid comfort, excellent sea-keeping qualities and respectable American-style food. When the *Dorchester* and her sister ships came along, Merchants & Miners had moved up-market to become one of the big operators in the coastwise passenger service. The new ships were flush-deckers, with riveted steel hulls and wooden upper-works, and powered by four-cylinder, triple-expansion steam engines supplied by four oil-fired Scotch boilers, giving them a service speed of 12 knots. They had no cargo-handling gear on deck, but were capable of lifting up to 6,000 tons, loaded and discharged through side doors in the hull. The passenger accommodation was of a high standard, catering for 302 first-class and twelve second-class. Merchants & Miners' reputation grew and they prospered, but when war came to America at the end of 1941, the US Government was quick to see the potential of their ships. Very soon, the entire fleet was in the hands of the Government and on active service.

The *Dorchester* was assigned the role of troop transport, and suffered the indignity of having her luxurious, predominantly first-class accommodation gutted, and transformed into spartan quarters for up to 800 troops. She retained her 120-strong Merchant Marine crew, led by Captain Hans Jorgen Danielson, and was fitted with one 4-inch, one 3-inch and four 20-mm guns. This armament was manned by a squad of twenty-three US Navy Armed Guard seamen, under the command of Lieutenant William Arpaia.

When the *Dorchester* sailed from Staten Island late in the evening of 22 January 1943, she had on board, in addition to her crew and Armed Guard gunners, 751 troops, giving her a total complement of 904. She also carried sixty bags of mail, and 1,069 tons of cargo, mainly constructional material. The *Dorchester* was heading north to relieve the US Army's garrison at Narsarssuak, Greenland. This cannot have been an inviting prospect for those on board, for they were leaving behind an America, although over a year into the war, which showed little sign of being affected by the conflict. For most of the inhabitants war was only newspaper talk. Food rationing was in force, but the weekly allocation per household would have been viewed in war-weary Britain as the height of gastronomic indulgence. Gasoline was in short supply, but even so, the ordinary driver was allowed a generous three gallons a week. The lights still burned brightly, hotels and nightclubs were packed with well-heeled revellers, and there was big money to be earned by any man or woman prepared to work in the defence industry. Edward R. Murrow, the distinguished war correspondent, who had experienced the dangers and hardships on the other side of the Atlantic, was moved to comment: 'We live in the light, in relative comfort and complete security'. However, the daily casualty lists coming from the Pacific theatre were a grim reminder that America really was in the war.

The majority of the GIs lining the rails of the *Dorchester* as she made her way past the Statue of Liberty, down the Ambrose Channel, and out into the open sea, had little conception of what awaited them at the end of their voyage north. Greenland, the world's largest island, is a cold and desolate place, all but a tiny coastal strip of which is covered by an ice cap 5,000 feet thick. In winter, with temperatures down to -9°F (-23°C), the sun does not rise until ten in the morning, and sets again at two in the afternoon. Few crops grow, and only a few sheep graze the scrubland in the extreme south. Storms with winds of up to 150 mph frequently sweep the frozen wastes, and it is often so cold that a man's breath freezes on his beard. In 1943, Greenland's small indigenous population of mixed Eskimo and Danish descent were a poor lot, plagued by venereal disease and alcoholism, and with the highest suicide rate in the world. Greenland certainly had little in the way of excitement to offer the fresh-faced young soldiers packed into the *Dorchester*. And yet, the island was of vital strategic importance to the United States. Right from the outset of the war, German parties had been landing to set up weather bases on its remote eastern shores, but the last of these had finally been cleared out by Coastguard patrols, and now military airfields were under construction, which could change the face of the war in the North Atlantic.

Leaving the Ambrose Light astern, the *Dorchester* was clear of the Long Island shore by nightfall, and feeling the push of a long northerly swell. She took on a slow, gentle roll, hardly enough to disturb the crockery in her pantries, but quite sufficient to inflict misery on her passengers, most of whom had never been to sea before. Packed like sardines below decks, with the stench of fuel oil and cooking food pervading over all, they soon began to suffer the agonies of seasickness, for which the small medical staff on board had no magic cure. Lying wretched in their narrow cots, their misery matched their fear of the unknown as they embarked on the first stage of the *Dorchester*'s four and a half day passage to St John's, Newfoundland, where she would join a convoy for the voyage north.

It was late afternoon on the 26th, with the light fading fast, when the trooper arrived off St John's, and picked up a pilot to guide her into the harbour. The entrance to St John's is one of the world's worst navigational hazards. The gap – for it is little more than that – in the 500 feet-high cliffs must be approached at full speed, and with a firm hand on the wheel. Once inside, the pull of the tide and wind is lost, but with the towering cliffs closing in on either side, the approach gets even more frightening. The half-mile-long channel, aptly named The Narrows, is only 220 yards wide in places, which left very little margin of error for a ship the size of the *Dorchester*. For those GIs who managed to make it up on deck, this was the first taste of the excitement they had dreamed of. For Captain Danielson, standing nervously at the pilot's shoulder, it was nail-biting.

The *Dorchester* emerged unscathed from The Narrows, carefully negotiated the final hazard, the right-angled bend that led into the harbour, and brought up to an anchor amongst a motley collection of merchantmen awaiting convoy. The engines were rung off, and an unaccustomed quiet descended on the ship. It was peaceful here in this landlocked haven, one of the oldest settlements in North America. First colonized by Sir Humphrey Gilbert, half-brother of Sir Walter Raleigh, in 1583, St John's has ever since been an important outpost of the Americas. Home port of the vast Grand Banks cod fishing fleet, it was here, on Signal Hill, that Marconi received the first transatlantic wireless message in 1901, and from here Alcock and Brown took off to make the first non-stop transatlantic flight in 1919. In January 1943, a slimmed-down fishing fleet, with its ever-present stink of decomposing fish and flocks of wheeling gulls, was still there, but the port of St John's had taken on another role. It was now the main Atlantic base for the escort destroyers and corvettes of the British and Canadian navies, as well as a meeting point for the convoys they guarded.

There was no shore leave for the *Dorchester*'s passengers in St John's, but they were at least able to go on deck, to breathe clean air, to stretch their cramped limbs and, above all, to sleep without fear, and free of the debilitating curse of seasickness. On the afternoon of the 29th, the American troopship made her way out through the Narrows, past the Chain Rock and Pancake Island, to once again meet the challenge of the restless Atlantic. But this time she was not alone as she continued her voyage to the north. In company were the two small Norwegian steamers *Biscaya* and *Lutz*, both of around 1,400 tons gross, and loaded down to their marks with Army stores for Greenland. The escort for this three-ship convoy consisted of the US Coastguard cutters *Tampa*, 1,780 tons, *Comanche*, 1,005 tons, and *Escanaba*, 1,005 tons. The twenty-one-year-old *Tampa*, the senior escort, was armed with two 5-inch and two 3-inch guns, while the other cutters, younger by thirteen years or so, carried only two 3-inch guns. *Tampa* had a top speed of 15 knots, while *Comanche* and *Escanaba* could only manage 13. This was not a force to strike fear in the heart of any enemy, nor would it instill great confidence in merchant ships, but it was all the US Navy deemed necessary to protect Convoy SG 19, as the *Dorchester* and her two companions were designated.

Once clear of St John's, the three merchantmen formed up in a line abreast, with the *Dorchester* in the middle, the *Biscaya* to port, and the *Lutz* to starboard. The escorts then took station around them, *Tampa* in the lead, *Comanche* on the port beam, and *Escanaba* to starboard. This left the rear of the convoy unguarded, and as *Escanaba* had no radar and her sonar covered only 180 degrees from beam to beam forward, the starboard quarter was left dangerously exposed to attack·by submarine. And to further increase the vulnerability of this little convoy, the *Lutz*, a coal-burning steamer of indeterminate age, was sending up a tall plume of black smoke from her funnel, and would continue to do so throughout the passage, despite the protests of the S.O.E in *Tampa*. This is how Convoy SG 19 set out to head north towards the infamous Torpedo Junction, the area off Cape Farewell where Admiral Dönitz's U-boats reigned supreme. The final destination of the ships was Narsarssuak, on the south-west coast of Greenland.

In April 1941, the United States Government, alarmed at the news that the Germans had set up weather reporting stations on the east coast of Greenland, decided to take remedial action. An agreement was signed with the Danish Government in exile allowing the US to set up military bases on the island. The largest base, codenamed *Bluie West One*, was built at Narsarssuak, a small fishing village at the head of a fjord 100 miles north-west of Cape Farewell. By 1943, Bluie West One had assumed major strategic importance as a landing place for stores brought in by sea, while its airfield had become the main departure point for aircraft being ferried across the Atlantic to Britain.

The short respite from the disagreeable habits of the North Atlantic enjoyed by the *Dorchester*'s passengers came to an end soon after she left St John's and emerged into the open sea. The wind was in the north, and blowing fresh. At first, the ship rose and fell gently on the oncoming waves, but before long she was digging her bows into big, green-topped rollers, shuddering each time she dropped into the trough. The agony was beginning all over again for the unfortunate GIs crammed below decks. It was no consolation to them that the other ships were faring worse. The two tiny Norwegian freighters were burying their foredecks and lifting their sterns high, propellers racing as they rode the roller-coaster of the waves. The even smaller Coastguard cutters were built with the Atlantic weather in mind, but for the most part they were invisible as they wallowed in the deep troughs. SG 19's progress slowed to a painful crawl.

Seven hundred and fifty miles to the north, *U-223* was experiencing even worse weather conditions. She was all but hove-to on the surface ninety miles south-south-east of Cape Farewell, riding out a force 7 north-westerly, battered by twenty feet waves, under a grey forbidding sky heavy with sleet and snow. As ordered, *Oberleutnant* Wächter was making a pretence of seeking out the enemy, but to him the likelihood of making contact in the prevailing weather seemed very remote.

It had been much the same story over the previous seven days since clearing Iceland, a constant battle against the foul Atlantic weather. Late on the 23rd, Wächter had received a message from BdU warning that a U-boat returning to base had sighted British destroyers, or sloops, possibly a hunter-killer group, but more likely the remote screen for a New York-UK convoy believed to be passing about 500 miles south of Cape Farewell. The *Haudegen* pack had already been ordered south to intercept the convoy, and *U-223* was instructed to join them at all possible speed. Wächter duly altered course to the south-west, but an increase in speed was beyond his capability. The wind was blowing south-easterly, force 6, and rising, the sea and swell running high, and short of damaging his boat, Wächter could manage no more than 4½ knots.

The convoy in question, coincidentally HX 223, was sighted by another U-boat, but owing to poor radio reception, a by-product of the weather, she was unable to get her sighting report through to BdU until eighteen hours later. The *Haudegen* boats were ordered to form a patrol line across HX 223's estimated track, but by the time they were in position the convoy had slipped past. Wächter was then ordered to resume his original westerly course, by which time he was in the midst of a whole gale blowing from the south, with precipitous seas and visibility reduced to near-zero by driving hail and snow, with heavy ice forming on *U-223*'s casing. Ship hunting in such weather was a useless exercise, and Wächter contented himself with coasting along on one diesel, thereby saving fuel and avoiding damage to the boat. For his crew, flung, from bulkhead to bulkhead by the violent rolling, there was no relief.

By the afternoon of the 25th, *U-223* had fought her way to within 350 miles of Cape Farewell. Surprisingly, the wind had backed and eased to a mere force 5 to 6, and visibility was dramatically improved. There was still a big swell on the beam, but it was possible to post lookouts without fear of them being washed overboard. The lookouts quickly proved their worth, sighting mast-heads on the horizon to the north just as the last of the daylight was fading. As the boat lifted on the swell, Wächter saw a funnel, and having concluded that this must be an east bound merchantman, he altered towards her.

U-223 was now going into the wind, and her progress towards the target ship was slow. It was almost dark when Wächter took aim and fired a single torpedo. Not surprisingly, considering the range and the motion of the boat, the torpedo missed, and within half an hour the ship was out of sight, gone on her way without even realizing she had been under attack. The exercise might be considered by many to be a waste of an expensive torpedo, but Wächter judged the attempt to not be without merit. While the attack was on, and the adrenaline running, it had provided a much-needed boost for his bored and weather-beaten crew.

The adrenaline was running again next day. The wind had dropped further to force 3, no more than a gentle breeze, and there were patches of blue sky overhead. In the late afternoon, a twin-engined aircraft suddenly appeared, heading to the north-east. The aircraft was obviously too far away to sight the U-boat, but its appearance did provide Wächter with an excuse to hit the alarm and exercise his crew in an emergency crash dive. He came back to the surface half an hour later, and soon after dark received a radio signal instructing him to join up with Gustav Poel who, in *U-413*, was shadowing the east-bound convoy SC 117. Poel had sunk one ship in the convoy, but the escorts were hounding him and he needed help. Given the fine weather,

Wächter was confident of reaching Poel's position within five or six hours. *U-223* turned southwards, and quickly worked up to 16 knots, her thundering diesels matching the heartbeat of all on board. The chase was on.

It was a false start. Two hours after receipt of the first message, BdU (C.-in-C. U-boats) cancelled the rendezvous, and ordered Wächter to make haste to join the *Haudegen* pack. It was a group signal reading:

(1) Rosenberg, Drewitz, Gretschel, Wächter, Thater to join the old *Haudegen* Group, at the moment consisting of Heydemann, Graf, Huth, Clausen, Köhler, Mengersen, Borchers, Hesemann, Kremser, Heine, Franzius, Soden, Kessler, Köppe and *U-752*. Patrol from FE4555 to OS9183 with 20 miles separation between boats.

(2) From 0800 27/1, Rosenberg to take up station between Mengersen and Borchers and Drewitz between Borchers and Hesemann, etc. Gretschel, Wächter between the two nearest boats. Thater between Heine and Franzius.

Wächter was about to join a very powerful hunting pack which, when assembled, would consist of twenty-one Type VIIC boats, some of them under the command of men who had considerable experience and success in the on-going battle of the Atlantic. On this occasion, the pack was to be deployed against the slow east-bound convoy SC 118. Under escort by the all-British Escort Group B 2, SC 118 consisted of sixty-one ships, many of them loaded with arms and supplies for Russia. This was a prize worthy of *Haudegen*.

Chapter Three

Rendezvous at Cape Farewell

It was early afternoon on the 30th before *U-223*, navigating by dead reckoning again, arrived in a position Wächter estimated to be 200 miles south-west of Cape Farewell, where she was to rendezvous with other boats of the *Haudegen* pack. There was no one in sight, or even in radio contact. Not that Wächter had really expected otherwise. The ocean was vast, and it was blowing a gale from the north-west, with a very rough sea, and frequent snow and hail squalls reducing the visibility to no more than the bow of the boat for long periods. *U-223* was once again just holding her own and rolling horribly in a beam sea. As usual, those who suffered worst were the men who kept watch in the conning tower, their faces lashed raw by the stinging hail and spray, their hands and feet numb with impending frostbite. They could see nothing but the grey heaving waves, and with no opportunity to take sights for days on end, they had only a vague idea of where they were. It all seemed a pointless, masochistic exercise. They were, however, marginally better off than those confined to *U-223*'s hull, who were not even able to taste the salt and sniff the fresh air. With everything battened down except the conning tower hatch, the boat stank of unwashed bodies, stale food and diesel oil. As for *U-223* herself, she was no longer the smart, newly-painted boat that had made her way confidently out of the Kieler Bucht only eighteen days earlier. Her casings and conning tower were thick with ice, but this did not hide the scars of her long and hard-fought outward passage. Her once-immaculate paintwork was streaked with red rust. To an outside observer, if there had been one in this God-forsaken sea, she must have looked a sorry sight.

The *Dorchester* was 400 miles to the south, and steaming north with the other ships of SG 19 in steadily deteriorating weather. Conditions below decks in the trooper were, if possible, even worse than in *U-223*. After a full day at sea, her GI passengers, many of them accustomed to a very different life on the farms and in the cities of the USA, now faced an uncertain future in a foreign land, and meanwhile all they had to look forward to was another three or four days of seasickness and boredom. There was some relief for those who had not taken to their beds. Captain Danielson fully appreciated the danger he was sailing into, and called for volunteers to stand watch with the Armed Guard gunners who were manning the guns day and night. He also used some of the volunteers as extra lookouts, so that at all times forty-four pairs of eyes were scanning the sea for the enemy. As for the others, their welfare was looked after by the four Army chaplins sailing in the *Dorchester*. George Fox, a Methodist preacher from Vermont; Alexander Goode, a rabbi from Pennsylvania; Clark Poling, an Anglican pastor from New York; and John Washington, a Roman Catholic priest from New Jersey, put aside their religious differences to try to maintain morale amongst the troops. It was a thankless and demanding assignment, but they did produce significant results.

At the same time, morale was getting a boost aboard *U-223*. In the early hours of the morning of 31 January, a message was received from BdU informing all boats that Karl Dönitz had been appointed Commander-in-Chief of the German Navy, with the rank of *Grossadmiral*. This followed the departure of Admiral Raeder, who had 'retired' after a row with Hitler over his proposal to scrap Raeder's big ships and bring their guns ashore. The move had little real significance, as most ships of the German surface fleet were either crippled, or holed up in the Norwegian fjords and the Baltic with no immediate prospect of returning to sea. It did, however, mean that Dönitz now had a free hand to concentrate all resources on his beloved U-boat arm, with which he still believed he could win the war. The U-boat men, riding out the storms of the North Atlantic couldn't have wished for better news.

Later that day, Karl Wächter received orders to join with four other boats to form an offshoot of *Haudegen* codenamed

Nordsturm. The other boats were *U-268* (Ernst Heydemann), *U-358* (Rolf Manke), *U-186* (Siegfried Hesemann) and *U-707* (Günter Gretschel). *Nordsturm* was to remain in the vicinity of Cape Farewell to intercept a small Greenland-bound convoy, which had been reported sailing from St John's by German agents in Newfoundland. Meanwhile, the rest of the *Haudegen* pack was to spread out in a long north-west/south-east patrol line to trawl south-westwards at 3 knots across the intended track of Convoy SC 118. B-Dienst, the German decoding service, had been listening in to radio traffic from SC 118, and was able to plot the convoy's progress with a fair amount of accuracy.

Nordstrum formed its own patrol line, with Wächter in the middle, and the others spread out on either side within visual signalling distance. Strict radio silence was maintained, for it was estimated that the reported Greenland-bound convoy – SG 19 in other words – was only 200 miles to the south. The weather was slowly improving again, but speed was reduced to the bare minimum required to maintain steerage way. *Nordstrum* would wait for the enemy convoy to steam into its net.

The hours went by slowly, but there was an air of excitement in *U-223*'s conning tower that permeated deep into her hull. The improved weather helped to put a new face on things, and the passing snow showers failed to dampen the new air of optimism. At long last, *U-223* and her highly-trained, but untried, crew were going into action.

As they rode out the night, Wächter submerged at regular intervals to listen for hydrophone effect, the tension mounting each time a possible target was reported. But it was only the sounds of the sea, passing shoals of fish, a cruising whale, perhaps, or the movement of the ice flows now gathering all around them.

At dawn on 2 February, hastily snatched star sights showed *U-223* to be 225 miles south-west of Cape Farewell and, according to Karl Wächter's calculations, very close to the northbound convoy. The visibility was good, up to six miles between snow showers, but nothing had yet been sighted. The routine continued, scanning the horizon with binoculars while on the surface, listening carefully with hydrophones while submerged. Nothing. Then, when it was full daylight, a smudge of black smoke was seen on the horizon, not ahead as had been anticipated, but to the west, well out on *U-223*'s starboard beam.

SG 19 came so very near to slipping past the *Nordstrum* patrol line, and would have done so if it had not been for the coal-fired *Lutz* trailing her plume of smoke across the horizon. Wächter increased to full speed and altered course to intercept. An hour later, a cluster of masts and two more plumes of smoke were visible. The ships appeared to be on a northerly course, and moving slowly to starboard, drawing ahead. A snow squall blotted out the scene for a while, but when it had passed, Wächter was able to make out three steamers and two smaller ships; the latter he assumed to be the convoy's escorts. His range finder put them at between fourteen and sixteen miles away, and they were steering a steady course, not zig-zagging, which in the vicinity of the infamous Torpedo Junction seemed downright careless of the enemy.

Wächter's first duty was to report to BdU and warn the other *Nordstrum* boats, none of which were now in sight, and to do so he was obliged to break radio silence and risk bringing the convoy's escorts down on him. Using the *Kurzsignale* (Short Signal) code, which took only a few seconds to transmit, he reported the convoy sighting, giving its estimated course and speed. He then gave chase. Sixty years on, *U-223*'s War Diary makes compelling reading:

1629	Sent radio message FT 1606/834
	Convoy in AJ1687 bearing 000 degrees.
	Wind SW 3–4, good visibility, snow showers.
	Still only three steamers seen.
1716	Received radio message FT 1651/836
	U-boat Command requires to know whether convoy is large England-bound one or small Greenland-bound.
1857	Enemy in AJ1654. Steering between 010 degrees and 020 degrees.

1932	Intend to attack convoy in AF1625. Run into thick snow squall and alter course to 290 degrees. When visibility clears again convoy bearing 200 degrees.
1934	Dived for underwater attack. Wind has dropped right away and sea is flat calm. According to hydrophones convoy steering between 030 degrees and 040 degrees. Snowing again.
2000 AJ1389	Visbility now good.
2010	One escort at 1000 metres. Patrol boat of Kingfisher type with one gun aft and one mast. Very light grey paintwork.
	I listen but can hear no asdic transmissions. Nothing heard from the steamers. Listening all round horizon with hydrophones.
2020	One escort sighted right ahead. She is coming in very fast. She cannot fail to see us. Then at 400 metres she turns away. I fear that the English lookouts will see my periscope in this weather.
2030	The escort is now well clear and I can again use my periscope with caution. I can see the steamers to starboard. They are steering due north. Three steamers, two small 4000 tonners and one big 6–7000 tons. This appears to be passenger ship. Painted light grey, almost white. This is probably camouflage for the Greenland area. Fore and aft she has a high deck cargo. Abeam and astern of steamers is another escort similar to first. As they are 6000 metres off it would be pointless to shoot.

Wächter decided it was now safe to surface, and *U-223* emerged onto a sea that was 'as still as a duckpond'. Some twilight remained, and the convoy was clearly visible but with the boat trimmed down so that little more than her conning tower was above water, Wächter was confident that he would not be seen by the enemy. He set off cautiously in pursuit of the convoy, his primary target the passenger ship, which in these waters was almost certainly carrying troops. He intended to get as close to her as possible, before diving for an underwater attack.

The U-boat, her throbbing diesels sounding dangerously loud in the still air, edged closer to her quarry. Then, without warning, the visibility began to go, first with drizzle, and then snow. The convoy was lost to sight, and as darkness was not far off, Wächter feared he might lose contact altogether. He dived again, and listened with the hydrophones. The propeller noises were still there, very clear and moving north. He came back to the surface again, for with a top speed submerged of 6 or 7 knots, he had no hope of overhauling the convoy underwater. He resigned himself to a long chase, making as much speed as possible on the surface, and diving from time to time to listen. Several times, perhaps unwisely, he broke radio silence to report his progress to BdU, but received no acknowledgements. The enemy, it seems, was equally deaf to his signals, for no escort came chasing after him.

As pursuer and pursued moved north, so the weather took another turn for the worse, and by midnight it was blowing force 4 to 5 from the north-north-east, and the white horses were galloping again, providing good cover for *U-223* on the surface. The visibility was still being marred by passing snow showers, but when Wächter surfaced at 01.43 on the 3rd, the convoy was clearly visible as a cluster of dark shadows ahead and to port. The nearest ship, she looked like an escort, was less than a mile away. Wächter got ready to dive, but there was no need. By pure chance, he was approaching the convoy on its starboard quarter, which was covered by the *Escanaba*, the only escort with no radar and only a forward searching sonar.

On board the *Dorchester*, there was a new air of optimism. Word had gone round that they were within 150 miles of the coast of Greenland, that air cover was expected at daylight, and they would enter Narsarssuak fjord next afternoon. For those confined to the airless, vomit-spattered troop decks, the news could not have been more welcome. The buoyant mood was tempered by orders from the bridge that all troops must sleep fully clothed and keep their lifejackets handy. *Tampa* had passed the word to Captain Danielson that a U-boat was believed to be in the area. Unfortunately, such was the expectation in the troop decks that the voyage was drawing to a safe conclusion, that Danielson's orders were largely ignored.

Astern of the *Dorchester*, in the snow-filled dark of the night, Karl Wächter was even then manoeuvring *U-223* into position to strike. His War Diary continues:

0440   Enemy now bearing 220 degrees. I hold back because the steamer is in a patch to the north. Ahead and astern it is dark. More snow squalls are coming in.

     The big steamer is ahead of the others. I can see one escort to starboard at about 1500 metres.

     Suddenly I see one escort between 020 and 030 degrees, also three others to starboard.

     There is no way I can get through. Also I am not yet in position to fire, even though I am only 4000 metres off. I think I have a good chance of sinking two steamers, as one is overlapping the other. They are steaming in line abreast.

     I fire tubes 1 and 3 at these two and tube 2 at the third ship. I then turn very slowly to starboard to present my smallest silhouette to the second escort. I think he must have spotted my wake, as he is turning towards me. He is about 1200 metres off. All three targets are now right ahead. The distance is slowly opening and I am going into the shadows.

     After 5 minutes and 30 seconds (5300 metres) two torpedoes hit the big ship, one in the region of her foremast, the other near her funnel. A great cloud of flame and smoke is thrown up and she sinks almost right away, going down bow-first with her stern rising high in the air. There are ten to twenty small detonations. Probably ammunition exploding.

     I get a third hit after 5 minutes and 30 seconds on the ship behind the big one. She is hit in the

> forward cargo hold and started to burn right
> away. I think I can just get across her bow. I go
> hard to starboard.

Although Karl Wächter was on his first war patrol in command, and in an, as yet, untried boat, his attack on SG 19 was both audacious and faultlessly executed. However, Lady Luck must have been on his side. Without knowing it, he had come in on the blind side of the convoy – due to the *Escanaba*'s deficiencies – and he had approached to within 1,000 yards of the cutter without being discovered. Furthermore, the convoy was steering a steady course, and not zig-zagging, as it should have been in this extremely dangerous area. Also, since first sighting SG 19 on the morning of the 2nd, Wächter had sent no fewer than ten radio reports. Admittedly, these were in the *Kurzsignale* code, lasting only seconds, but they should have alerted the escorting Coastguard cutters to the immediate danger. It seems that if these signals were heard by the cutters, they were ignored. Captain Carl V. Petersen, commander of the *Escanaba*, wrote in his report: '. . . it is evident that the submarine made its approach from the starboard quarter of the convoy astern of the *Escanaba* and thereby protected by our wake . . . If the *Escanaba* had been equipped with radar, it is believed that the enemy could not have made his approach without being detected. In fact, it is considered very likely that he selected this position since by observation he could determine that this vessel was not equipped with radar.' This seems to be a poor excuse for not keeping a good lookout astern.

Wächter's claim to have scored three hits with three torpedoes was an exaggeration, although an understandable one given that it was a dark night and the three steamers were overlapping in his sights. One report states that the other ships, the *Biscaya* and *Lutz*, collided with each other following the torpedoing of the *Dorchester*, thus adding to the confusion. What is certain is that Wächter scored a direct hit on the *Dorchester*, thereby setting in train a terrible chain of events.

Third Officer Harold W. Beach, who was keeping the 12 to 4 watch on the trooper's bridge, had not really been at ease since taking over the watch at midnight. Beach, who hailed from

Savannah, in the sunny southern state of Georgia, was not at home in these frigid latitudes, and although he was wearing an alpaca-lined parka, several heavy jumpers and thick woollen underwear, the cold was troubling him. Further to that, he had misgivings about steering a steady course in these waters, where it seemed to him so obvious that a zig-zag pattern was called for: Torpedo Junction did not earn its reputation lightly. The next alteration of course, as per Captain Danielson's night orders, was not due until 03.00, which was surely tempting Providence. The night was dark, the visibility good; ideal stalking weather for the U-boats, and with only three escorts in attendance, the convoy's rear was dreadfully exposed. Beach was sweeping the horizon astern with his binoculars when the torpedo hit the *Dorchester*. The 12 to 4 watch was not yet an hour old.

Contrary to some lurid press reports which emerged after the war, there was no 'thunderous explosion' when Wächter's torpedo ploughed into the *Dorchester*'s hull, no 'blinding flash', only a muffled thump and a heavy concussion that was felt throughout the ship. Second Officer Samuel W. Dix, who was asleep at the time, reported being woken by the shock wave, but had no idea that the ship had been torpedoed. He concluded that she had struck a small iceberg, for there were many in the area. Most of the *Dorchester*'s passengers were also asleep, and although some were thrown from their cots, none of them thought anything serious was amiss. It may have all been a terrible misunderstanding, but in this way mass panic was avoided.

An official report compiled from survivors statements details the real extent of the damage:

At 0355 GCT (0055 Ship's Time) something exploded without warning just abaft of midships in the vicinity of the engine-room; the explosion was muffled; there was very little noise, but considerable concussion. The vessel swung to starboard and lost way, the engines having apparently been stopped by flooding of the engine-room, the ship listed sharply to starboard. The shell of the ship was ruptured in the vicinity of the engine-room, and just under the refrigerator plant a few feet aft of amidships; some of the bulkheads were distorted since some of the doors tended to jam; both

37

generators and an auxiliary gas generator above the waterline shorted or failed to function. Flooding was very rapid; some flying debris, No. 4 lifeboat believed holed by fragments, No. 7 lifeboat reported smashed beyond use.

The sum of it all was that the *Dorchester* had been dealt a mortal blow. Just one torpedo had blasted open her engine-room below the waterline, thus laying open her main watertight compartment to the sea. Within minutes, water rushing in had doused the boiler fires, stopped the main engines, and swamped the generator flat. The emergency petrol-driven generator on the main deck, which should have cut in automatically when the other generators failed, for reasons unknown, possibly lack of maintenance, did not function, and the ship was plunged into complete darkness. As the water poured into her hull, the *Dorchester* began to list heavily to starboard, eventually going over to about 30 degrees and staying there. Added to all that, ammonia fumes from the damaged refrigeration plant were seeping into the accommodation.

There is no record of how many men were killed in the engine-room by the explosion and subsequent rapid flooding, but it is almost certain that none of the watch below survived. Their end will have been mercifully sudden, but for those in the crowded troop decks the nightmare was only just beginning. Suddenly finding themselves in complete darkness, with the ship leaning over at a crazy angle, and loose gear flying in all directions, no one could have blamed the young enlisted men for panicking. They had turned in on the previous evening with a sense of relief that their uncomfortable sea journey would soon be over, only to be rudely awakened with death staring them in the face. There was, of course a scramble to find the ladders leading to the upper decks, but by and large, order was maintained.

The chaos came later when, with the *Dorchester* lying over on her beam ends, Captain Danielseon gave the order to abandon ship. The prearranged signal for abandoning was a series of blasts on the ship's whistle, but as the steam supply had been cut off, only a brief whimper was heard when the whistle lanyard was pulled. The alarm bells were likewise out of action, leaving word of mouth as the only means of passing the order to take to the boats. The Navy Department report states:-

Some of the crew and passengers left the ship; many others remained on board and went down with the ship . . . Of the 14 boats aboard, only No. 6 and No. 13 were successfully used in abandoning ship. No. 2 boat was lowered successfully but was soon swamped by the excessive number of persons in or trying to get in it. No. 4 boat was capsized almost as soon as it was lowered (It is not clear whether this was due to excessive crowding or damage to the boat). No. 9 boat was left hanging by a davit. No. 8 boat was probably not lowered (One of the seamen who was supposed to lower this boat found no one else to assist him so he joined No. 6 boat and assisted in lowering it). Apparently, No. 2, 4, 6, 11, 13 and 14 boats were lowered. Some davits were damaged in the explosion. Several liferafts were cut loose by the ship's crew, but left on deck to float clear if the vessel sank. Other liferafts were reported to have been dropped over the side (probably by inexperienced personnel), and injured persons who were in the boats or in the water. Several liferafts were still aboard when the vessel sank . . . There was apparently no panic during the abandoning ship operations. Some lifeboats swamped due to overcrowding. Many of the passengers did not realise the seriousness of the situation. When the vessel went down, many persons were seen standing motionless on deck and apparently making no effort to leave the ship . . .

There is some confusion as to how long the *Dorchester* stayed afloat after being torpedoed, but best estimates are that she went down in twenty minutes, which gave precious little time to organize the evacuation of the 904 souls on board. Contrary to good practice when sailing in enemy infested waters, none of the trooper's watertight doors were closed when she was hit. When belated attempts were made to close them, it was found that the explosion had distorted some bulkheads and many of the doors were jammed open. Water poured into the holds from the engine-room, the *Dorchester* quickly lost her reserve buoyancy, and she went to the bottom bow-first.

The torpedoing of the *Dorchester* had happened without a sound being heard or a flame being seen by the other ships. Her casualty list might have been far longer, had it not been for the keen eyes of an officer on the bridge of Coastguard cutter *Escanaba*. The cutter's commander, Carl V. Peterson, reported:

Just after 0400 on 3 February, the officer of the deck reported a white light showing on the *Dorchester*. At this time the *Escanaba* was on station about 3000 yards distant with the *Dorchester* bearing about a point abaft the port beam. Right after this the OOD reported what seemed to be a fire on board the *Dorchester*. The Commanding Officer went out to the pilot house from the emergency sleeping quarters and received another report that there was one white light in the water. When the Commanding Officer reached the pilot house, the time by the bridge clock was 0105 (0405 Zebra) and the OOD had altered course 30 degrees to port. The *Dorchester* had swung around stopped, heading in a south-westerly direction with a few white lights, apparently flashlights, showing, and one white light in the water astern. Course was altered to port and the *Escanaba* ran in to investigate the picture which indicated that there was a man overboard and the *Dorchester* was attempting to make a pickup. Within a minute's running time it became apparent that the *Dorchester* had been torpedoed since the red lights attached to survivors dropping over the side and swimming in the water became visible. General Quarters was sounded, the *Tampa* advised, and the ship went to full speed, swung out and around the stern and bow of the *Dorchester*, and back to station. Fired star shells as ordered. The *Escanaba* had to go around the wreck since survivors were on the port hand, *Lutz* drifting on the starboard hand. After firing star shells, the *Escanaba* returned to the scene of the wreck to pick up survivors in accordance with orders.

The sinking of the *Dorchester*, linchpin of the convoy, caused confusion in the ranks of SG 19, ships scattering in all directions, the escorts firing starshell at random and circling at high speed in search of an enemy they could neither see nor hear. When the real situation became apparent, order was restored. The *Biscaya* and *Lutz*, presumably having recovered from their collision, which can have caused little damage to either ship, were rounded up by the *Tampa* and set off for Narsarssuak at best possible speed. *Comanche* and *Escanaba* were detailed to pick up survivors, an unenviable task, for it was still highly likely that enemy submarines were in the vicinity. When the rescue operation started, weather conditions were good, with light winds and a calm sea, but as night turned to morning, the

North Atlantic reverted to type, and a fresh gale was blowing by the time the sun came up. Captain Petersen, of the *Escanaba* reported:

At the beginning of operations, a large portion of the survivors were hysterical, shouting for help (this same condition was evident during rescue operations performed by this ship 15 June 1942) and could not or would not help themselves when we took them on board. To get these men on board it became necessary to put members of the crew in the water to secure a line around each survivor after which he was hauled on board. During this period and while they lasted, rubber suits were used, the procedure being to stuff a member of the crew into this suit, tie a stout line around his chest, pick him up bodily and lower him over the side. These retrievers would then swim out from the ship, tow in life rafts and single survivors in the water. After a while, these rubber suits became so damaged that their use had to be discontinued and men had to go into the water protected only by their clothing and a lifejacket. During these operations, two crew members fell overboard and were promptly rescued by these men. As the survivors recovered from their hysteria, action of the cold water set in, stiffened their joints, and made it impossible for them to help themselves so that the only way to get these men on board was to put members of the crew in the water to assist. These men were constantly exposed to the danger of being injured between the life rafts and the ship's hull and to avoid this careful handling was required. At one time a group of survivors were removed from a life boat and the life boat then secured to the ship's side by fore and aft painters. Men were stationed in the boat and pulled survivors off the life rafts into the boat from where they were easily hoisted on board. This system worked very well until the sea made up, making it necessary to cut the boat adrift. The performance of the officers and crew of the *Escanaba* was excellent.

Discipline of the survivors while afloat, with one exception, was very poor which slowed up operations. In one case, 17 men were picked off a box-type life raft where one man had taken command of the situation and had all of the men under control. These men were in the best physical condition of all the men rescued. In general, all men who were riding box-type rafts were in a better physical condition than those who rode the doughnut type . . .

41

The *Escanaba*'s Medical Officer, Assistant Surgeon Ralph R. Nix, reported on the condition of the survivors:

> The principal etiological factor present was exposure to the elements, particularly cold. The temperature recorded during the entire rescue work was 40 degrees Fahrenheit for the water and 30 degrees Fahrenheit for the air. Traumatic injuries surprisingly a very minute and trivial problem. The first survivor was taken aboard approximately thirty minutes after the *Dorchester* disaster, the last some seven hours later. The survivors were picked up at a fairly constant rate during these seven and one half hours of exposure. They arrived aboard in ones, twos or threes, fairly evenly spaced throughout the rescue. They were taken from lifeboats, doughnut rafts, box liferafts, and from the water itself, all in very close contact with the water. The first to arrive aboard were able to walk aboard unhelped. These men were less than twenty in number and were comparatively dry. The remainder of the men were all soaked with water and oil and all had to be assisted or carried bodily aboard and down to the mess deck where treatment was instituted. Approximately fifty percent of the entire number were unable to assist themselves in any respect, the others could move without support. About ten men arrived semi-comatosed. The exposure to the cold air and water seemed to literally 'freeze the men stiff'. The extremities were the sites most involved, the lower more so than the upper . . .

When the final count was made, it was found that the *Comanche* had rescued ninety-seven survivors, while the *Escanaba* had on board 132 survivors and thirteen bodies. Other ships, called in to continue the search, found only abandoned liferafts and hundreds of bodies floating in the area where the *Dorchester* had gone down. Of her total complement of 904 passengers and crew, 675 had lost their lives on that dark, cold January night off Greenland's Cape Farewell. Among those who lost their lives were Captain Hans Jurgen Danielson and the four Army chaplins, Reverend George Fox, Rabbi Alexander Goode, Reverend Clark Poling and Father John Washington. It is said that the padres, having given up their lifejackets to men who had lost theirs, were last seen at the ship's side rail offering up a prayer for the survivors in the water. To the last, the welfare of their troops was their first concern.

As a sad footnote, the Coastguard cutter *Escanaba*, which had raised the alarm when the *Dorchester* was torpedoed, and had pulled so many of her men from the water, was herself lost four months later when an unexplained explosion suddenly ripped her apart while she was patrolling off Greenland. Only two survivors were picked up from her crew of 105 men.

Chapter Four

The Hardest Battle

U-223 was a long time gone from the scene of her first victory when ships of the US Navy arrived in force to hunt her down. At first, Wächter had every intention of pursuing the convoy to inflict further damage, but the weather turned against him. With visibility reduced to around 500 metres in snow and hail squalls, and small icebergs, some of them big enough to cause serious damage to his boat, becoming more numerous, he decided to abandon the chase. After sending off a signal to BdU reporting his success, he dropped back. When daylight came, he dived to reload his forward tubes, resurfacing again shortly before noon. By this time, the weather had improved substantially, and he decided to mark time awaiting orders from BdU.

U-223 lay hove to on the surface for two hours, with Wächter becoming increasingly uneasy as the time passed. The visibility had increased to 2,000 metres, was improving steadily, and the cloud ceiling was lifting, leaving the U-boat uncomfortably exposed. Then, at last, Wächter heard the rattle of morse coming from *U-223*'s tiny radio room. BdU's message was brief and to the point:

Your signal FT 1118/858 received.

Carry on towards coast. Attempt to attack again.

This was not the answer Karl Wächter was looking for. As the man on the spot, he considered it was far too late and too dangerous to go after SG 19 again, but he was obliged to comply with the order. Reluctantly, he turned north again. Eight hours later, he was not surprised, and considerably relieved, to receive a second signal from BdU instructing *U-223* and the other *Nordstrum* boats – none of which he had yet seen – to abandon the chase and go south to join the *Haudegen* pack, then somewhere to the north-east of Newfoundland.

Meanwhile, far to the east, in mid-Atlantic, momentous events were taking place. The thirty-eight-ship eastbound fast convoy HX 224 was under attack. Sighted three days earlier by Max-Martin Teichert in *U-456*, this convoy of thirty-eight heavily escorted ships happened to be in an area where only five other U-boats were patrolling, and they were too scattered and too far away to answer Teichert's call to battle. Eventually, Teichert had no alternative but to go in alone. He met fierce opposition from HX 224's escorts, but succeeded in sinking two ships, the US-flag Liberty ship *Jeremiah van Rensselaer*, and the 9,456-ton British tanker *Inverillen*, before being beaten off. On the evening of 3 February, Hans Karpf, in *U-632*, came across a straggler from HX 224, another British tanker, the 8,190-ton *Cordelia*, and torpedoed her. The *Cordelia* blew up, leaving only one survivor out of her crew of forty-seven. This man was picked up by Karpf, and on interrogation revealed that a slow convoy was following on forty-eight hours behind HX 224. This vital piece of information was immediately radioed to BdU, thereby sealing the fate of Convoy SC 118.

SC 118 had left New York on 24 January, sixty-four ships sailing in thirteen columns and bound for Loch Ewe, on Scotland's north-west coast. This was an important convoy, most of its ships carrying arms and supplies for the Russian front, and it was escorted by the British Escort Group B 2. Under the command of Lieutenant Commander F.B. Proudfoot, B 2 was a scratch group, hastily cobbled together for SC 118. It consisted of the old Campbell-class destroyers *Vanessa* (S.O.E) and *Vimy*, the equally old Town-class destroyer *Beverley* and the Flower-class corvettes *Abelia*, *Campanula* and *Migonette*. Temporarily attached to the group were the US Coastguard cutter *George M. Bibb* and the Free French corvette *Lobelia*. In support was the first of the specially equipped rescue ships, the ex-River Clyde pleasure steamer *Toward*, under the command of the experienced Captain G.K. Hudson. The *Toward* remained a merchant ship, but carried a surgeon and full medical staff, special rescue equipment, and had accommodation for 100 survivors. Her primary function was to allow the escorts to concentrate on the defence of the convoy, rather than dropping back to pick up survivors. *Toward* also carried the latest HF/DF, so that she played a role in the fight against the U-boats. SC 118 was therefore covered for most eventualities – except the indiscretions of the *Cordelia*'s lone survivor.

SC 118 started out badly. Hours after sailing from New York, the German *B-Dienst* had intercepted and successfully decoded the Convoy Commodore's sailing message, sent in code to the Admiralty. This, along with *U-632*'s information, enabled the German plotters at BdU to pinpoint the position of the convoy with some accuracy, and a reception was prepared. Two U-boat packs were available, *Haudegen* to the north and *Landsknecht* to the east. BdU ordered thirteen boats from *Landsknecht* and five from *Haudegen* to form a new pack named *Pfeil* with the express purpose of finding and attacking SC 118. The designated boats were to form up in a north-west/south-east patrol line some 600 miles to the east of Newfoundland, and wait for the enemy to come to them. The line consisted of *U-89* (Dietrich Lohmann), *U-135* (Otto Luther), *U-187* (Ralph Münnich), *U-262* (Heinz Franke), *U-266* (Ralf von Jessen), *U-267* (Otto Tinschert), *U-402* (Siegfried Freiherr von Forstner), *U-413* (Gustav Poel), *U-454* (Burkhard Hackländer), *U-465* (Wolf), *U-594* (Friedrich Mumm), *U-608* (Struckmeier) and *U-609* (Klaus Rudloff), all from the *Landsnecht* pack. The five *Haudegen* boats were, *U-438* (Rudolf Franzius), *U-613* (Helmut Köppe), *U-624* (Ulrich Graf von Soden-Fraunhofen), *U-704* (Horst Kessler) and *U-752* (Karl-Ernst Schroeter), and two boats which had been involved with HX 224, Max-Martin Teichert's *U-456* and *U-614* (Wolfgang Sträter). Some of the boats, including *U-187* and *U-267*, who had sailed in company with Karl-Jurgen Wächter's *U-223* when breaking out into the Atlantic from Kiel, were yet to fire a shot in earnest.

While the *Pfeil* boats were taking up their positions in the path of SC 118, the convoy was already fully occupied with another dangerous enemy, the North Atlantic in an evil mood. Since passing north of 50 degrees North SC 118 had run into a severe gale, which scattered the low-powered merchant ships over a large area. Lieutenant Commander Proudfoot fought hard to keep some semblance of order, but his destroyers and corvettes, themselves taking heavy punishment at the hands of the sea, could do little more than hover on the fringes of the loose formation and watch over the chaos. However, while the ships of the convoy were experiencing difficulties, the U-boats spread out across their predicted track were faring even worse. Careering from crest to trough, conning towers awash, they were often unable to see past the next wave as it came crashing down on them. Keeping a watch for enemy ships had become a bad joke. Yet they persisted, out of sight of each other, but somehow maintaining a ragged line into which they hoped the convoy would steam.

Initially, the weather was marginally on the side of the Allies, and SC 118, although well spread out, slipped through *Pfeil*'s net during the night of the 3rd under the cover of the rampaging wind and waves. And this stroke of good luck could have spelled the end to any serious danger for this vital convoy. The ships were then in mid-Atlantic, and would soon come under the umbrella of long-range Liberators flying from Iceland, and it was these big, lumbering planes with their airborne radar that the U-boats feared most. But it was not to be.

Disaster happened a little before dawn on the 4th when, possibly because of the heavy rolling, someone on the bridge of the Norwegian steamer *Vannik* accidentally fired a snowflake rocket. The rocket soared high into the air, to burst in a brilliant blaze of white light that lasted long into the dawn. It was unfortunate that at that time Ralph Münnich's *U-187*, a latecomer from the *Landsknecht* pack was twenty miles ahead of SC 118, and battling her way through heavy seas, heading west to join the *Pfeil* line.

Twenty-seven-year-old Münnich, was twenty-four days into his first war patrol, and eager to make his mark. When one of the conning tower lookouts reported the *Vannik*'s rocket, Münnich immediately altered towards it, calling for more speed. *U-187* began to nose-dive into the seas, throwing up a wall of green water on either bow as she headed for the beacon in the sky. At the same time, Münnich instructed his radio operator to send off a sighting report. This was transmitted on short wave using coded letter groups, and was very brief, lasting at the most twenty seconds. But this was long enough for a wide-awake HF/DF operator on board the rescue ship *Toward* to get a quick bearing. One bearing does not make a fix, but it was enough for the destroyers *Beverley* and *Vimy* to home in onto *U-187*.

Racing ahead of the convoy, the British destroyers sighted the U-boat at seven miles, still on the surface, and apparently unaware of the danger she was running into. When Münnich did finally become aware of *Beverley* and *Vimy* bearing down on him, he crash-dived at once. *U-187* almost got away, for at that crucial moment *Beverley*'s Asdic failed. *Vimy* was more fortunate, her Asdic gaining and holding a firm contact. While *Beverley* circled around the contact dropping single depth charges, *Vimy*, commanded by Lieutenant Richard Stannard, VC, RNR, carried out four running attacks on the target. *U-187* was forced to the surface, and a short, one-sided gun battle followed. The U-boat put up a gallant fight with her 88mm but she was heavily outgunned by the destroyers. *Vimy* scored a direct hit with a 4-inch shell, which blew a hole in the submarine's pressure hull. She took on a pronounced port list, and then began to sink slowly by the stern, her crew spilling up on deck and hurling themselves into the rough seas. The destroyers picked up forty-five survivors; Ralph Münnich and eight others were lost. So came to an end *U-187*'s brief and inglorious career. She had survived for just twenty-four days from leaving her berth in Kiel, and went to the bottom with all her torpedoes unfired.

SC 118 steamed on, tightening up its ranks, for more HF/DF contacts were being reported by *Toward* and USS *George M. Bibb*. The bearings came from astern of the convoy, indicating that *U-187*'s sacrifice had not been entirely in vain. The *Pfeil* pack, now swollen to twenty boats, had scented blood, and was rapidly overhauling the slow-moving merchantmen. Proudfoot resisted the temptation to send any of his ships back to challenge the U-boats, preferring to keep a defensive ring around the convoy, while urging his flock to cram on all speed. His urging was in vain, for this had not been designated a slow convoy without good reason. It was made up of tramps of various flags, many of them more than a quarter of a century old, and built to roam the trade routes of the world at a fuel-saving speed of 7 or

8 knots. They could no more outrun the approaching U-boats than compete for the Atlantic Blue Riband.

As soon as night fell, SC 118 made an emergency alteration of 45 degrees to starboard, hoping to shake off the U-boats during the hours of darkness. The usual practice for making an alteration of this magnitude in convoy was for the Commodore's ship to display a pre-arranged light signal from her signal mast – red, white, green, or similar. This would be acknowledged by each ship displaying the same signal. When all ships were showing their coloured lights, the Commodore would extinguish his. This was the signal for all ships to alter course simultaneously, rather like a military parade turning on the command of the drum major. In practice, this usually worked well, the merchant ships holding their ranks and, except on the odd occasion, avoiding colliding with each other. However, due to the known presence of U-boats, rather than use the give-away lights, the Commodore decided to use a sound signal for SC 118's alteration of course. While this method may have worked perfectly well in the quiet of a flat calm, it proved highly unsuitable for use with a force 7 howling in the rigging and substantial waves slamming against the hull. The ships of the three port columns, and some of those in the rear of the convoy, failed to hear the signal, and maintained their original course.

It was not until around midnight that it was realized that the convoy had split, and the two separate sections were fifteen miles apart, and on diverging courses. With a U-boat attack expected at any moment, this was a most unwelcome state of affairs, and on being made aware of the situation Lieutenant Commander Proudfoot sent the corvettes *Abelia* and *Lobelia* to round up the missing ships. Fortunately for SC 118, and largely down to the aggressive sweeps made by Proudfoot's escorts, the U-boats were unable to take advantage of the chaotic situation. By dawn on the 5th, the convoy was one unit again and steaming to the east with the escort screen around it. SC 118 was now just over 500 miles from the west coast of Ireland, and would soon be within reach of continuous air cover. Furthermore, Proudfoot had been advised that US Navy ships were due to join him from Iceland at sometime during that night. It was becoming more and more evident that the *Pfeil* boats had missed the opportunity to do any real damage to SC 118. But this was no time for complacency, and Proudfoot's escorts did not relax their vigilance.

At around 10.30 that morning, HMS *Beverley* spotted a surfaced U-boat fifteen miles astern of the convoy, and raced back to attack, opening fire with her Hedgehog as soon as she was within range. The Hedgehog, a 24-barrelled mortar mounted on the destroyer's forecastle head, straddled the surfaced U-boat with small 35lb charges designed to explode on impact, but most of the bombs exploded prematurely. The U-boat made a hurried exit below the waves. *Beverley*'s Asdic failed to make contact, and the destroyer carried out an extensive box-search, but with no results. At 11.15, *Beverley* was about to rejoin the convoy, when another U-boat – it might have been the same one – was sighted on the surface six miles away. HMS *Vimy* joined in the attack, but again the U-boat dived before it could be reached. The two destroyers, now separated from the convoy by twenty-two miles, carried out a painstaking Asdic search, but their efforts were in vain.

There now appear to have been four U-boats in contact with the convoy, *U-267*, *U-402*, *U-608* and *U-609*. Three of these, *U-267*, *U-402* and *U-608*, were driven off by the aggressive actions of *Beverley* and *Vimy*, but *U-609*, commanded by Klaus Rudloff, had escaped the destroyers attentions and was shadowing from a safe distance.

The weather was again worsening, and during the course of the morning the 5,376-ton American steamer *West Portal*, a long way from her home port of San Francisco, already straggling, fell further astern, until she was out of sight of the other ships. Nobody saw her go, for at that time the other ships were all struggling against the weather to keep on station. The *West Portal* fell easy prey to Gustav Poel in *U-413*, who sank her with a single torpedo. Fifty-two men went down with the American ship.

The *West Portal* failed to send an SOS and, quite unaware of the tragic happenings astern, SC 118 sailed on, enjoying the rest of the day in peace. Klaus Rudloff was still following at a discreet distance, but the other *Pfeil* boats had lost contact. Their chances of mounting a concerted attack on the convoy were diminishing with every hour that passed. During the night, the first of Proudfoot's promised reinforcements arrived, in the shape of the

US Coastguard cutter *Ingham*. On the morning of the 6th the American destroyers *Babbitt* and *Schenck* also joined from Iceland. To complete SC 118's improved defences, daylight air cover was being provided by Liberators of 120 Squadron RAF Coastal Command.

With five destroyers, four corvettes and aircraft patrolling overhead, SC 118 was no longer an easy target, but the U-boats were not ready to give up. In contact now, in addition to *U-609*, were *U-135* (Otto Luther), *U-266* (Ralf von Jessen), *U-267* (Otto Tinschert), *U-438* (Rudolf Franzius), *U-454* (Burkhard Hackländer) and *U-465* (Wolf), and others were closing in. Throughout the rest of the hours of daylight, the Liberators overhead were kept busy investigating HF/DF contacts made by the escorts. They caught a number of the U-boats on the surface, and used their depth bombs to good effect, but whenever one U-boat was forced down, another would surface to take its place. A little after 09.00, one of their number, Wolf's *U-465*, was surprised by a diving Liberator, and so severely damaged that she dropped out of the fight.

The game of hide and seek went on all day, but with no other real successes for the escorts or the Liberators. Then, an hour before sunset, one of the aircraft reported a U-boat on the surface dead astern of the convoy. Proudfoot sent *Vimy* to investigate, the destroyer obtaining an Asdic contact at 17.23. *U-267* had gone deep when she was spotted from the air, but Tinschert had since brought her back to periscope depth to see if the coast was clear. *Vimy* made a sustained depth charge attack, which drove Tinschert deep again, and contact was lost. As darkness was coming on, and *Vimy* was by that time twenty-three miles astern of the convoy, Lieutenant Commander Stannard decided to return to his station on SC 118. He left the scene unaware that his charges had inflicted heavy damage on *U-267* and the boat was limping away under water, Otto Tinschert having decided to give up the fight and return to base for repairs.

After dark, the attacks petered out, but Proudfoot, not without some justification, concluded that the respite was only temporary. There would be no air cover during the night, so he reorganized his now considerable escort force to meet all eventualities. *Babbitt* and *Ingham* were sent to sweep ahead of the convoy, while *Lobelia* and *Bibb* dropped back to cover the rear. The other escorts then formed a tight ring around the merchantmen. The convoy was now on a course of 053° and making 7½ knots, running before a force 6–7 south-westerly wind and with visibility at one to two miles. It would not be a comfortable night in the ships, but all the indications were that it would be a quiet one.

Amidst all the excitement of the day, no one had seen the little Greek tramp *Polyktor* fall astern. Built at the start of the First World War, after a lifetime of hard steaming around the world, the *Polyktor* had done well to maintain convoy speed this far. The combination of the need to produce those few extra revolutions and the heavy following sea that set her propeller racing out of control at times, had proved too much for her ageing engine. She dropped further and further behind until she found herself completely alone and barely able to keep steerage way in the huge following sea. That was how Ralf von Jessen found her. One torpedo was all that was necessary to send the Greek ship to her lonely grave and give *U-266* her first victim.

The 'quiet' night ended for SC 118 just after the watches changed at 20.00, when *U-262* penetrated the escort screen on the port side, and unseen, fired five torpedoes. Her commander, Heinz Franke, claimed three hits on a tanker, which broke in two and sank in twenty minutes. In reality, the 'tanker' was the small Polish cargo ship *Zagloba*, of 2,864 tons. The *Zagloba* had her engines and accommodation right aft, which would account for Franke reporting a tanker sunk. Yet again, the loss of another member of the convoy went unnoticed by the others. There were no survivors to tell the tale of the *Zagloba*'s last moments. *U-262*, however, did not get away scot-free. She was sighted by the Free French corvette *Lobelia*, which was keeping station astern of the convoy. *Lobelia* picked the U-boat up with her Asdic when she dived and mounted a determined depth charge attack which left *U-262* so badly damaged that she was also forced to quit the fight and make for Biscay.

Two hours passed without further incident then, at 22.45, the USS *Babbitt*, a 1918-vintage four-stacker, screening some five miles ahead of the convoy, obtained a firm radar contact on her port bow. The echo, which by its size was obviously a U-boat, was closing, and *Babbitt* altered to intercept. The ageing destroyer was slow to manoeuvre, with the result that the U-boat got inside her turning circle, and made good her escape. However, it appeared that Proudfoot's escort force had a firm control of the situation – then a man destined to be one of Germany's top U-boat aces entered the fray.

Kapitänleutnant Siegfried Freiherr von Forstner, born in Hanover in 1910, was Old Navy, having begun his career in 1930 as a midshipman in surface ships. He served in the light cruiser *Nürnberg* for the first year of the war, and in April 1940 transferred to the U-boat arm. His introduction to undersea warfare was with the legendary Otto Kretschmer in *U-99*, under whom the baron learned his trade well. Forstner took command of the newly-commissioned Type VIIC *U-402* in April 1941, but was not to score his first success until January 1942, when he torpedoed and damaged the 12,053-ton British troopship *Llangibby Castle* north of the Azores. In the twelve months that followed, Forstner proved to be an aggressive hunter cast in the same mould as his mentor, Kretschmer, sinking no less than eight ships of 30,963 tons. He was awarded the Iron Cross 2nd Class in February 1942, and the Iron Cross 1st Class in August of the same year.

Baron Forstner slipped into the ranks of SC 118 from the starboard side just after midnight, and opened the new day by sinking one of the most important ships in the convoy, the rescue ship *Toward*. A total of fifty-eight men, including Captain Hudson and his naval surgeon, perished in the cold waters as the little Clyde-based steamer went down. She left a dangerous gap in SC 118's defences, for Lieutenant Commander Proudfoot's ships would from then on have to carry the extra burden of picking up survivors.

Five minutes after delivering the death blow to the *Toward*, Forstner had the 6,625-ton US-flag ship *Robert E. Hopkins* in his sights. His first torpedo hit home, failing to sink the American, but twenty minutes later he delivered the *coup de grâce* with a second torpedo. *U-402* then retired to reload her tubes, but was back again within the hour and manoeuvring to take a shot at the Norwegian motor tanker *Daghild*.

The 9,272-ton *Daghild*, commanded by Captain Olaf Egidius,

would not have been with SC 118 but for a series of misfortunes going back over the previous five months. On 12 September 1942, whilst westbound to New York in Convoy ON 127, the *Daghild* was torpedoed by Otto von Bülow in *U-404*, sustaining major damage to her hull. She was able to reach St John's under her own power, where temporary repairs were carried out, enabling her to carry on to New York. She lay there for two months while her damaged hull plates were renewed, and a further month while she was fitted with an extra deck to carry a cargo of aircraft. It was not until January 1943 that she was ready to go to sea again, when she joined Convoy HX 224 bound for the UK. The convoy ran into bad weather off Newfoundland, and the *Daghild* soon found herself in trouble, the built-on deck severely restricting her ability to manoeuvre. Things went from bad to worse, and she lost the convoy in a snowstorm, and was unable to find it again. Captain Egidius decided to return to New York. The *Daghild* eventually sailed with SC 118, having on board 13,000 tons of diesel oil, a 143-ton landing craft on deck, along with as many aircraft as the rest of the deck would carry. This time she experienced no problems with her steering.

The *Daghild*, fifth ship in Column 11 of the SC 118, was lagging behind when she came into Siegfried von Forstner's cross-wires, a target most U-boat commanders could only dream of. Few, if any, were lucky enough to come across a deep-laden tanker with a huge landing craft perched forward of her bridge and a deck full of aircraft. Forstner took careful aim, and put a torpedo in the *Daghild*'s engine-room. The explosion ripped open her hull, and she slowly came to a halt, to lay stopped and listing heavily.

Judging the condition of the *Daghild* to be terminal, Captain Egidius gave the order to abandon ship, and all the tanker's crew got away safely in two lifeboats. Luckily, the corvette *Lobelia* was to hand, and despite the heavy seas, the boats were brought alongside and the men rescued. *Lobelia* then tried to sink the *Daghild* with gunfire, but she stubbornly refused either to go down or catch fire. She was last seen drifting forlornly astern, beam on to wind and sea and rolling her rails under, with her valuable deck cargo still lashed securely in place, and obviously destined to go to the bottom with her. She was found next day by Wolfgang Sträter in *U-614*, who wasted a torpedo on her, for she still refused to sink. Sträter lost sight of the *Daghild* in poor visibility, and she was not seen again until the early hours of the 8th, when *U-608* found her fifty-seven miles astern of the convoy, still afloat, but very low in the water. *Kapitänleutnant* Struckmeier's torpedo broke the sturdy old ship's back, and she finally succumbed to her enemies, slipping beneath the waves before the dawn came. *LCT 2335* went with her, still sitting expectantly on her foredeck.

SC 118, in spite of its formidable escort force, had meanwhile been suffering more losses. During the morning of the 7th, *U-614* sank the 5,730-ton British steamer *Harmala*, which had by then so nearly completed her long homeward passage from Rio de Janeiro. Then Siegfried Forstner dispatched yet another, the Danish East Asiatic Company's 8,597-ton *Afrika*, sailing under the British flag. It was a bad night for SC 118, a night seemingly without end.

Pausing only to search around the horizon for any escorts that might be threatening, Forstner turned his attention to the 6,063-ton American merchantman *Henry R. Mallory*. Owned by Clyde-Mallory Lines of New York, and commanded by Captain Horace Weaver, the twenty-seven-year-old *Henry R. Mallory*, like the ill-fated *Dorchester*, was a passenger liner requisitioned by the US Navy and converted for trooping. She had on board, in addition to a crew of seventy-seven, thirty-four US Navy Armed Guards, who manned her guns, and 227 troops, along with a cargo of trucks, tanks and Army supplies. At 04.59, Forstner's torpedo struck her on the starboard side in way of No. 3 hold, blowing a large hole in her hull and fracturing her main steam line. She quickly lost way and began to settle by the stern. Captain Weaver passed the word to abandon ship. This was not an easy operation, as two of the *Mallory*'s ten lifeboats had been destroyed by the explosion, and one other badly damaged. Furthermore, there appears to have been a great deal of confusion, possibly due to the fact that the troops had not received much in the way of lifeboat drill. Two boats capsized in the rough seas, and in the end only three boats, with 175 men on board, cleared the sinking ship's side. Many men were left struggling in the water, and most of them would die. There was no organized rescue attempt, for once again one of SC 118's ships had gone down unnoticed by the others. It was not until four hours later, when the *George M. Bibb* was searching astern for survivors from the *Toward*, that she stumbled on the *Henry R. Mallory*'s lifeboats. In all, the *Bibb* picked up 203 men from the trooper, three of whom later died, while the USS *Ingham* pulled twenty-four men from the water, and two of those died on board. Captain Horace Weaver, forty-eight of his crew, fifteen Armed Guards and 208 US Army personnel were lost from the *Henry R. Mallory*.

Siegfried Forstner rounded off the night by sinking the 4,965-ton Greek steamer *Kalliope* and, in the small hours of the 8th, the British tramp *Newton Ash* of 4,625 tons. In the space of twenty-four hours, Forstner had succeeded in sinking six ships totalling 32,466 tons gross, during the process of which *U-402* had been subjected to no less than seven prolonged depth charge attacks. For this remarkable achievement, Baron Siegfried von Forstner was awarded the Knight's Cross.

While the *Newton Ash*, deep-loaded with grain from St John's, New Brunswick for Hull, was spiralling to the bottom, *Lobelia*, sweeping astern on the lookout for more survivors, came across the final casualty in the battle for Convoy SC 118, this time not a victim of the U-boats, but of sheer bad luck. The Greek steamer *Adamas* was out of station somewhere between Columns 6 and 7, when an unidentified U-boat was seen between Columns 7 and 8. A minor panic occurred, during which ship No. 73 made a sudden alteration to port to run away from the danger. The *Adamas*, which was then close on No. 73's port side, was obliged to make a similar emergency alteration. In doing so, she inadvertently put herself squarely across the bows of ship No. 63, the American freighter *Samuel Huntingdon*, and was promptly rammed. The Greek ship was badly holed and began to sink. *Lobelia* picked up thirteen survivors, but the rest of the *Adamas*'s crew, who jumped overboard, died in the icy waters.

SC 118 reached home waters on 10 February, having lost to the U-boats eleven ships of 59,765 tons, and one other, the unfortunate *Adamas*, to collision. The Free French corvette *Lobelia*, which had taken on the *Toward*'s role of rescue ship and had 100 survivors on board, suffered an engine breakdown, and was towed into port by one of the destroyers. On the other side, three U-boats, *U-187* (Ralph Münnich), *U-609* (Klaus Rudloff) and *U-624* (Ulrich Graf von Soden-Fraunhofen) were sunk, and at least four others badly damaged. All concerned, the merchantmen, the escorts and the U-boats, had taken a severe battering from the weather.

Viewed in retrospect, the battle for SC 118 can hardly be seen as a victory for the Allies. Admittedly, fifty-two ships got through to Loch Ewe with a huge amount of vital cargo, but despite an unprecedently strong escort of five destroyers, two Coastguard cutters and four corvettes, and with significant air cover for much of the time, the U-boats managed to inflict very heavy damage. An inquiry held in Liverpool by the Admiralty had these comments to make:

The main lesson to be learnt from this experience is clear. That the ships in the escort were individually efficient is proved by the numbers of encounters that they had with the enemy and the amount of damage they inflicted. Had the escort been equally well trained as a group the encounter might well have been one of the highlights of the U-boat war. As it was, eight ships were torpedoed while in convoy, seven in a period of three hours. Even so, the price the U-boats had to pay in losses inflicted both by aircraft and surface ships was a heavy one. At least two U-boats were sunk and about six damaged.

The inability of the escorts to fend off the attacks on the convoy on the night of the 6th/7th was due to the fact that it was a scratch team. There were present at this time ten escorts, with two more in the vicinity; six of these were destroyers. A force of this size, drilled as a team, understanding the Senior Officer's ideas and intentions, should be ample to compete with a situation such as this. In this case, however, the ships had not worked together and were led by a Senior Officer whom they did not know. A further handicap was the fact that a proportion of the force joined after the main escort. There are various criticisms which can be made of the conduct of operations during this period, but the point is that the things which went wrong on this occasion are those which can always be expected to go wrong when escorts are made up of a miscellaneous collection of ships which have no previous experience of each other. . .

The battle for SC 118 was fought in the most atrocious weather conditions, with high winds, rough seas, and visibility often down to a few hundred yards in fierce sleet, hail and snow squalls. That the convoy held together at all when under attack was a remarkable achievement. But there can be no doubt that the U-boats were still on top. On the other hand, Grand Admiral Dönitz described SC 118 as 'perhaps the hardest convoy battle of the war'. Could the tide be turning against the U-boats?

Chapter Five

The Running Fight

U-223 arrived too late to take part in the attack on SC 118. Since sinking the *Dorchester*, she had been battling her way south against force 10 winds, snow storms and very rough seas and her progress was slow. On some days, it was all Wächter could do to hold her head to wind and sea with the diesels ticking over. Any attempt to force the boat through such weather would have been to court disaster. On a good day, *U-223* made fifty miles, but no more. The other *Nordstrum* boats were somewhere in the vicinity, also under orders to join up with the *Haudegen* pack, but they were all lost to each other in the welter of wind and sea.

The weather relented briefly on the 11th, by which time *U-223* had made her way to a position some 280 miles to the north-east of Newfoundland, but the temporary lull almost ended in the loss of the boat. The sheer relief of being able to stand watch in a conning tower not rolling wildly from side to side and free of the lash of icy spray may have induced a sense of euphoria in the look-outs that dulled their senses. The enemy destroyer was over the horizon and heading straight for them before the warning shout went up. Wächter, fortunately, had not dropped his guard, and crash-dived at once. He came back to periscope depth to see the destroyer still shouldering the waves aside and closing fast. He decided to seize the initiative with a snap torpedo shot, but as he lined the destroyer up in his sights, she opened fire, her shells pitching uncomfortably close. Realizing his periscope must have been seen, Wächter dived deep and waited for the crash of the depth charges that must follow. The expected assault did not materialize, and the beat of the enemy ship's propeller was clearly audible as she passed overhead at speed. When Wächter came back to the surface half an hour later, the destroyer was nowhere to be seen. It must have been that she had other more important fish to fry.

The wind was back up over gale force by daylight on the 12th, bringing with it an unpleasant mixture of rain, hail and snow, but *U-223* made fair progress, reaching the rendezvous position 220 miles east of Belle Isle by 1,600 on the 13th. Wächter stopped and lay hove to for the next twelve hours awaiting fresh orders. It was a sleepless night, with the boat fighting to hold her own against a south-westerly gale and thirty-feet seas. At 04.00 next morning, having seen nothing and heard nothing from BdU, Wächter decided to push on to the south on his own.

On the afternoon of the 15th, the weather remaining foul, the ocean dark and empty, Wächter was ready to believe that he had been abandoned to his own devices then, at 16.50, the radio burst into life. The orders from BdU were to proceed south-east to join up with three of the old *Nordstrum* pack, *U-186* (Siegfried Hesemann), *U-358* (Rolf Manke) and *U-707* (Günter Gretschel), to form another pack codenamed *Taifun*. They were to meet with other boats and mount an attack on a convoy reported west-bound across the Atlantic. The convoy in question was ONS 165, earlier sighted by *U-69* (Ulrich Gräf) which, with a number of other old *Haudegen* boats had been ordered to rendezvous with the U-tankers *U-460* and *U-462*, then on station 500 miles north of the Azores, to refuel. All the *Haudegen* boats in the area, those heading for the refuelling rendezvous and some others to the north-east of Newfoundland, were well placed for an attack on ONS 165, and they were ordered to move in at once. The scene was set for yet another triumph for the U-boats

On his way south to join the attack, on the 17th Karl Wächter fell foul of another patrolling enemy destroyer, which kept *U-223* submerged for several hours. Thereafter, the weather began to deteriorate rapidly, and by early morning on the 18th the boat was again hove to, this time in a force 10 southerly, with visibility down to 100 metres in torrential rain. Progress was minimal, and to add to Wächter's frustration, heavy atmospheric interference made radio communication impossible. Once again he was on his own. Having not seen the sun or stars for many days, the boat's position was uncertain, but Wächter pushed south whenever the weather allowed. But once more *U-223* was too late to join the *Haudegen* boats, and along with the rest of the *Taifun* pack, she was reduced to transmitting regular reports on the weather, which in view of the poor reception, may or may not have been received by BdU.

The bad weather worked in ONS 165's favour, the forty-feet seas, torrential rain and poor visibility providing a natural cover. Ulrich Gräf held on to the convoy for two days, sending in regular reports to guide the other U-boats in, but they were hampered by the poor radio reception and the inability to accurately fix their own positions, and any concerted attack on ONS 165 proved impossible. Only three other boats, *U-201* (Günther Rosenberg), *U-403* (Heinz-Ehlert Clausen) and *U-525* (Hans-Joachim Drewitz) were able to make contact with the convoy. Clausen sank the Greek steamer *Zeus*, while Drewitz found the 3,454-ton British ship *Radhurst* straggling astern and promptly dispatched her. However, this brief and relatively unproductive engagement had a high cost for the U-boats. Destroyers of ONS 165's escort sank both Gräf's *U-69* and Rosenberg's *U-201*.

While the attack on ONS 165 was in progress, the German Radio Intercept Service in Paris was busy taking long-range HF/DF bearings of radio traffic from aircraft believed to be escorting another westbound convoy. The bearings indicated that the convoy was 300 miles to the west of the North Channel, and on a westerly course. Later, the convoy altered to the south-west, and on 20 February the boats of the *Ritter*, *Knappen*, *Taifun*, and the newly formed *Neptun*, packs were ordered to take up positions in an extended north-south line along the meridian of 35° West. In all, a total of thirty-three U-boats were involved, backed up by the two U-tankers, *U-460* and *U-462*. The tankers, 1,700-ton Type XIVs, each carried 700 tons of diesel oil, sufficient to refuel up to twelve Type VIICs. They also carried fresh water, torpedoes, spare parts, a doctor, and a number of relief wireless operators and technicians. They had already supplied a number of the *Haudegen* pack boats, and much to the surprise of Paris, in view of the amount of radio traffic involved in the operations, they had not yet been discovered by the Allies.

The expected convoy, ON 166, a fast convoy of sixty-three ships bound for New York, had formed up off Belfast on the 12th, and sailed the same day. All but a few of the merchant ships, a mixture of British, American, Norwegian and Panama flags, were flying light in ballast, but they were, nevertheless, empty holds to be filled for the return passage across the Atlantic, and as such worthwhile targets for the U-boats. ON 166 was therefore well escorted by the American-led Escort Group A 3 under the command of Captain Paul R. Heineman USN. Heineman, in the Coastguard cutter *Spencer*, had with him a second cutter, USS *Campbell*, the Canadian corvettes *Chilliwack*, *Dauphin*, *Rosthern* and *Trillium*, and the British corvette *Dianthus*. Despite its multi-national make up, this was an experienced group, and commanded by an experienced Senior Officer, their work together having earned them the title 'Heineman's Harriers'. With A 3 was the rescue ship *Stockport*, a small steamer of 1,683 tons built in 1911 for the London & North-Eastern Railway Company, but well equipped for the job assigned to her. Also in the convoy were three part-loaded oil tankers capable of refuelling escorts at sea. The only thing A 3 lacked was a destroyer. Although the Coastguard cutters were larger and more heavily armed than the average British destroyer, they were 10 to 15 knots slower, and unable to produce the high-speed dash often needed to fend off U-boats.

Given fair weather, ON 166 would have been expected to cover the 3,000 miles to New York in twelve to thirteen days, but the weather was anything but fair. In fact, when the convoy, steaming two abreast, rounded Malin Head on the night of the 12th and entered the open Atlantic, the ships sailed into what was later described as the worst weather of the war. They were confronted by an ocean gone mad, with westerly winds blowing in excess of 50 knots and gigantic waves riding on the back of a long heaving swell that radiated outwards from a huge depression centred 1,000 miles out in the Atlantic. This was a time when not only first-trippers, but hardened seamen were throwing up as they fought to stay on their feet.

Forming up into steaming order for the ocean crossing was a hair-raising operation, with the slow, awkward merchantmen, harried by the tiny corvettes, drifting in all directions as they tried to manoeuvre in the teeth of the storm. Tempers frayed, and near-collisions abounded, but eventually Convoy ON 166 was in eleven columns abreast, and covering the sea as far as the eye could see. The barometer was plummeting, and there were few aboard the ships, merchant and naval, who were not aware that the voyage ahead, the attentions of the enemy apart, would be a test of endurance.

One week later, on 19 February, ON 166 was still only 600 miles to the west of Ireland, having fought constantly against a force 10 westerly, averaging a speed of around 4 knots, which is only a fast walking pace for a man. And there was, as yet, no sign of the weather letting up. Acting on information from the Admiralty, the convoy had altered onto a south-westerly course, a diversion that would add 700 miles to the passage, but with the wind and sea now on the bow, the ships were riding a little more easily. Nevertheless, the columns of the convoy were ragged, and a number of ships, unable to keep up, were strung out astern like a long tail. This presented a serious problem for Captain Heineman, who was obliged to send one of his corvettes back to watch over the stragglers.

The constant roar and crackle of atmospherics interfered seriously with radio communications, but it did not prevent the German Radio Intercept Service from taking bearings of the convoy, presumably on traffic between the S.O.E and the Admiralty, from which it was deduced that the convoy had made a diversion. Advised of this, BdU decided to extend its U-boat patrol line further to the south, but the weather was affecting friend and foe alike. It soon became obvious that the fourteen *Neptun* boats coming from the north would be too late to join in the interception.

The foul weather had also caused a temporary suspension of ON 166's air cover, but the British aircraft based in Northern Ireland were not standing idle on their runways. On the 19th, a Liberator of 172 Squadron, patrolling over the Bay of Biscay, surprised *U-268* on the surface and sank her. *U-268*, commanded by *Oberleutnant* Ernst Heydemann had been with the *Haudegen* pack in the attack on SC 118, but had failed to make her mark. After refuelling from one of the U-tankers off the Azores, she was ordered to return to St Nazaire, and was on her way back when the British Liberator put an end to her. She left no survivors.

Moving to the west-south-west at a pitifully slow pace, ON 166 had progressed to a position 880 miles from the Irish coast, less than a third of the way into its long ocean passage, by noon on the 20th. Nine ships were now straggling astern, labouring in the heavy seas, and adding to Heineman's worries. But the German net was still not yet fully in place, and the convoy might well have eluded the U-boats if it had not been for a chance sighting by *U-604*, under the command of *Kapitänleutnant* Horst Höltring. Only twelve days out of Brest, Höltring was on his way to join the *Knappen* pack when he sailed right into the untidy mess of ships that constituted Convoy ON 166. The U-boat was spotted by USS *Spencer*, and Höltring was forced to dive and beat a hasty retreat. He surfaced later, and tucking himself in behind the last of the stragglers, settled down to shadow the convoy. BdU was contacted, and the wolves began to gather.

News that a U-boat had been seen went round the convoy like wildfire, and for the first time the weather assumed secondary importance. Guns were manned, lifeboat readiness checked, and life jackets kept close at hand. When darkness came, the Commodore signalled two evasive alterations of course, one of 20 degrees and another of 28 degrees.

U-225, commanded by *Oberleutnant* Wolfgang Leimkühler, a lone wolf not attached to any of the packs in the vicinity, was first to sight the convoy, in mid-morning on the 21st. Sunday, 21 February, had opened much as any other day in the voyage, with a dark, overhanging sky and the wind howling out of the west, bearing rain and sleet on its wings. Unfortunately for Leimkühler and his crew, *Spencer* and two corvettes were sweeping astern of the convoy on the lookout for shadowers. *U-225* was spotted on the surface, and as she dived *Spencer* came racing in to smother the area with depth charges. A large oil patch appeared on the surface, dampening down the restless waves, but Paul Heineman did not have the satisfaction of confirming his kill. In fact it was a kill, U225 had gone to the bottom, taking Wolfgang Leimkühler and all his crew with her. But their sacrifice was not made in vain. Leimkühler's sighting report had been heard, and the pack was moving in.

U-332 (Eberhard Hüttermann) and *U-603* (Hans-Joachim Bertelsmann), two of the *Ritter* boats, were first to arrive. They came from the west while *Spencer* and the two corvettes were still nine miles astern and ploughing through heavy seas as they fought to regain station on the convoy. With only the cutter *Campbell*, commanded by Captain T.L. Lewis, USCG, and three corvettes covering sixty-three merchant ships, the two U-boats were able to slip through the screen with comparative ease. Hüttermann lined up on the leading ship of the port column, the Norwegian motor tanker *Stigstad*, a substantial target of 6,000 tons. One torpedo was sufficient to bring the tanker to a halt then, six minutes later, Bertelsmann unleashed another two torpedoes on the same target. The *Stigstad*, her back broken, sank fifteen minutes later. The battle had commenced with the score even.

A lull followed, during which the *Stockport* dropped astern to pull a few half-drowned survivors from the sea, all that was left of the *Stigstad*'s crew. The missing escorts rejoined, Captain Lewis handed the convoy back to Paul Heineman, and peace reigned again. There were some of the opinion that the sinking of the Norwegian tanker had been no more than an opportunistic act by a passing U-boat. They would soon be proved wrong.

The fight started in earnest an hour after darkness had fallen, when at 19.35 the first of the *Knappen* boats made its rendezvous with ON 166. Adolf Oelrich, in *U-92*, on his second war patrol and still with only one Allied ship to his credit, was eager to improve his score. He pounced on the 10,000-ton *Empire Trader* when he found her straggling behind the convoy. She was so obviously old and tired that Oelrich used only one torpedo on her. He had miscalculated, the thirty-five-year-old British ship was a product of an age when ships were built to outlast their owners, and she stayed afloat. She was low in the water, but her engines still functioned, and Heineman decided to send her to the Azores for repairs. The Canadian corvette *Dauphin* was detailed to accompany her which, under the circumstances prevailing – it being quite obvious that ON 166 was the target of a number of U-boats – seems like a grave mistake, for it left an already meagre escort force even weaker. As it was, the attempt to get the *Empire Trader* into port turned out to be a wasted gesture. Long before she reached the safety of the Azores, the Admiralty intervened, ordering the *Dauphin* to take off the damaged merchantman's crew and sink her by gunfire.

When the flurry of starshell that followed the torpedoing of the

Empire Trader had subsided, relative peace returned to the convoy once again. In the face of the angry response of Heineman's Harriers, Oelrich withdrew, but he was back again soon after midnight. This time he penetrated deep into the convoy to fire a fan of three torpedoes at the 9,348-ton Norwegian whale factory ship NT *Nielson Alonso*. Two of the three torpedoes found their mark, but again, much to Adolf Oelrich's disgust, the ship did not sink. She was still afloat two and a half hours later when one of the *Ritter* boats, *U-753*, under the command of *Korvettenkapitän* Alfred Manhardt von Mannstein, moved in to finish her off. Mannstein left the *Nielson Alonso* with her decks awash, but she was another stubborn old ship, and refused to die until she was dispatched by one of the escorts next day.

The remainder of the night passed without further incident, and when the dawn came on the 22nd it brought with it a welcome improvement in the weather. The wind backed to the south-west and eased to a moderate force 4; the seas were still rough, and the swell big and menacing, but for the first time since leaving home waters the cloud was lifting and breaking up. The air of gloom that had settled over the convoy lifted with the cloud, and when the Polish destroyer *Burza* joined later in the day and news came that *Dauphin* was returning after disposing of the *Empire Trader*, morale began to climb.

The euphoria did not last the day. Although the wind had dropped considerably, the evening brought with it a thick, clinging drizzle that wrapped its cold, miserable blanket around the bridge watchkeepers and lookouts. Now, with visibility limited to less than a ship's length, station-keeping became a nightmare. The merchantmen being without radar, were sailing blind. As far as the U-boats were concerned, the drizzle was an unexpected blessing, a cloak under which they could shelter while they made their stealthy approach to the convoy. Hans Bertelsmann in *U-603*, Hans Döhler in *U-606* and Heinrich Hasenschar in *U-628* were were in position before darkness fell. They were soon joined by Adolf Oelrich in *U-92*, Siegfried Hesemann in *U-186*, Rolf Manke in *U-358* and Alfred Manhardt von Manstein in *U-753*.

Hans Döhler was the first to move in to attack. At 19.20, he scored a hat trick with three torpedoes fired simultaneously, hitting the 6,615-ton British steamer *Empire Redshank*, the US-flag *Chatanooga City* of 5,687 tons and another American, the 4,959-ton *Expositor*. The *Chatanooga City* went down in nine minutes and both the *Empire Redshank* and the *Expositor* were badly damaged and abandoned. Döhler's audacious attack brought a prompt response from the ON 166's escorts. He was immediately set upon by USS *Campbell*, quickly supported by the destroyer *Burza* and the corvette *Chilliwack*. Döhler was in such a hurry to dive that U-606's conning tower was not properly sealed, and as she went down water poured into the boat. She sank like a stone, until Döhler managed to hold her at 230 metres, very near to maximum depth. In desperation, for the boat's crew thought their last moment had come, every cubic metre of compressed air remaining on board was pumped into the main ballast tanks. The reaction was predicable, *U-606* shooting to the surface like a rocket.

Campbell was closest when the U-boat broke the surface with a rush. Captain Lewis immediately opened fire with all guns able to bear and charged in at full speed to ram. The collision rolled the U-boat over on her side, but she came upright again, her crew spilling out of the conning tower onto the casing. Her scuttling charges exploded, and she sank seconds later taking Hans Döhler and 37 of his men with her. Twelve others were taken prisoner by USS *Campbell*.

While Lewis' action in ramming *U-606* was perfectly acceptable, an action most escort commanders would have taken under the same circumstances, it turned out to be a major disaster for ON 166. *Campbell*, her bow reduced to a tangled mess of torn plates, was forced to withdraw from the convoy and call for a tug. She was later towed into St John's and was out of the Atlantic battle for some months.

Hans Döhler's attack, which cost ON 166 the loss of two ships – the *Empire Redshank* was sunk later that night by HMS *Trillium* – and left another drifting astern abandoned, resulted in the convoy being bathed in the light of starshell and flares visible far out over the horizon, and was seen by *U-223*'s lookouts. Hurrying south with the newly-formed *Taifun* pack Karl-Jurgen Wächter had passed ahead of the convoy during the day, and was then steering north-east on a bearing given by *U-628*. When, at

19.45, Wächter saw the gunflashes reflecting on the clouds, he knew he was near to his goal. He adjusted course and raced on through the night. His War Diary takes up the story:

22.2.43	
2245	Shell bursts bearing 060 degrees. Far off.
	On two engines and steering 060 degrees
23.2.43	
0000 BD4654	I must be careful to avoid the escorts. It is a dark night with light drizzle.
	Keeping sharp lookout between 000 and 180 degrees.
0030	Dived to listen. Hydrophone effect between 040 and 050 degrees.
0048	Surfaced. Course 040 degrees
0145	Dived to listen. Ship hydrophone effect from 310 to 350 degrees
0150	Surfaced and going ahead.
0215	Now on westerly course. Keeping sharp lookout.
0220	German U-boat sighted on course 300 degrees.
0246	Destroyer bearing 290 degrees. Quite close. The bridge is very damp with drizzle. Often have to make do with one pair of binoculars while the rest are being cleaned.
0255	Searching the horizon from 240 to 270 degrees.
0400 BD4642	
0455	Escort in sight.
0508	Convoy in BD4641. I am now astern of one of the escorts.
540	Convoy in BD4566 bearing 230 degrees 8 miles ahead.

0659	Flames from burning tanker light up the sky (May be hit by Hasenschar). Wild firing from convoy. The whole of the horizon ahead is lit up.
	Without binoculars I would not have seen them.
	I am close to the last column and manoeuvring to shoot.
	Target is tanker of 6000 BRT. All accommodation aft.
	She seems fully loaded.
	There is a damaged tanker with her afterpart missing in the same area.
	The tanker has seen me and opens fire with her gun while running in circles. Her aim is good. She runs away from me.
0750	A destroyer comes to the aid of the tanker. I put myself between the 'tanker and the escort. When it gets light enough I will attack.
0800 BD4559	
0928	Dived for underwater attack. Fired tubes 1,3 and 4 at tanker.
	The destroyer has moved away to about 1000 metres off.
	Three hits on tanker after 28 seconds (400 metres). First under bridge, second in after part, third forward of mast. Three plumes of flame and smoke.
	After the first hit the ship – she is 125-130 metres long – heels over to port and sinks stern first.

The recipient of Wächter's torpedoes was the 6,907-ton Panama-flag tanker *Winkler*, which had previously been damaged by Heinrich Hasenschar's *U-628*. The *Winkler*, commanded by Captain Arthur Gasso, was on charter to the US War Shipping

Administration, and en route from Avonmouth to New York. Her story is told in a report written by the commander of her Armed Guard detachment:

The *Winkler* left Belfast on February 11th. Extremely rough weather was encountered and on the 19th of February the convoy was only 600 miles from Ireland. On February 22nd at 2130 ship's time, one of the 4 diesel engines broke down causing the speed to be reduced to 8 knots while repairs were made. This caused the ship to fall astern of its original position (No.63). At 0410 on February 23rd she had become the last ship in the convoy. At this time a torpedo hit the ship on its port side between No.2 and No.3 tanks. This torpedo was fired by the *U-628* (Heinrich Hasenschar) in position 46-48 N 36-18 W. The ship was only damaged.

A survey showed the ship to be in good condition except for a slight list to port. At 0445, a sub surfaced about 500 yards directly ahead. The forward gun crew fired 5 shells at the conning tower scoring one possible hit, as an explosion was seen. The sub crash dived at once.

At this time, survivors in lifeboats from another ship (s.s. *Glittre*, a Norwegian tanker torpedoed by *U-628*) signalled with a light to pick them up. The Master decided to pick them up and spent about 2 hours maneuvering to rescue them. About 0630, a corvette, HMS *Dianthus*, came upon the scene and ordered the Master to rejoin the convoy and to zigzag. The *Dianthus* followed the *Winkler* after pick-up of the survivors in the boats.

At 0710 on February 23rd, with the gun crew still at battle stations and the crew at general quarters, two torpedoes struck the ship on the port quarter, blowing out the bottom of the ship and causing her to sink within 45 seconds. The ship was not zigzagging at the time of this attack. These torpedoes were fired by *U-223*.

It was impossible to launch any boats. Therefore all hands jumped overboard and clung to a raft which had been let go. The *U-223* dove under the survivors so the *Dianthus* was unable to drop any depth charges.

The *Dianthus* picked up all the survivors at 0755 and headed for St John's, Newfoundland, arriving there about 0800 on February 26th. All survivors were taken to Argentia on February 28 where they boarded the ss *Pontiac* for Boston.

The ship's complement was made up of 33 merchant crew and 18 US Navy Armed Guard. Of this number, 14 crew members and

5 Navy gunners were lost. Three of the crew members were Americans.

In stopping to pick up survivors, the commander of HMS *Dianthus* was disobeying the S.O.E's orders and giving the U-boats the advantage of one less escort to worry them. But the *Winkler*'s survivors could not have lasted long in the water in the conditions prevailing, and it was the humanitarian thing to do. The convoy's rescue ship, the *Stockport*, should have been there, but she was missing. It was only some time later that Captain Heineman discovered she had fallen victim to a U-boat. While astern picking up survivors from the *Empire Trader*, the *Stockport* had been torpedoed by Horst Höltring in *U-604*, first boat to sight ON 166. The loss of life in the rescue ship was very heavy. In addition to her crew of sixty-four, she had ninety-one survivors on board. All 155 men went down with the little ex-railway steamer.

Already hard-pressed to defend his convoy Captain Heineman now suffered another blow, when *Dianthus* signalled that she was running dangerously low on fuel. In view of the high swell still running, refueling while under way from one of the remaining tankers was out of the question. There was no other alternative but for *Dianthus* to make a dash for St John's, 650 miles to the west. This proved to be more of a gamble than anticipated. So low were the corvette's tanks that she ended up using every available drop of burnable oil on board, including the gun oil, engine lubricating oil, linseed oil from the paint stores, and 120 gallons of Admiralty compound. Her safe arrival in St John's was a very near run thing.

The departure of both *Campbell* and *Dianthus* left Heineman's Harriers seriously depleted. Without a rescue ship to help out, and more and more U-boats joining the ring around the convoy the consequences were predictable. In the next forty-eight hours ON 166 lost another seven ships. The last to go was the 7,264-ton British steamer *Manchester Merchant*. The report written by her master, Captain F.D. Struss, makes grim reading.

At 0500 0n 25 February, when in estimated position 45°10' N 43°23' W, steering a course of 255° at a speed of 10 knots, my ship

71

was struck by two torpedoes. There was a moderate sea and a SE wind force 3. The weather was fine and clear, and visibility good. It was just moonlight. A previous torpedo had been fired which missed the ship and passed under her bow.

The torpedoes struck practically simultaneously abreast of the foremast on the starboard side with a loud explosion, and two huge columns of water were thrown up. I did not see any flash or flame. The rush of water carried away one raft, but none of the lifeboats was damaged.

I was sitting on the after part of the bridge at the time, wearing my lifebelt, and on hearing the explosion, looked over the forepart of the bridge and saw water pouring over the forecastle head. The ship was settling rapidly by the head, and as she was obviously doomed I ordered 'Abandon Ship! Every man for himself'. The three lifeboats were lowered, but they capsized, as the ship was still under weigh. Some of the crew managed to get three rafts away; I managed to knock one clear, but before I could abandon ship on it I was washed off the bridge deck into the sea by the force of water rushing over the ship. I was pulled under by the suction, but rose to the surface quickly, just in time to see the ship slide under the water. She sank by the head, with the propellers still turning slowly, about 90 seconds after being hit. One SSS message was transmitted before the ship sank, and I understand this was received. We were not able to fire away any rockets, as they became wet when the column of water flooded the ship, and were useless. Although the boat's wireless was kept in the wireless room ready to be placed in the lifeboat, there was no time to get this away.

From my position in the water, I saw some men had climbed onto the rafts and upturned lifeboats, but a number of survivors were in the water, wearing their lifebelts. I found my lifejacket extremely uncomfortable. In my opinion the lifejackets are too short, and owing to the disposition of the kapok filling the centre of buoyancy, when afloat, is too low, and apt to capsize the wearer, bringing the feet up, and forcing the head down. I found it impossible to swim in my lifejacket, and I could not get to the rafts, so I stayed in the water without struggling, so as to reserve all my energy. My red lifejacket light would not work. I found two small pieces of wood, which I placed under each arm; these gave me some added buoyancy, and I was much more comfortable. I could hear men screaming and shouting all around me, and lots of small lifebelt lights bobbing about on the swell, but the situation was such that nobody could help anybody else.

After about half an hour, the destroyer HMS *Montgomery* came along and rescued fifteen men who were on a raft, but went away leaving the remainder of the survivors in the water. I suppose she had some reason for going away, but when the men in the water saw the destroyer going, their cries were terrible, and from the splashing in the water I imagine they must have tried to follow. It was then I think that most of my crew in the water were drowned, for after the destroyer had gone I could only hear moans for a while, and then silence.

Two hours later, just as dawn was breaking, the Canadian corvette *Rosthern* came to pick up the men still in the water. I heard her Commanding Officer shout 'Take the men out of the water first', then I saw a small boat approaching. I was pulled out of the water into the boat, then a sailor, Sorensen, and a fireman named Ince, who unfortunately died of exposure before we reached the corvette. Thirteen other men were picked up from upturned boats, and from rafts. I had by this time been in the water about 2½ hours, the temperature of which was 47°, and my body was completely numb when I was rescued. We were given every attention on the corvette, and soon recovered from our ordeal. The *Rosthern* took us to St John's, Newfoundland, where we arrived on Saturday 27th February. . .

In the running fight, which covered over 1,000 miles, and lasted from 21 to 25 February, ON 166 lost fourteen ships totalling 88,000 tons, while Heineman's Harriers sank two U-boats, one of these at the cost of one of the major escort ships so badly damaged that she had to withdraw from the fight. And all this went on while less than 100 miles to the south, other U-boats were queuing up to refuel from *U-460* and *U-462* so that they might join in the slaughter. The German High Command commented: 'It remains a mystery why this activity was not interrupted by the enemy, who must have known of it through the heavy but unavoidable radio traffic that it involved.'

Chapter Six

The Climax

In March 1943, the North Atlantic weather reached its equinoctial climax, each violent storm following so hard on the heels of the other that they appeared to merge into an ocean-wide anarchy of screaming wind and raging sea. Driving rain, sleet and snow, changing quickly to dense fog if the wind momentarily eased its fury, all too often marred the visibility and hid the frightening menace of icebergs drifting south in the spring thaw. And in this same month nature's turmoil was to be matched by the shuddering crescendo of the Battle of the Atlantic.

February had been a bad month for the Allies in the Atlantic, with a total of sixty-three ships being lost at a time when the build-up of supplies in Britain for the impending invasion of Europe was under way. More guns, tanks, ammunition, oil and food must continue to cross the Atlantic from the Americas if the landings on the Normandy beaches, now in the advanced planning stage, were to take place.

In answer to what was now becoming an insatiable demand, in the first week of March there was a total of no less than 250 Allied merchant ships at sea in the Atlantic at the same time. They were all deep-loaded and heading east in five separate convoys like flocks of heavily pregnant ducks majestically breasting the waves as they sailed determinedly towards their various destinations on the other side of the ocean. This was a dream of plenty come true for Grand Admiral Dönitz, an unparalleled opportunity to make history on the convoy routes and, possibly, to alter the course of the war in the favour of Germany. He had ninety U-boats at sea in the Atlantic, and he called on every one to go into battle.

The first of the convoys, SC 121, had sailed from New York

on 23 February, sixty-one ships in all, and once again it fell to Captain Paul Heineman to lead the ocean escort. Heineman, still in the Coastguard cutter *Spencer*, had with him on this assignment the destroyer USS *Greer* and four corvettes, two British and two Canadian. This was not an over-large force with which to defend sixty-one ships, but Heineman was a very experienced escort commander, and the bad weather was in his favour. On the other hand, three of his escort force had their radars out of action, and three had defective Asdics. Against this somewhat weakened opposition BdU had called in two wolf packs, *Westmark* and *Ostmark*, totalling between them thirty-one boats.

Sailing in fourteen columns abreast, presenting a front seven miles across, SC 121 ran into a force 10 as soon as it cleared the southern tip of Newfoundland. As usual, the storm was accompanied by rain, hail and snow which reduced the visibility down to a matter of yards at times. Heineman and the convoy commodore, Captain Burnie, RNR, in the Norwegian ship *Bonneville*, did their utmost to hold the convoy together but the ships were for the most part old tramps some of whom should not really have been at sea in such weather. Before many hours had elapsed there were ships straggling astern, some romping ahead, and others, barely able to steer in the grip of the powerful following seas, just went their own way.

The *Westmark* and *Ostmark* boats, labouring in the same tremendous seas, made their first contact with SC 121 on the afternoon of 6 March, when the convoy was 450 miles south of Cape Farewell. They moved in carefully to test the defences.

At some time before midnight, those on the bridge of USS *Spencer* saw red rockets soar skywards from the port side of the convoy. No distress signal was heard on 500 K/cs and no ship was reported missing by the Commodore or the other escorts. Conditions were so bad that a search was out of the question, and it was assumed that some ship or other had fired the rockets accidentally. But out there in the wild darkness of the night, the small Liverpool steamer *Egyptian*, torpedoed by Paul Siegemann in *U-230*, had gone down unseen and unmissed.

By some extraordinary feat of seamanship, the *Egyptian*'s crew had managed to get away in their lifeboats, and were sighted around dawn next day by another British ship, the *Empire Impala* which was weathering the storm well astern of the convoy. Strictly against convoy procedure, but in accordance with the unwritten rule of the sea, the *Empire Impala* stopped to pick up the *Egyptian*'s survivors, and in doing so she became a sitting target for Hans-Jurgen Zetzsche, who was coming up astern in *U-591*. Zetzsche used one torpedo to send the *Empire Impala* to the bottom, leaving her crew to join the *Egyptian*'s men in their fight for survival.

Being widely scattered and mostly out of sight and out of touch with their escort, the storm-bound ships of SC 121 were easy prey for the U-boats. The next to go was the 3,921-ton Hull-registered steamer *Guido*, sunk while romping ten miles off the starboard bow of the convoy by *U-633* (Bernhard Müller). She was followed by another British ship, the *Fort Lamy*, torpedoed while she was straggling astern by Herbert Uhlig in *U-527*. The *Fort Lamy* had a 143-ton landing craft on deck, which she took down with her when she sank. Later that day, three more stragglers fell victim to the U-boats, the Yugoslav-flag *Vojvoda Putnik*, another addition to Hans-Jurgen Zetzsche's score, and the British steamers *Empire Lakeland* and *Leadgate*, sunk by Max Wintermeyer in *U-190* and Herbert Brünning in *U-642* respectively.

There was an enforced lull in the fight lasting some twenty-two hours, during which the weather was so bad that even the U-boats were more concerned for their own survival than attacking the enemy. It was during this lull that SC 121's escort was reinforced by the arrival of two more Coastguard cutters and an American destroyer from Iceland. But this did nothing to blunt the U-boats' attack. They returned on the night of the 9th with a slight easing in the weather. Within the space of four hours they had sunk another five ships, the Swedish-flag *Milos*, the American steamer *Malantic*, the British ships *Rosewood* and *Nailsea Court*, and lastly, the Commodore's ship *Bonneville*. The latter also carried a tank landing craft on deck, and was lost with all hands, including the Commodore, Captain Burnie.

In the face of atrocious weather conditions, the *Westmark* and *Ostmark* boats had made a devastating attack on SC 121, sinking a total of twelve ships, who took down with them over 100,000 tons of cargo vital to the Allied cause. The loss of life among the men manning those ships was also heavy, for most of those who survived the enemy torpedoes died of exposure in the stormy sea. No U-boats were lost.

Convoy HX 228 left New York three days after SC 121. Made up of sixty merchantmen, HX 228 was under escort by the British Escort group B 3, commanded by Commander A.A. Tait in the destroyer *Harvester*. With *Harvester* was a second British destroyer, HMS *Escapade*, the Polish destroyers *Burza* and *Garland*, the British corvettes *Narcissus* and *Orchis*, and the Free French corvettes *Aconit*, *Renoncule* and *Roselys*. Also in attendance on HX 228, but acting independently, was the US Navy escort carrier *Bogue* with her two destroyers *Belknap* and *Osmond-Ingram*. Unlike its predecessor, this convoy was under heavy protection.

When the attack opened on SC 121, on the 6th, HX 228 was ordered to make a bold alteration of course to the south to avoid the concentration of U-boats, which had by then been detected by HF/DF. Unfortunately, and unknown to the Admiralty, their diversionary signal to HX 228 had been intercepted and decrypted by *B-Dienst*. A new pack, code named *Neuland*, was formed, made up of twenty-two boats, some of which had been in action against SC 121. The deployment of *Neuland* was almost too late and HX 228, which was 700 miles north of the Azores on the 10th, might well have slipped through the U-boats' net, had not the southernmost boat, Hans Hunger's *U-336* been to the south of her allotted station.

The weather was working in Hunger's favour, for it was too bad for the *Bogue* to fly off her aircraft, and he was free to shadow the convoy without fear of detection from the air. Hunger called in the other *Neuland* boats, the attack starting at dusk on the 10th with *U-221* (Hans Trojer) sinking the 5,412-ton Glasgow ship *Tucurina*. Five minutes later, Trojer fired a second fan of torpedoes, one of which sank the American steamer *Andrea Luckenbach*.

During the night of 10–11th, the *Neuland* boats, although attacking with determination, were not over-successful. *U-444* (Albert Langfeld) damaged the US Liberty ship *William C. Gorgas*, and *U-406* (Horst Dietrichs) hit, but failed to sink the

British fruit carrier *Jamaica Producer*. Although six men died in her engine-room, the rest of the crew of the Mobile-registered *William C. Gorgas* had a miraculous escape. Luckily for them, Langfeld's torpedo struck in the after part of the ship, for in her forward holds was stowed 900 tons of TNT. Had this gone up the ship and crew would have been vaporized. As it was, fifty-one survivors abandoned ship and were picked up by HMS *Harvester*.

Over the next two hours, try as they may, the U-boats failed to penetrate the escort screen. Then, half an hour after midnight, Friedrich Deetz in *U-757* slipped through and torpedoed the 5,000-ton Norwegian *Brant County* at close range. Deetz suffered for his audacity. The *Brant County* was loaded with ammunition, and the explosion that followed not only blew the Norwegian ship to pieces, but also severely damaged *U-757*. Deetz retired from the fight, but an hour later came across the abandoned wreck of the *William C. Gorgas*, which he promptly dispatched before setting course for home. *U-757* did not return to sea again for another four months.

The closing episode of the HX 228 action came in the small hours of 11 March, when HMS *Harvester* picked up a surfaced U-boat on her radar. Commander Tait immediately ran down the bearing, sighted *U-444*, and went in to ram. *Oberleutnant* Langfeld reacted equally quickly, diving before the destroyer reached him, but Tait depth-charged him to the surface again, and this time successfully rammed the U-boat, running right over her. This proved to be a mistake, for *Harvester*'s propellers were damaged, and she was reduced to crawling along on one engine at slow speed.

U-444 was still afloat, but the arrival on the scene of the Free French corvette *Aconit* sealed her fate. The stoutly-built little escort rammed the U-boat again, and this time she went down for good. Tait then ordered *Aconit* to return to the convoy, leaving *Harvester* to limp along astern. Unfortunately, during the course of the morning the destroyer lost her second engine, and was left drifting helplessly and unprotected. She was not alone for long, being found by Hermann Eckhardt in *U-432*. Eckhardt could not have wished for an easier target. Taking careful aim, he put two torpedoes into the *Harvester* which tore her apart. Commander Tait went down with his ship, as did seven of his officers, 136 ratings and thirty-nine survivors from the *William C. Gorgas*, who hours earlier had been so grateful for their rescue by the British destroyer.

There was swift retribution for *U-432*. *Aconit*, still striving to rejoin the convoy, had seen the column of flame and smoke shooting up from the *Harvester* when she was torpedoed and came racing back to investigate. Eckhardt was by this time attempting to creep away at periscope depth, but *Aconit*'s Asdic found her, and she was depth-charged to the surface. The corvette opened fire with her 4-inch at 7,000 yards, and eventually rammed and sank *U-432*. Later, *Aconit* rejoined the convoy, having on board sixty survivors from HMS *Harvester*, which included twelve from the *William C. Gorgas*, twenty survivors from *U-432* and four from *U-444*.

HX 228 suffered one other casualty, and that from causes unknown. Rolling in thirty-feet waves, the American steamer *Henry Wynkoop* hit a submerged object, and was thrown hard over to starboard. The ship righted herself, but as she slowed down to check for damage, thirty-three of her crew assumed the ship was about to be abandoned, and took to the boats. The *Henry Wynkoop*, now dangerously short-handed, got under way again and recovered eight of her men from one boat, but was obliged to leave the rest to their own devices. Of these, the corvette *Narcissus* picked up another sixteen and the British steamer *Stuart Prince* rescued five more. The search for the missing ten was taken up by HMS *Orchis*, and one more man was found alive in the rough seas. This left three men missing, and they were never found. It was a sad end to an incident that could have been avoided had the discipline of the ship held, but then these were tense days, and nerves were stretched like bow strings. As to what had been lurking below the waves when the *Henry Wynkoop* crashed down on it, no one will ever know. It might have been the wreck of one of the torpedoed ships floating just below the surface or, perhaps, could she have collided with a submerged U-boat – one of the *Neuland* pack that took one risk too many?

The weather improved sufficiently on the 12th for the *Bogue* to fly off her aircraft, and on the same day long-range Liberators of Coastal Command arrived overhead. There was no more opportunity for the boats of the *Neuland* pack to increase their score, and they were called off next day. Their action against HX 228 could hardly be defined as a brilliant success; only four out of the sixty merchant ships had been sunk, plus one destroyer. In return, two U-boats, *U-444* and *U-432*, had been lost, and two others, *U-221* and U757, sufficiently damaged to put them out of the war for a considerable time.

While SC 121 and HX 228 were under attack, three more convoys in the transatlantic supply chain had sailed from New York. SC 122, with fifty ships accompanied by four Canadian corvettes left on 5 March, and within twenty-four hours ran into a storm of gigantic proportions. By dawn on the 7th, the convoy was in complete disarray, the merchant ships scattered all around the horizon, and the tiny corvettes, beaten by the ferocity of the sea, unable to round them up. Several ships returned to port with heavy weather damage, and one, the 5,754-ton British steamer *Clarissa Radcliffe*, went missing, never to be seen again.

In spite of the weather, the remainder of SC 122's ships held together, and managed to maintain an average speed of 6 knots, meeting up with their ocean escort south of Newfoundland on the 12th. Escort Group B 5 was under the command of Commander R.C. Boyle in the destroyer HMS *Havelock*, and with her were the frigate HMS *Swale*, the British corvettes *Buttercup*, *Lavender*, *Pimpernel* and *Saxifrage*, the Belgium corvette *Godetia*, the US Navy destroyer *Upshur*, and the anti submarine trawler HMS *Campobello*. The 545-ton, coal-burning *Campobello*, newly built in a Canadian shipyard, was on her way to Britain to take up duties in coastal waters. She was not designed for deep-sea work, and those who sent her out into the North Atlantic at the equinox must have been possessed by some kind of madness. And last, but by no means least, strategically placed at the rear of SC 122, was the rescue ship *Zamalek*.

HX 229, a forty-ship fast convoy, sailed from New York three days after SC 122, and met up with its ocean escort on the 14th. Escort Group B 4 was very much a makeshift group, cobbled together at short notice. It consisted of four First World War vintage British destroyers, *Beverley*, *Mansfield*, *Volunteer* and *Witherington*, the two last named being ex-US Navy 'four-stackers' notorious for their poor sea-keeping qualities, and the

Flower-class corvettes *Anemone* and *Pennywort*. The Senior Officer Escort, brought in at short notice to command the group, was Lieutenant Commander G.J. Luther, RN, who sailed in HMS *Volunteer*.

A day after HX 229 sailed, on 9 March, a supplementary convoy, HX 229A, also left New York, thereby clearing up the backlog of loaded ships. This convoy was made up of thirty-seven fast cargo liners and tankers, escorted by another British group, Escort Group 40, under the command of Commander J.S. Dalison, RN, in the sloop *Aberdeen*, with three other sloops, *Hastings*, *Landguard* and *Lulworth*, and the frigates *Mayola* and *Waveney*. In the hope of avoiding the attentions of the U-boats, HX 229A was routed far to the north, within 200 miles of the Arctic Circle. There was a great deal of ice around in that area at the time of the year, and the voyage would be cold and uncomfortable for the men involved, but if they meant a safe passage, then these were small considerations.

At this time, the German intelligence organisation, *B-Dienst*, was reading the Allied naval codes without difficulty, and within hours of the sailing of HX 229, had full details of the convoy through signals sent to the Admiralty by the convoy commodore, Commodore M.J.D. Mayall, RNR, in the Norwegian ship *Abraham Lincoln*. Mayall's coded messages contained the convoy's sailing time, number of ships, the names of the escorts and the intended route, all of which were immediately passed to Berlin. Hard on the heels of this priceless intelligence followed similar information on SC 122. BdU quickly gathered together three wolf packs, code named *Dränger*, *Raubgraf* and *Stürmer*, a total of forty-four boats, and ordered them to lay an ambush for this vast armada of enemy shipping crossing the Atlantic from west to east.

The element of surprise was not to be all in favour of the U-boats, however. British Intelligence was playing the Germans at their own devious game, and BdU's signals to the U-boats were being read by Ultra, and passed to the Admiralty Submarine Tracking Room on the banks of the River Mersey. Plans were laid to frustrate the U-boats.

It had been proposed that the faster HX 229 would not overtake SC 122 until both convoys were within 200 miles of the west coast of Ireland, and under the protection of destroyers of Western Approaches Command and round-the-clock air cover. But, as so often happens at sea, where so many differing elements are at work, careful planning has a habit of coming to naught. Twenty-four hours out from the Nantucket Light, SC 122 was overtaken by a tremendous storm, with westerly winds of force 9 to 10 and seas reported to be 'very high to precipitous'. This was not unusual for the North Atlantic, but running before the wind and sea the ships were in constant danger of being pooped or broaching to, either of which could have had disastrous consequences. Progress was slow. Sailing in the wake of the storm, HX 229 was making good time. By 14 March, when SC 122 was 600 miles to the east of Newfoundland, HX 229 was only 300 miles behind, and closing the gap steadily. Both convoys were by then in comparatively good weather, but this was not to last. Next day, another deep low pressure system came sweeping up from Cape Hatteras to envelop both convoys in a tumult of wind and waves, rain and sleet.

For an observer able to look down from 10,000 feet, the scene below would have been an impressive sight; the ocean covered by eighty-nine merchantmen of diverse shapes, sizes and flags. They ranged from the great 12,156-ton whale factory ship *Southern Princess*, one of Christian Salvesen's a long way from her Antarctic cruising grounds, to the tiny Icelandic-flag *Selfoss*, 745 tons gross and out of her depth in more ways than one in the broad Atlantic. They were a motley bunch, with the smart Dutch East Indies cargo liner *Terkoelei* sailing beam to beam with the down-at-heel Greek tramp *Carras*, which had passed through half a dozen owners and flags since her launch twenty-five years earlier. In and around this half-disciplined multi-national fleet roamed a total of fifteen escort vessels, mainly British, the diminutive Flower-class corvettes, who were in the majority, spewing green water from their scuppers as they tried to roll their masts out. Limping along in the rear was the even smaller armed trawler *Campobello*, now looking suspiciously low in the water.

On the 15th, the Admiralty, unhappy with so many vulnerable ships at sea in mid-Atlantic without the benefit of air cover, signalled instructions to the convoys for a series of alterations of course to confuse any potential attackers. But the Admirals might just as well have saved their counsel. With a force 10 north-westerly howling in the rigging, for the majority of the ships in SC 122/HX 229 any radical change of course would prove to be difficult, if not downright dangerous. Two of their number, not built to withstand this extreme weather, were already in dire straits. Early on the 16th, the battered little *Selfoss* signalled the Commodore that she could take no more, and quietly dropped out of the ranks. She would carry on alone at her own pace. The *Campobello*, with a serious leak in her coal bunkers, fell further and further astern, eventually heaving to with her main deck awash. Her crew were taken off by HMS *Godetia*, which then put an end to the trawler's short career with depth charges dropped close alongside. Ironically, the *Selfoss*, steamed alone through 1,000 miles of U-boat infested waters without being molested, and arrived safely in Reykjavik six days later.

Advised of the flood of radio traffic emanating from the convoys, BdU signalled the waiting U-boats to close in, to find the enemy ships and attack. Only 150 miles now separated SC 122 and HX 229, and although they would never actually merge to become one huge convoy – a myth peddled by some historians – they would from now on be only just over the horizon from each other in terms of a 17-knot U-boat. The tail-enders of HX 229 were discovered by chance at 04.00 on the 16th, when *U-653* came across them as she was on her way to rendezvous with one of the U-tankers. Her commander, Gerhard Feiler, decided to put off refuelling for a while, and tagged on behind the convoy, reporting his find with a *Kurzsignale* to BdU. Within a few minutes, the general call went out:

ALL U-BOATS PROCEED WITH MAXIMUM SPEED TOWARD CONVOY GRID SQUARE BD 14. OVER SIXTY SHIPS COURSE NORTHEAST NINE KNOTS.

That night, as if to set the scene for the drama about to be enacted, the weather suddenly relented. The wind dropped, the seas lost their fury, the grey clouds rolled back, and all was bathed in bright moonlight. For the convoy escorts this was the beginning of a nightmare they had hoped would never happen; for the U-boats it was an opportunity not to be missed.

The first to arrive in response to *U-653*'s signal was Hans-Joachim Bertelsmann in one of the *Raubgraf* boats, *U-603*. At 21.00, Bertelsmann approached HX 229 and fired a spread of four torpedoes, one of which hit the 5,214-ton Norwegian ship *Elin K*, under the command of Captain Robert Johannessen. The *Elin K*, carrying a cargo of 7,000 tons of wheat, a quantity of manganese ore and 339 bags of mail, sank quickly, but not before her crew took to the lifeboats. They were promptly picked up by the corvette *Pennywort*. Meanwhile Lieutenant Commander Luther's destroyers closed ranks to protect their charges. They would be very quickly outnumbered by the gathering U-boats.

The next attacker on the scene was Helmut Manseck in *U-758*, who crept in on the starboard side of the convoy while *Pennywort* was still astern picking up survivors. Manseck fired a four-torpedo spread into the massed ranks of merchantmen, two of which found their mark. The 6,813-ton Amsterdam steamer *Zaanland*, carrying a cargo of meat, wheat and zinc, was hit in the engine-room and started to sink right away. Captain Gerardus Franken ordered his men into the boats, and disciplined seamen that they were, the Dutchmen cleared the ship's side before she took a sudden plunge to the bottom.

It was a different story aboard the American Liberty ship *James Oglethorpe* in the adjacent column of HX 229. One of Manseck's torpedoes slammed into her starboard side at the fore end of her No. 2 hold. Loaded with 8,000 tons of steel, her decks crammed with aircraft, tractors and trucks, she took a list to starboard and began to settle by the head. For reasons unknown, her rudder jammed hard over to port, and she began to run in wide circles. A fire in No. 1 hold was brought under control, but panic set in, and forty-three of her complement of seventy four men abandoned ship prematurely in two lifeboats. As the ship was still under way, and steaming ahead at 8 knots, tragedy followed. One of the boats capsized on launching, and thirteen men were drowned. Another fell to his death between the ship's side and the boat, while thirty others got away, to be picked up by HMS *Pennywort*.

The *James Oglethorpe*'s master, Captain Albert W. Long, and twenty-nine of his crew stayed with the ship and made an attempt to reach St John's, but their brave gesture was in vain, and cost them their lives. The *James Oglethorpe* either foundered on the way to St John's, or she was picked off by another U-boat, for she was not seen again.

More than satisfied with his night's work, Helmut Manseck sped away from the convoy at full speed on the surface, and was out of sight before Luther could mount a counter-attack with his depleted force. *Pennywort* was still astern on rescue work, and HMS *Mansfield* was away chasing a U-boat, probably *U-653*, believed to be shadowing the convoy. *U-758*, with no more torpedoes left, and low on fuel, was under orders to top up his tanks from the U-tankers, and then return to her pen in St Nazaire.

Over the next hour, two other boats, Dietrich Lohmann's *U-89* and Adolf Graef's *U-664*, made repeated efforts to infiltrate the convoy, but were beaten off, largely due to the aggressive actions of the corvette *Anemone*. The tough little escort damaged both U-boats, and put them out of the fight for a while. Unfortunately, in doing so *Anemone* knocked out her own radar and radio-telephone, thereby handing herself a severe handicap.

While *Anemone* was heavily engaged with *U-89* and *U-664*, *Pennywort* was still away, and the destroyer *Mansfield* still chasing shadows, *U-435* took the opportunity to close in and fire a two-torpedo spread. One torpedo hit and damaged the US-flag *William Eustis*. The 7,196-ton Liberty, loaded with 7,000 tons of sugar, fell astern, developing a starboard list. Her damage was not terminal, but her crew refused to stay with her, much to the annoyance of Lieutenant Commander Luther, who was obliged to take *Volunteer* to their assistance.

SC 122, now just over 100 miles ahead of HX 229, had so far escaped the attentions of the U-boats, but by 01.05 on the 17th, undetected by Commander Boyle's escorts, Manfred Kinzel penetrated deep into the convoy and was in the midst of the merchant ships. At 01.06, he fired two torpedoes at the ships in Column 5. Two British steamers were on the receiving end, the lead ship the London-registered *Kingsbury*, and immediately astern of her, the *King Gruffydd*. The 4,898-ton *Kingsbury*, commanded by Captain William Laidler, sank stern first within minutes, but all except one of her crew got away in the boats.

Those aboard the Welsh ship were less fortunate. The *King Gruffydd* was a veteran ship, built in 1919 as a wartime replacement, and had enjoyed a brief career as the naval auxiliary in the present war. Now she was back to her old trade, and loaded perilously near to her marks with 5,000 tons of steel, 500 tons of tobacco, and 493 tons of high explosives. Mercifully, the latter did not explode and blow her apart, but the weight of steel in her holds took her down so fast that Captain Hywell Griffiths and twenty-three of his fellow Welshmen were lost with her.

Taking full advantage of the chaos he had caused, Kinzel aimed and loosed off another two torpedoes from his bow tubes, and then slewed hard round to fire his stern tube. Once again, Kinzel's torpedoes caused havoc. The first hit the 7,886-ton Dutch steamer *Alderamin*, commanded by Captain C.L. van Os, and carrying a cargo of seeds and oil. Most of the *Alderamin*'s crew got away before she sank, but one of their lifeboats subsequently went missing with fifteen men. Three other men died after being picked up by SC 122's rescue ship *Zamalek*.

Kinzel's second torpedo missed its intended target and detonated harmlessly at the end of its run, but his stern shot, passing astern of the sinking *Alderamin*, blew a hole in the hull of the British ship *Fort Cedar Lake* in Column 12. She was a brand new wartime replacement ship, built in Canada, and had come a long way with her cargo of general supplies from Vancouver, via the Panama Canal and New York, before her short career came to a sudden end. Abandoned by her crew, she drifted astern, to be dispatched later by Hans-Jurgen Haupt in *U-665*.

After an unexpected, but welcome, breathing space, HX 229 was again under attack. Siegfried Strelow, having hastily reloaded his tubes, had been joined by Heinz Walkerling in *U-91*, both opening fire within minutes of each other just after 01.30 on the 17th. Strelow's spread of four all missed, but two of Walkerling's torpedoes went home, stopping the New York-registered *Harry Luckenbach* dead in her tracks. Under the command of Captain Ralph McKinnon, and carrying 8,381 tons of general cargo for an unnamed British port, the *Harry Luckenbach* was hit in her engine-room and sank in three minutes. An unknown number of her crew got away in three lifeboats, which were later sighted by HMS *Pennywort*, but the corvette already had 108 survivors on

1. Heading for the killing ground. Two Type VIICs outward bound in the Atlantic.

Photo: Lothar-Gunther Buchheim

2. *Kapitänleutnant* Karl-Jürgen Wächter.   *Photo: The Conning Tower*

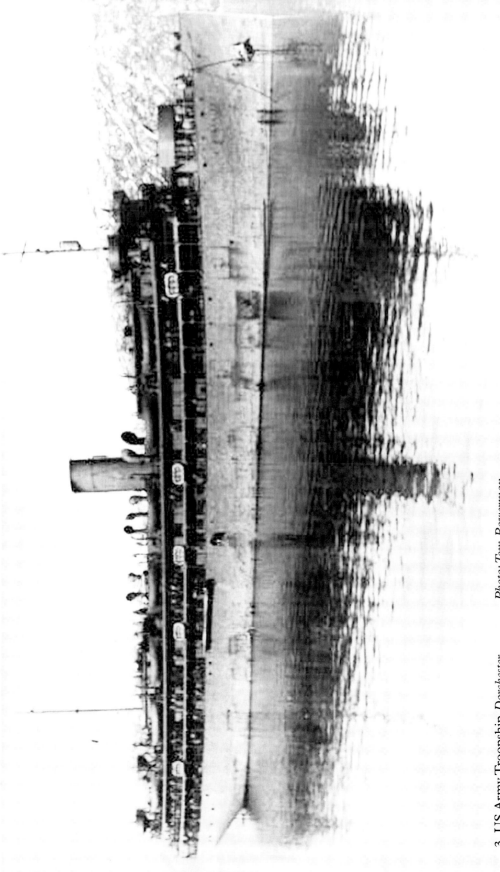

3. US Army Troopship *Dorchester*.   *Photo: Tom Bowerman*

DRAFTER	EXTENSION NUMBER	ADDRESSEES	PRECEDENCE
FROM CTF 24			PRIORITY
RELEASED BY	FOR ACTION		ROUTINE
DATE 3 FEB 1943			DEFERRED
TOR CODEROOM 1643	INFORMATION	CINCLANT COMINCH	PRIORITY PPP
DECODED BY KINERK			ROUTINE
PARAPHRASED BY GILBERT			DEFERRED

INDICATE BY ASTERISK ADDRESSEES FOR WHICH MAIL DELIVERY IS SATISFACTORY.

ROBINSON   #31523   NCR 200

UNLESS OTHERWISE INDICATED THIS DISPATCH WILL BE TRANSMITTED WITH DEFERRED PRECEDENCE.

ORIGINATOR FILL IN DATE AND TIME	DATE	TIME	GC

TEXT

ACTION

| F-00 |
| F-01 |
| F-015 |
| F-0015 |
| F-05 |
| F-07 |
| F-1 |
| F-11 |
| F-2 |
| F-3 |
| F-30 |
| F-31 |
| F-32 |
| F-33 |
| F-34 |
| F-35 |
| F-37 |
| IG-00 |
| VCNO |

SS DORCHESTER (747 PASSENGERS) ENROUTE GREENLAND IN
SG-19 TORPEDOED AT 0446Z/3 POSITION 59-22 N 48-42 W.
ESCANABA COMANCHE CONDUCTING RESCUE OPERATIONS. DUANE
DETACHED ON-163 AND ORDERED TO ASSIST IN RESCUE EXPECTED
ARRIVE PRIOR DARK FEBRUARY 3. TAMPA (CTU 24.8.3) ENROUTE
DESTINATION ESCORTING REMAINING 2 SHIPS OF CONVOY ORDERED
RETURN TO COORDINATE RESCUE OPERATION. SANDPIPER, NOGAK,
RARITAN AKLAK, AMAROK ENROUTE FROM GREENLAND TO ASSIST.
SOPA GREENLAND CONDUCTING AIR SEARCH.

COMINCH....COG
16....F37....39....23....20C....C.G....19....19C....
FILE:20OP...CNO...

SECRET

Make original only.   Deliver to communication watch officer in person.   (See Art. 76 (4) NAVREGS.)

NCR—15   16—22000-2

4. Signal reporting loss of the US Army troopship *Dorchester*.

Photo: National Archives, Washington

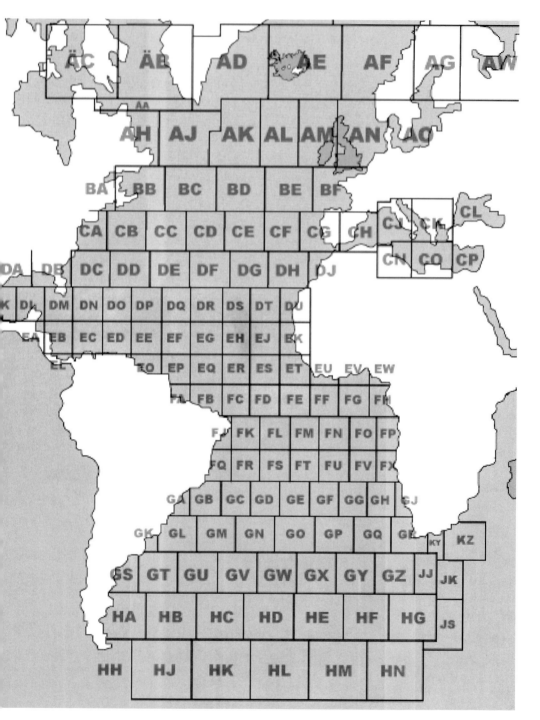

Grid system used by U-boats for reporting position.   *Photo: The Conning Tower*

6. U-boat refuelling at sea.   *Photo: Cajus Bekker*

7. Rescue ship *Stockport* ex-London & North Eastern Railway.

Photo: The Messenger, Stockport

8. The Belgian-manned Flower-class corvette HMS *Godetia.*

Photo: World Ship Photo Society

9. U-boat trimmed down and running at full speed. *Photo: Horst Bredow*

H&A 782

1943

Subject :   RECOMMENDATIONS FOR AWARDS - CONVOY S.C.129

Be pleased to lay before Their Lordships the enclosed recommendations for Honours and Awards to Officers and men of H.M.S. HESPERUS for the destruction of one U-Boat (known sunk), and for damaging two more (assessed as probably slightly damaged and probably damaged (B) respectively) whilst escorting Convoy S.C.129.

2.   The circumstances in which these successes were achieved are set out in the Report of Proceedings from H.M.S. HESPERUS forwarded under cover of my No. W.A.2345/61/16 RP. of 22nd June 1943.

3.   I fully concur in these recommendations and propose the following order of merit.   H.M.S. HESPERUS has played a leading part in the defence of convoys in the Battle of the Atlantic and I consider that the services of her Officers and men deserve full recognition.

Officers.

(1)   Commander D.F.G.W.Macintyre, D.S.O., and Bar,
          Royal Navy - Decoration

(2)   Mr. W.H.Pritchard, Gunner (T), Royal Navy -
          Decoration

Ratings

(1)   E.T.J.White, Able Seaman (S.T.) D/J.86569 -
          Decoration

(2)   L.G.Green, Chief E.R.A. D/MX. 38776 -
          Decoration

(3)   A.F.Lilley, Petty Officer (G.M.) D/J.107751 -
          Mention in Despatches

(4)   C.A.Edwards, Leading Seaman (RADAR) P/JX.299057
          Mention in Despatches

(5)   H.H.Moffatt-Bailey, Ordinary Telegraphist, P/JX. 206822-
          Mention in Despatches

(6)   A.Pilling, Able Seaman, (RADAR) P/JX. 256806 -
          Mention in Despatches

(7)   L.Read, Ordinary Seaman (RADAR) P/JX. 321197-
          Mention in Despatches

Max Horton.

10. Award to HMS *Hesperus* for her work with Convoy SC 129.

Photo: Public Record Office

11. HMS *Drumheller* rescues survivors from *Fort Concord*.   *Photo: Bill Bowen-Davies*

13. American Liberty ship hit amidships by torpedo and sinking by the stern.

Photo: George Young

12. Long range Liberator of RAF Coastal Command over the Azores.

14. HMS *Laforey*. Sunk by *U-223* off Sicily, 30 March 1944.

Photo: The Conning Tower

Photo: Cajus Bekker

15. A new Type XXI U-boat puts to sea.

16. Entrance to Kiel Harbour. 'The fog rolls in from the Kattegat...'   *Photo: Author*

17. U-boat War Memorial, Möltenort.   *Photo: Author*

18. U-boat War Memorial, Möltenort. A record of the price paid for Germany's bid to win control of the seas.

19. Kiel Harbour today. Cruise liners berth where the U-boats once gathered.

board and could take no more. The *Anemone* was later sent out to find the boats, but failed to locate them. None of the *Harry Luckenbach*'s crew of eighty survived.

With both his corvettes involved in rescue work, Lieutenant Commander Luther used his destroyers to force Stretlow and Walkerling to break off their attack, but there were others waiting in the wings. A little before 04.00, Bernhard Zurmülhen brought *U-600* in on the starboard side of HX 229, and fired off four torpedoes with spectacular effect. The 8,714-ton Royal Mail cargo liner *Nariva*, loaded with 5,600 tons of refrigerated meat, and nearing the end of her long voyage from Buenos Aires, was hit squarely amidships. Simultaneously, two more of Zurmülhen's torpedoes slammed into the US-flag *Irénée Du Pont*, which in addition to 5,800 tons of general cargo and 3,200 tons of oil in drums in her holds, had eleven medium bombers lashed down on deck. *U-600*'s fourth shot found the largest target in the convoy, the 12,156-ton whale factory ship *Southern Princess*. Both the *Nariva* and the *Irénée Du Pont* remained afloat, but the *Southern Princess* caught fire and capsized, thus ending a career that had begun in the Antarctic in 1915. The *coup de grâce* was administered to the *Nariva* and *Irénée Du Pont* by *U-91* as, abandoned by their crews, they drifted forlornly astern of the convoy.

Many of the U-boats had by now exhausted their supply of torpedoes, or were in need of refuelling, and for the next eight hours HX 229 enjoyed a quiet spell, before others came in to renew the attack. At five minutes after noon on the 17th, *Oberleutnant* Hans-Achim von Rosenberg-Gruczszynski in *U-384* infiltrated the columns of the convoy unobserved, and fired a spread of three torpedoes. Donaldson Brothers' *Coracero*, another frozen meat carrier out of Buenos Aires, was hit and sank with the loss of five lives. A few minutes after the *Coracero* went down, and before the escorts were able to interfere, Jurgen Kruger's *U-631* had found an opening and sank the 5,158-ton Dutch steamer *Terkoelei*. Her crew abandoned ship, but thirty-eight men were lost when two lifeboats capsized.

Eighty miles to the east, SC 122 was also again under attack. Manfred Kinzel was back, having reloaded *U-338*'s empty tubes, and had the Panama-flag *Granville* in his sights. Managed by the

US War Administration, the 1913-vintage coal burner carried a crew of mixed nationality, and was under the command of Captain Friedrich Maltzen, a Dane. Her cargo consisted of 3,700 tons of Lease-Lend goods, US Army stores and mail, with a large landing craft across her Nos. 2 and 3 hatches.

At 11.56, one of the three torpedoes fired by Kinzel struck the *Granville* on her port side in way of her No. 2 hold. Unfortunately, when the torpedo hit, the engine-room crew had been in the process of transferring coal from the bunkers to the stokehold, and the watertight door between the two compartments was open. As a result of this, the *Granville*'s engine-room was flooded, and she broke her back, sinking fifteen minutes later. Fifteen of her crew were lost, and another man died after being rescued.

Both convoys were now less than 800 miles from the west coast of Ireland, and long-range Liberators and Sunderlands were beginning to arrive overhead from their bases in Northern Ireland. Their presence drove the U-boats beneath the waves for the rest of the daylight hours.

SC 122 was back in the firing line after dark. Rudolf Bahr in *U-305* used a well aimed two-torpedo spread to hit two British ships, the *Port Auckland* and the *Zouave*. The 8,789-ton *Port Auckland*, loaded with a refrigerated cargo from Australia and New Zealand, took one torpedo in her engine-room killing seven men who were on watch below at the time. The ship stayed afloat for another hour, allowing the *Godetia* to take off the rest of her crew. The London-registered *Zouave*, weighed down under 7,000 tons of iron filings, went straight to the bottom ninety seconds after Bahr's torpedo hit. Fortunately, most of her crew got away and were picked up by *Godetia*. While the corvette was so engaged, Bahr used another torpedo to put an end to the *Port Auckland*.

It was not until 14.00 on the 18th that the attack was renewed on HX 229, by which time Luther had both the corvettes *Anemone* and *Pennywort* back with him. However, the escort being back up to strength did not stop Hans Trojer's *U-221* breaking through to try a stern shot on the *Walter Q. Gresham*, lead ship of Column 2. The torpedo blew a large hole in the American Liberty's stern, and she sank taking her cargo of 9,000 tons of powdered milk and twenty-seven of her crew with her. This was a sad ending to the steamer's maiden voyage.

Trojer used his bow tubes on the 8,293-ton *Canadian Star*, stationed two ships astern of the *Walter Q. Gresham*. The Blue Star liner, under the command of Captain Robert Miller, and carrying 7,806 tons of meat, cheese and butter from Sydney, Australia, was hit by two torpedoes and sank in fifteen minutes. Captain Miller, twenty-two of his crew, and nine passengers lost their lives.

With SC 122 and HX 229 now less than fifty miles apart, more British naval ships were arriving to support their escorts, while air cover was increasing. It was time for the U-boats to bow out while they still had the upper hand. But before they finally broke off the engagement they made an attempt to deliver a parting gift. Early on the morning of the 19th, Klaus Hartmann in *U-441* tried hard to break through the reinforced escort screen, but failed. The five torpedoes he fired before giving up, all missed. Struckmeier's *U-608* also moved in, but had similar bad luck when attempting to sink the newly-arrived destroyer HMS *Highlander*. An hour later, *U-666* had a partial success, when she came across the ex-SC 122 ship *Carras*, straggling in the no man's land between the two convoys, and damaged her with one torpedo. The 5,234-ton Greek ship, loaded with a full cargo of wheat, remained afloat until she was finally sunk that evening by *U-333*. All thirty-three men of the *Carras*'s crew were saved.

Later that morning, Herbert Uhlig in *U-527* sighted the *Mathew Luckenbach* some miles ahead of HX 229. The 5,848-ton American ship was carrying a cargo of 8,360 tons, which included steel, grain, ammunition, mail, and trucks on deck. It appears that, after witnessing at close quarters several ships being sunk, Captain Atwood N. Borden took the unprecedented step of calling for a vote amongst his crew to decide whether the ship stayed with the convoy or went on alone at full speed. The latter course was agreed and, not unexpectedly, the *Mathew Luckenbach* paid the price for this unwise action. Uhlig used two well-aimed torpedoes to put an end to her flight. Captain Borden and his crew of sixty-seven were lucky to get away in their lifeboats. They were picked up later by the cutter *Ingham*, whose commander, seeing that the *Mathew Luckenbach* was still afloat, called for volunteers from among her crew to reboard and attempt to get the ship to port. Not one man was prepared to go back. The derelict ship was sighted that night by *U-523*, and again torpedoed. This time she sank.

On 22 March SC 122 and HX 229, now to all intents and purposes one convoy, came in sight of Inishtrahull lighthouse, which stands on the lonely islet off the north coast of Ireland, marking the entrance to the North Channel. It was journey's end for the men who had survived one of the greatest sea battles of all time, which involved ninety Allied merchant ships and twenty escorts under attack by forty-four U-boats. For the Allies, the cost had been heavy; twenty-two merchantmen totalling 146,596 gross tons lost, and with them in excess of 160,000 tons of cargo; food, guns, ammunition, aircraft, all of which were sorely needed for the prosecution of war in Europe. The cost in lives had been equally heavy, 360 seamen and twelve passengers having found lonely graves in the deep Atlantic. For Grand Admiral Dönitz and the men of the U-boat arm it was a major victory at the cost of only one U-boat, and that away from the main battle. *U-384*, commanded by Hans-Achim von Rosenberg-Gruczszynski, was on her way back to St Nazaire when she was surprised on the surface by a Fortress of 201 Squadron RAF, and sunk. All forty-seven crew went down with their boat.

In the first three weeks of March 1943, German U-boats sank ninety-seven Allied merchant ships of more than half a million gross tons. The war in the Atlantic had now reached a crucial stage, for the Allies were losing on a monthly basis almost twice the number of ships being produced by the shipyards on both sides of the ocean. If something was not done soon to redress the balance, then Karl Dönitz might well achieve his avowed ambition to cut the Atlantic supply lines.

Chapter Seven

The Turning Point

After her successful attack on the Panamanian tanker *Winkler*, *U-223* only narrowly escaped the wrath of ON 166's escorts. Karl-Jürgen Wächter's War Diary for the morning of 23 February reads:

	. . . the destroyer approaches at full speed. I dive and turn under full helm. There is complete silence in the boat as we listen to the roar of her engines as she comes in. Depth charges dropped: six at 30 metres and six at 10 metres.
1005	Another at 50 metres. After each attack the destroyer searches with her asdic. We can hear the double pulse like pistol shots.
1015	I come around onto a northerly course and creep away. Six to eight depth charges heard exploding every four to ten minutes up until 1103 They are getting further away. I go to periscope depth to look around.
1115	Can hear more depth charges. There are now three destroyers dropping charges one after the other. But they are all astern of me and getting further away.

In all, over a period of an hour and a quarter, *U-223* was subjected to a total of 219 depth charges, 126 of which were close

91

enough to give the boat and her crew a thorough shaking up. Other than that, no serious damage was done but, having survived thus far, Wächter decided it was time to make an exit. Notwithstanding the enemy's attentions, he was down to his last two torpedoes, and running short on fuel. A brief radio message to BdU reporting the tanker's sinking and his current predicament, brought instructions to make for the refuelling rendezvous off the Azores, and thereafter return to St Nazaire.

With only two ships sunk, U-223's first war patrol had not been a spectacular success, but it had been largely carried out in the most dreadful weather, and with a new boat and a new crew, it had been a testing time. Neither Wächter, nor any of his men voiced a complaint when they were ordered home.

The rendezvous was made with the U-tanker U-460 on the morning of the 25th, and weather conditions being excellent – a light southerly wind and low swell – U-223 was on her way again within two hours, having topped up her tanks, and taken on sufficient fresh water and stores to see her to Biscay.

Wächter was aware that the dangers of the voyage were not yet finished. Ahead of them lay a stretch of water heavily patrolled by British long-range aircraft, specifically on the lookout for U-boats bound in and out of the French ports. Perversely, the weather remained fine, with good visibility and broken cloud, ideal conditions for marauding aircraft. Extra lookouts were posted day and night, and running on one engine to conserve fuel, U-223 continued eastward on the surface. As they neared the Bay of Biscay, there were frequent sightings of enemy planes, mainly big Sunderland flying boats and four-engined Liberators of RAF Coastal Command carefully searching the sea below for their prey. By diving at the first hint of danger, Wächter avoided being sighted until, on the morning of 1 March, his luck ran out. U-223 was then 600 miles due west of St Nazaire.

Fortress FL463D of 59 Squadron RAF, captained by Flying Officer N. Barson, was five hours out from her base and cruising at 2,000 feet on the easterly leg of her Biscay patrol. It was a fine morning, with the cloud base at 3,000 feet and visibility between twelve and fifteen miles. They had left at dawn, and glancing at his fuel gauges, Flying Officer Barson decided it would soon be time to turn for home. Then, at 12.47, the port beam gunner saw the long frothing wake of the U-boat snaking across the cobalt blue of the sea below. Alerted by the intercom, Barson threw the Fortress into a diving turn to starboard, to get up-sun of the U-boat and lose height rapidly. His co-pilot opened the bomb doors.

U-223's Second Watch Officer had the watch in the conning tower. All guns were loaded and manned, the three lookouts alert, their keen eyes ceaselessly quartering the sky for the first glimpse of an approaching enemy aircraft. The Metox was switched on, but giving no warning buzz indicating incoming radar impulses. The sky appeared to be empty.

The Fortress came diving out of the sun unannounced, the deep-throated roar of its four Pratt & Whitney engines rising to a piercing scream.

The Second Watch Officer was first to come alive to the danger. It was too late to dive, and in desperation he shouted for all guns to open fire. The quadruple 20mm on the lower gun platform and the two twin 20mms on the upper platform opened up simultaneously with a deafening clatter, eight guns throwing up a hail of tracer and high explosive shells that took Barson by surprise, causing him to swerve violently. Seven depth bombs, released as the Fortress roared over the U-boat at a height of seventy feet, fell wide and to starboard. The sea erupted and *U-223* was lifted bodily, but she suffered only superficial damage and no casualties, other than a few bruised ribs.

Barson's aircraft, although possessing the element of surprise, came off worst in the encounter. *U-223*'s 20mm fire damaged her hydraulic system, causing oil to gush into the cockpit, the throttle control of her No. 4 engine was shot away, and the auto pilot smashed. Black smoke filled the interior of the aircraft but, as with the U-boat, the damage was largely superficial. When the smoke cleared, Barson came in for a second attack, but by this time Wächter had taken his boat down. The laconic entry in his War Diary reads:

1242   BE5554 A four-engined Boeing suddenly appeared out of the clouds at 1000 metres. Crash dive. The boat was saved by the prompt action of the II WO, who immediately opened

fire with all anti-aircraft guns. This caused the
enemy plane to veer off course and all five
depth charges dropped well away to starboard.
Plane then flew away.

The boat suffered no damage of any
consequence and there was no further attack.

In resisting the impulse to dive as soon as the enemy aircraft was
seen *U-223*, was following BdU's recommended practice for all
U-boats under attack from the air. The reasoning behind this was
– and it was certainly vindicated in this case – that it was far better
to stay on the surface and attempt to shoot the attacker down
with the formidable battery of guns carried than to risk an emergency crash dive. No U-boat was able to dive deep enough to
escape the blast of depth charges dropped by an aircraft swooping
out of the skies at 300 mph.

Over the next five days, *U-223* suffered almost continuous
attacks from the air. The sky above seemed to be alive with
British planes day and night, all intent on depth charging her to
the bottom. More time was spent below than on the surface, and
the average daily run was never much more than 100 miles.
There was no release for the purgatory until, early on the
morning of 6 March, Wächter made a rendezvous with an escort
vessel off St Nazaire. *U-223* found shelter in her concrete pen at
14.29 that day, the last few miles to the French port being
covered on the surface without fear of attack. Her first war
patrol had lasted fifty-three days, during which she had sunk
only two enemy ships totalling 12,556 tons. This was a poor
return for the millions invested in her, but it was the coming
trend for the Dönitz's U-boat arm. In summing up the voyage,
Karl Wächter wrote:-

1.) As we were in bad weather for most of the time, and without
the means of fixing our position for three to four days at a time,
the actual position was frequently in doubt. This was especially
the case during the operation from 17 to 19 February. The only
accurate sighting report sent was from Drewitz (*U-525*). I did
not receive this until the 19th.

2.) When we were attacked from the air on 1 March, we were

saved only by opening fire at once with all guns. Even in the open sea, a good defence against aircraft is required.

3.) Even though the weather was so bad, this did not effect morale on board. Spirits were high, and the behaviour of the officers and men during the depth charging was excellent.

U-223 spent the next six weeks in St Nazaire, sheltered from the incessant raids of RAF Bomber Command by a roof of reinforced concrete sixteen feet thick. While she was being refitted by dock-yard workers, there was leave for some, but there was a rude shock in store for these men when they reached the homeland. Germany was a country under siege from the air, with a contin-uous stream of American bombers overhead by day, and British bombers by night. German anti-aircraft defences were still strong, but the Allied planes came over in such numbers – up to 500 at a time – and the bombs rained down with such ferocity that there was no escape from them. Many German cities, particularly those in the industrial Ruhr, lay in ruins. And all this against a back-ground of the German armies being forced relentlessly back on the Russian Front, and in danger of complete annihilation in North Africa as British and American troops closed in on them from two sides.

It was with some unspoken relief that, on the morning of 15 April 1943, Karl Wächter took *U-223* out through the locks of St Nazaire and headed west into the Bay of Biscay. Repaired, refu-elled and rearmed, she was re-entering the one theatre of war where Germany was still dominant. Since they had returned to St Nazaire a little over a month earlier, more than 100 Allied merchantmen had fallen to the U-boats. Of this period, the Admiralty later expressed the opinion that 'the Germans never came so near to disrupting communications between the New World and the Old . . . it appeared possible that we should not be able to continue convoy as an effective form of defence'.

Enemy air activity over Biscay had not diminished, and Wächter was forced to spend the greater part of the daylight hours underwater, surfacing only at night to push westwards at full speed under the cover of darkness. But even this was not without great risk. The British and American aircraft that cruised overhead were equipped with the new ASV II centimetric radar and Leigh Light, a lethal double threat to any U-boat caught on the surface. It was a threat that for *U-223* failed to materialize. By the morning of the 20th she was 500 miles to the west of Ushant, and Wächter estimated they had run clear of the the Allied air patrols. The weather was fine, with a light northwesterly breeze and good visibility, and the U-boat was making good speed on the surface. As yet, no specific orders had come through from BdU, and they were heading in the general direction of the New York – UK convoy route.

Far to the east, the British ship *Harperley* was disembarking her pilot off St Ann's Head on her way out from Milford Haven, where she had been at anchor for some days awaiting a convoy. The 4,586-ton *Harperley*, under the command of Captain J. E. Turgoose and owned by J. & C. Harrison of London, was bound for Buenos Aires with a cargo of 6,000 tons of Welsh coal and 200 bags of mail. She was manned by a crew of forty-nine, which included seven DEMS gunners, and was armed with one 4-inch gun, one 12-pounder, four 20mm Oerlikons, two twin-Marlin machine guns, and an assortment of anti-aircraft rockets.

The *Harperley* joined Convoy ONS 5 off Liverpool next day, taking up position as No. 13, third ship in the outside port column. ONS 5 consisted of thirty-nine ships under the protection of Commander Peter Gretton's Escort Group B 7. Gretton, in the destroyer *Duncan*, had with him the frigate HMS *Tay*, the corvettes *Sunflower*, *Snowflake*, *Loosestrife* and *Pink*, the armed trawlers *Northern Gem* and *Northern Spray*, which were to act as rescue ships, and the fleet tanker *British Lady*.

The weather was fair on sailing, but the barometer was falling steadily, and when the convoy emerged from the North Channel on the morning of the 22nd, it sailed straight into a rising gale. It was not unexpected – the North Atlantic in April is still in a belligerent mood – but this was a slow convoy, made up of a collection of elderly ships in ballast. In no time many of them were finding it hard to maintain station. And, of course, things went from bad to worse. The rising gale became a whole gale, with the usual mountain-sized Western Ocean swell, and the waves running high and breaking green. By the 24th, ONS 5 was reduced to inching forward at a painful 2 knots, with eight or nine

96

stragglers limping along in its wake. In the struggle to maintain station, two ships collided, one of which was so badly damaged that she had to make for the nearest port for repairs.

In the hope of avoiding the U-boats, and in order to take full advantage of air cover from Iceland, the Admiralty routed ONS 5 far to the north, reaching almost to the Arctic Circle. Viewed from the comfort of the Admiralty's Operations Room, this may have seemed a sensible strategy, but it must inevitably lead the convoy into a grim world that most seamen would prefer to avoid. The further north they went, so the weather must deteriorate, the thermometer falling to new bone-chilling depths, with pack-ice and icebergs shrouded in fog adding to the menace of the unrelenting storms. And the enemy had even worse to offer. In the area through which ONS 5 would eventually pass four U-boat packs were on station; *Star* to the south-west of Iceland, *Specht* north-east of Newfoundland, and two others, *Amsel* and *Dressel* east of Newfoundland. They comprised a total of forty-five boats, with three U-tankers in support, and they were lying in wait for three UK-bound convoys, HX 235, SC 128 and SC 129, which were known to be at sea.

Unaware of, and probably not concerned by the enemy threat in its path, ONS 5 sailed on, much more occupied with day to day events. The weather was at its worst, and in the midst of the storm the lead destroyer, HMS *Duncan*, was running short of fuel. All efforts to refuel her from one of the accompanying tankers were frustrated by the heavy rolling of the ships in the high seas. Only one ray of hope broke through the gathering gloom on that day: a Fortress of 206 Squadron from Iceland, scouting ahead of the convoy, surprised *U-710* on the surface and promptly sank her. ONS 5 was saved from discovery, but that day also saw the end of all air cover for a while. Conditions had become so bad in Iceland that all aircraft were grounded until the weather improved.

It did seem that things could only get worse for ONS 5, then, on the 26th, Gretton got the second destroyer he so badly needed. During the day, HMS *Vidette* joined from Iceland with three more merchant ships in company. *Vidette* was of First World War vintage, four 4-inch guns and 28 knots, but to the Commander Gretton she was pure gold. On the following day, the weather improved sufficiently for both *Duncan* and *Vidette* to top up their tanks while under way. Gretton now felt better equipped to meet the U-boats, and the convoy having reached the furthest point north of its planned route, the omens were good.

So intent were the wolf packs on searching for the eastbound convoys that ONS 5 almost escaped their attention. It was unfortunate that the most northerly boat of the *Star* pack, Ernst von Witzendorff's *U-650*, happened to sight the fringe of the convoy on the morning of the 28th. Witzendorff resisted the temptation to make a lone attack, and began shadowing the Allied ships, transmitting position reports at intervals. Other U-boats homed in on *U-650*'s signals, which also served to alert Gretton to the threat to his convoy. After dark that night, he ordered a radical change of course, but the merchantmen were making so little progress against the heavy seas that the alteration amounted to no more than a gesture. *U-650* was still in contact, and other boats were closing in. Made aware of the danger to the convoy, the Admiralty ordered the 3rd Escort Group out from St John's to support Gretton. Under the command of Captain J.A. McCoy in HMS *Offa*, 3rd Escort Group consisted of four ex-Home Fleet destroyers, and was to be joined by a fifth destroyer from Iceland, HMS *Oribi*. When these reinforcements arrived, Gretton would be able to put a defensive ring around ONS 5 that the U-boats would find hard to penetrate.

By midnight, despite having to fight their way through heavy seas, four more boats had joined *U-650*. At 02.00 on the 29th – only two hours before dawn in those high latitudes – they moved in to the attack. Of the four newcomers, only Ottoheinrich Junker's *U-532* succeeded in launching her torpedoes, all of which missed. The U-boat was seen by the escorts, and the corvettes *Snowflake* and *Sunflower* charged in to attack. Junker crash-dived but his boat was heavily damaged by the corvettes' depth charges. *U-386* (Hans-Albrecht Kandler) also attempted to pick off a target, and she was likewise set upon by *Snowflake* and *Sunflower*. Both boats were forced to abort their attacks and return to Biscay for repairs. HMS *Duncan* dealt with the other U-boats, driving them off as they tried to move in. The brief engagement, fought in storm-force conditions, was a brilliant example of seamanship and sheer dogged determination on both sides. That the U-boats, dwarfed by the huge waves, were able to mount any sort of attack was to defy the impossible, while the skill displayed by the British escorts, their depth charge parties working up to their waists in water as the sea climbed aboard, was magnificent to behold.

Sunrise on the 29th saw a slight improvement in the weather, which offered an opportunity for *U-258* (Wilhelm von Mässenhausen), approaching from the south-east, to penetrate the escort screen unseen. At 06.24, she was well placed outside the port wing column of ONS 5, and von Mässenhausen fired a fan of three torpedoes. Two went wide, although one of these passed only three or four feet ahead of the *Harperley*, much to Captain Turgoose's consternation. The third went home in the engine-room of the American steamer *McKeesport*. It was a mortal blow, the *McKeesport*'s bulkheads were cracked and her engine spaces flooded. Only one of her crew was killed, the others abandoning ship half an hour later. They were picked up by the trawler *Northern Gem*. With the improvement in the weather, air cover was back over the convoy, and this prevented other U-boats emulating *U-258*'s success. Only one other boat, *U-528*, managed to get into position, but she was seen from the air and severely damaged by depth bombs. She followed *U-386* and *U-532* back to Biscay for repairs.

Commander Peter Gretton now had some cause for optimism. In the space of a few hours, with the help of the RAF, he had driven off five U-boats, damaging three of them so badly that they would not return, and in the process had lost only one merchant ship. But there was still the other enemy to contend with. Later that day, the North Atlantic resumed its onslaught on the convoy. It was soon blowing a full gale again, with poor visibility, and pack-ice and small icebergs drifting in and out of the murk. Most of the merchant ships were virtually hove to, reduced to holding their heads up into wind and sea, while the line of lame ducks straggling astern grew ever longer. As before, the U-boats fared even worse, their casings submerged by the pounding seas, their conning towers awash. For the moment, all thought of attacking the enemy ships was brushed aside by the fight to avoid being overwhelmed by the sea.

Some 450 miles to the south-south-west, Karl Wächter was a

very distant participant in the events surrounding ONS 5, listening in to the rattle of morse as the other *Star* boats communicated their frustration to each other. *U-223* had the benefit of more kindly weather, the wind being no more than force 5 from the south-west, the visibility good, the sun shone through broken cloud, and it was pleasantly warm. The *Amsel* pack, of which she was a now member, had been split into two groups, *Amsel I* and *Amsel II*, *U-223* being with the latter, along with *U-266* (Ralf von Jessen), *U-377* (Otto Köhler), *U-383* (Horst Kremser), *U-634* (Eberhard Dalhaus), and two other homeward bound boats which had been called in to make up the numbers. With *Amsel I*, six boats strong, *Amsel II* was in an extended line, each boat twenty miles apart, and moving in a north-easterly direction towards ONS 5 at 7 knots.

Blissfully unaware of the danger ahead, ONS 5 continued to inch its way to the south and west, battling against weather that was worsening by the hour. HMS *Oribi* arrived from Iceland during the day, making a welcome addition to Commander Gretton's force, but there was no sign of the Home Fleet destroyers from St John's. And the situation was rapidly getting out of hand. Gretton wrote in his memoirs after the war:

> The convoy was almost stationary and ships were heaving to as best as they could, gradually spreading all over the ocean as they drifted almost out of control. Two ships had to turn and run before the wind and we never saw them again, although I believe they reached Iceland safely . . . At noon this day, 1st May, one of our old friends from 120 (Liberator) Squadron turned up from Iceland, a magnificent effort in the shocking weather. But the U-boats were all sitting comfortably below the waves, waiting for the gale to stop, and he could do no more than confirm our worst fears about the convoy and give us the unwelcome news that there were icebergs thirty miles ahead of us. He added for good measure that if we continued on our present heading for fifty miles, we would be well inside the Greenland ice pack . . .

Luckily for Gretton, by dawn on 2 May, there was a marked improvement in the weather, the sea moderating sufficiently for him to round up his scattered flock, some of whom were over thirty miles off station. Even with the help of a Liberator spotting overhead, the gathering together of the wayward took many hours, by which time Gretton was horrified to see the ice pack in sight to starboard. Before long, growlers and large ice floes were sailing through the freshly-formed columns of the convoy. All attempts to refuel the *Duncan*, which was again running danger-ously low on oil, were frustrated by the need for the tanker to take constant evasive action to avoid the ice. By the time they were clear of the drifting ice, the wind and sea had risen again, and any idea of refuelling had to be abandoned.

Later in the day, the destroyers *Impulsive, Offa, Panther* and *Penn* joined from St John's, and for the first time Commander Gretton had the satisfaction of being in charge of a well organ-ised, well defended convoy. The screen was impressive, with the frigate *Tay*, the four corvettes and two trawlers in close atten-dance on the merchantmen, while the six destroyers formed a distant ring around them, their Asdics and radars searching for U-boats. This happy situation was not to last long. *Duncan*'s fuel tanks were running dry, and soundings revealed she had only just enough fuel left to reach St John's, 630 miles to the south-west, at economical speed. The weather continued to preclude the possibility of refuelling at sea, and neither was Gretton able to transfer to one of the other escorts and remain as S.O.E. He had no alternative but to hand over command to Lieutenant Commander Sherwood in HMS *Tay*, and go with *Duncan* to St John's. No sooner had *Duncan* disappeared over the horizon than the newly-joined destroyers *Impulsive, Panther* and *Penn* and the trawler *Northern Gem* signalled *Tay* that they also must leave for St John's to refuel. Sherwood could not deny them, and they went, leaving ONS 5 with *Tay* (S.O.E), the three destroyers *Offa, Oribi* and *Vidette*, the corvettes *Loosestrife, Pink, Snowflake* and *Sunflower*, and the other trawler *Northern Spray*. In terms of the North Atlantic in the early summer of 1943, this was still a considerable escort force, but the wolves were gathering in strength. A new pack, *Fink*, twenty-eight boats strong, had been formed, and this was ordered to make all speed towards ONS 5, and to join the *Amsel* boats in a combined attack. Together, the three packs would form one of the largest concentrations of U-boats ever to gather in the North Atlantic. It boded ill for ONS 5.

The weather joined on the side of the U-boats, moderating considerably, so that the attack was able to begin on the evening of the 4th. It proved to be not the easy success expected. Sherwood's escorts responded with such vigour that the U-boats retired with a bloody nose. Combined attacks by *Oribi* and *Vidette*, backed up by *Snowflake*, resulted in *U-270* (Paul-Friedrich Otto) and *U-732* (Klaus-Peter Carlsen) being so badly mauled that they set course for home without firing a torpedo. *Vidette* also depth charged *U-514* (Hans-Jürgen Aufferman) out of the fight, although she was able to rejoin the pack a few days later.

A lull followed, during which the convoy, which had again become scattered, reformed, although a few stragglers remained astern. One of these was the 4,737-ton *Lorient*, an ex-French ship, British manned, and with Captain Manley in command. Ulrich Folkers in *U-125*, who was approaching the convoy from astern stopped her with one torpedo. The *Lorient* was abandoned by her crew and quickly fell back out of sight of the other ships. She was found two days later by the US Coastguard cutter *Manhassetts*. Empty lifeboats were nearby, but there was no trace of her crew. The *Lorient* probably sank that night, as no trace could be found of her next morning.

Another unfortunate straggler was the British steamer *North Britain*, six miles astern of the convoy and striving to make up lost ground when Günter Gretschel's *U-707* caught up with her. The Newcastle-registered ship was broken in two by Gretschel's torpedo, and sank in two minutes, taking thirty-one of her forty-two-man crew with her. The survivors were picked up by the *Northern Spray*.

The sinking of the *North Britain* was the signal for the assault on ONS 5 to begin in earnest. Twenty minutes after she went down, Heinrich Hasenschar in *U-628* had manoeuvred into a favourable position to starboard of the convoy and fired all four torpedoes from his bow tubes. Three of them missed, but one went home into the London steamer *Harbury*, loaded with 6,820 tons of anthracite for St John's, New Brunswick. Seven of her crew were killed, and the rest taken off by the *Northern Spray*. *U-264* (Hartwig Looks) sank the abandoned ship four hours later.

The torpedoing of the *Harbury* was witnessed by those on the bridge of the *Harperley*, which was then unwittingly steaming into *U-264*'s line of fire. Hartwig Looks used a stern shot, and Captain Turgoose soon found himself compiling a survivor's report for the Admiralty. He wrote:

The convoy continued until the afternoon of May 4th, when a warning was received that enemy submarines were in the vicinity, and during the night s.s. *Harbury* was torpedoed on her starboard side. Our alarm was given for '*Action Stations*' immediately, and the 2nd Engineer, who was not on watch at the time, voluntarily went down into the engine-room to assist the 4th Engineer as necessary. Ten minutes later, at 2256 when in position 55°00' N 42° 58' W, whilst steaming at 7½ knots, on a course of 192° (approximately) we were struck by two torpedoes. The weather was overcast, visibility good but very dark, rough sea with heavy swell, SW wind, force 5.

Both torpedoes struck almost simultaneously on the port side, the first one in the vicinity of the engine-room, whilst the second torpedo struck in way of the foremast. The explosion was not very violent, and there appeared to be more of a dull thud. I did not notice a flash, neither was there a column of water thrown up, although I later learned from the survivors of another vessel that they saw a big flash. Neither the submarine, nor the track of the torpedoes was observed.

I was in the wheelhouse at the time, and was surprised to find that apparently there was practically no visible damage. Even the glass of the windows of the wheelhouse was unbroken, the only visible damage being that one of the port boats was destroyed, the hatches from No. 1 hold were blown away, No. 4 hatches were damaged, and No. 4 raft had carried away. The ship listed very heavily to port, submerging the holes in the ship's side, thus making it impossible to see the extent of the damage.

Owing to the heavy list I ordered 'abandon ship'. A W/T message was sent out, and the rockets fired, one of which failed to function. I endeavoured to ring the engine-room telegraph but found that it was jammed, although the engines must have stopped when the first torpedo struck, as it was the first torpedo which flooded the engine-room and caused the deaths of the 2nd, 3rd and 4th Engineers. I did not consider there was sufficient time to put the boat's wireless set into a lifeboat so it was left behind.

We carried four lifeboats, so having lost one port boat, the three remaining ones were manned and launched successfully, being clear of the ship within 8 minutes. The only trouble experienced was that the painter of my boat was blown away, and the boat drifted away from the ship's side, so we had to jump for it. We had been in the boats 10/15 minutes when I saw the ship disappear. She went down by the head, and sank approximately 20 minutes after the first torpedo struck . . .

In all, ten men of the *Harperley*'s crew of forty-nine lost their lives. The survivors were to spend some three and a half hours drifting in the boats before being rescued, as the battle for ONS 5 was then in full swing, all escorts being fully engaged in beating off the attacking U-boats. Eventually, the *Northern Spray* came along and took them on board.

The attack on ONS 5 went on for another eighteen hours, nine more merchant ships being sent to the bottom. Hartwig Looks made another kill, putting two torpedoes into one of the *Harperley*'s immediate neighbours, the 5,561-ton American steamer *West Maximus*, and the British ship *Bristol City* fell to Rolf Manke in *U-358*, who also sank the Dalgleish Steamship Company's 5,212-ton *Wentworth* a few minutes later. There was a short breathing space while the U-boats reloaded their tubes and the merchantmen adjusted their tattered ranks. Then the enemy came back again, *U-638* sinking the British motor ship *Dolius* and *U-584* (Joachim Deecke) picking off a straggler the American *West Madaket*. Ralf von Jessen in *U-266* scored a hat trick by sinking in quick succession the British steamers *Selvistan* and *Gharinder*, and the 1,570-ton Norwegian *Bonde*.

During the six days ONS 5 was under attack, a total of thirteen merchantmen were lost, comprising nearly 70,000 tons of irreplaceable shipping. The convoy was saved from further decimation by the onset of dense fog and the arrival of ships of the 1st Support Group from St John's. In exacting their heavy toll the U-boats did not escape retribution. Seven of their number, U125 (Ulrich Folkers), U-192 (Werner Happe), U-438 (Heinrich Heinsohn), U-531 (Herbert Neckel), U-630 (Werner Winkler), U-638 (Oskar Staudinger) and U-710 (Dietrich von Carlewitz) were sunk. Eight other boats received major damage and ran for home.

Neither side in the battle was justified in claiming victory, for both had suffered serious losses, but most contemporary observers see ONS 5 as the turning point in the Battle of the Atlantic. The British naval historian Stephen Roskill wrote: 'The seven-day battle fought against 30 U-boats is marked only by latitude and longitude and it has no name by which it will be remembered; but it was in its own way as decisive as Quiberon Bay or the Nile.' Grand Admiral Dönitz wrote in his memoirs: 'The enemy lost 12 ships with a total tonnage of 55,761 tons, but we had to mourn the loss of seven U-boats. Such high losses could not be borne. Notwithstanding the fact that 12 ships had been sunk I regarded this battle as a defeat . . .'

Twenty-three-year-old Petty Officer Sydney Kerslake, coxswain of the trawler *Northern Gem*, recorded a poignant memory of ONS 5 that perhaps best sums up how desperate and hard-fought the battle was: 'Our next really bad one, although on each trip we picked up one or two crews, was the ONS 5 when we finished with over 300 men packed on board, and it was on this one also that I nearly lost my mind. I had sewed up several bodies, but the last one I had no sail twine left and had to resort to lashing the canvas round him with ordinary twine. As we tipped the body over the side after the usual service, I was very upset by seeing the fire bars slip out from around the feet, and for several nights I felt afraid to go on the deck, with the thoughts that he would come back for me for botching up his burial. I just could not shake the incident from my mind.'

Chapter Eight

A Lucky Escape

Late on 4 May, *U-223* and the other *Amsel* boats were ordered by BdU to close on ONS 5 at maximum speed. The weather was holding fair, with a fresh north-westerly wind and good visibility, and Karl Wächter pushed *U-223* to her utmost limits, but could average no more than 13 knots on the surface. Sailing in company with Horst Kremser in *U-383* and Eberhard Dahlhaus in *U-634*, he had the misfortune to run into ships of the 1st Support Group, a British hunter-killer group. Under the command of Commander G.N Brewer, RN, in the Black Swan-class sloop *Pelican*, with the ex-US Coastguard cutter *Sennen* and the frigates *Jed*, *Rother*, *Spey* and *Wear*, the 1st EG was steaming at full speed to the rescue of ONS 5.

Wächter's first intimation of danger was when he sighted a single mast-top on the horizon. This spelled warship and, sure enough, when the ship came hull-up, she had the lines of a destroyer. Wächter assumed her to be one of ONS 5's escorts. Remaining on the surface, he broke radio silence to report his sighting to BdU, a move which proved to be tempting providence. The enemy warship, one of Brewer's hunter-killer group, came at *U-223* with the speed of an express train, forcing Wächter and Kremser, who was close astern of him, to batten hatches and crash dive. Both boats were then subjected to a severe depth charging, Wächter alone counting thirty-nine dropped on him. However, neither U-boat suffered any more damage beyond a rude shock to their crews, and a reminder that over-confidence can be dangerous.

Surfacing again four hours later, Wächter found the horizon empty, and altered onto a south-westerly course, following a hydrophone bearing of his attacker in the hope that she would lead him to the convoy. His hopes were realized shortly after dark, when the silhouette of a large merchant ship was seen on the starboard bow. Wächter closed on the steamer until the range was down to 3,000 metres, manoeuvring into position to attack. Then, suddenly, there were shadowy shapes all around him. He had blundered into the middle of a convoy, and it could only be ONS 5.

Fortuitously, it now began to drizzle, and with the visibility down to just over 2,000 metres, and the night very dark, Wächter decided it would be safe to stay on the surface. Another mistake. It must have slipped his mind that the convoy escorts would be equipped with radar, for U-223 was soon under attack again, a destroyer appearing out of the mist at high speed. It was too late to dive, so Wächter could only take advantage of his low silhouette and small turning circle to outmanoeuvre the enemy and slip away into the darkness.

Wächter returned at midnight, and with the visibility then down to 1,000 metres, he disengaged his diesels, and crept through the escort screen on his electric motors. Like a wraith sliding silently through the drizzling rain he had just lined up on a steamer, when another U-boat, possibly Kremser or Dahlhaus, suddenly shot across his bows no more than 100 metres off. Wächter avoided a collision by throwing the helm hard over, and when he resumed course, the steamer had gone, and the drizzle had turned to fog.

For the next three hours, Wächter tried to re-establish contact with the convoy, running silent on the surface, and diving at regular intervals to listen for hydrophone effect. It was not until the greying of the black night that passed for dawn was his patience rewarded. A large shadow loomed up in the murk to port, and Wächter brought his tubes to bear in preparation for firing. At that moment, a destroyer appeared only 150 metres of U-223's starboard bow. Wächter took the boat down at a run, the first salvo of depth charges following him down.

As Wächter twisted and turned in an effort to escape, his attacker was joined by a second destroyer, and for the next four hours the enemy ships took turn and turn about to rain down death on the U-boat. Wächter tried every trick in his book of manoeuvres to shake them off, but like the bulldogs they were, the British held onto him. For *U-223*'s frightened crew it was like being trapped in a tin can being ceaselessly battered by a giant hammer. Deafened by the exploding charges, covered in powdered glass from the shattered gauges, they crouched in the eerie glow of the emergency lighting and prayed for escape, or a swift death.

Their prayers went unanswered, but gradually, very gradually, the terrifying crash of the depth charges moved further away, and the high-pitched whine of the avenging destroyers' turbines was no longer overhead. They had survived again, but when Wächter made to put some distance between himself and the enemy, the starboard engine coupling began to vibrate violently, a result of the pounding the boat had received. *U-223* crept away on one motor, the sound of the detonating charges fading astern.

Another four hours passed before Wächter deemed it safe to resurface. When he threw open the conning tower hatch and emerged into the fresh air, the fog around him was heavy with the acrid stench left by the exploding depth charges, a grim reminder of the fate that had almost overtaken them. A detailed examination of the boat revealed that, in addition to the smashed gauge glasses, two battery cells were broken, and more worrying still, *U-223* was trailing a very noticeable oil slick astern. Investigation showed that Nos. 2 and 4 outer diesel tanks were leaking. Nothing could be done at sea to stem the leaks, which left the possibility of the boat running short of fuel. Wächter's first instinct was to go after the convoy again, in the hope of sinking at least one ship, but common sense warned that the leaking tanks and the persistent oil slick were too serious a handicap to carry. The decision was taken out of his hands by a timely signal from BdU ordering the *Amsel* boats to break off operations against ONS 5 and to steer east at an economical speed. Another more lucrative target was on offer.

On 8 May, German Intelligence had intercepted and decrypted a signal giving details of two eastbound convoys, the fast convoy HX 237 out of New York, and the slow convoy SC 129 out of Sydney, Nova Scotia. Between them, these two convoys contained seventy-two ships, all fully loaded with stores and equipment for Russia and the planned Allied invasion of mainland Europe through Sicily. German High Command considered it essential that maximum damage be inflicted on these convoys, and Dönitz, no longer interested in ONS 5, was calling in all U-boats in the area. Three new packs were formed, *Rhein*, made up of twelve boats, *Elbe I* of eleven boats, and *Elbe II* also of eleven boats.

The slow convoy SC 129, twenty-six ships in all, sailed from Halifax on 3 May, and was joined by its ocean escort when south of Newfoundland on the 4th. B 2 Escort Group comprised the two destroyers HMS *Hesperus* and HMS *Whitehall*, with the five Flower-class corvettes *Campanula*, *Clematis*, *Gentian*, *Heather* and *Sweetbriar*. The S.O.E was Captain Donald Macintyre, who commanded *Hesperus*, and the rescue ship *Melrose Abbey* was in support. The fast convoy HX 237, with forty-six merchantmen, had sailed from New York a day earlier, escorted by C 2 Escort Group under the command of Lieutenant Commander E.H. Chevasse. C 2 consisted of the destroyer HMS *Broadway* (S.O.E), the frigate *Lagan*, the British corvette *Primrose*, and the Canadian corvettes *Chambly*, *Drumheller* and *Morden*. Steaming within handy reach of both convoys was E 5 Support Group, an independent hunter-killer group under the command of Captain Connolly Abel Smith, and made up of the three first-rate destroyers *Obdurate*, *Opportune* and *Pathfinder*, with the escort carrier *Biter*. HMS *Biter* was the first of five 'Woolworth' aircraft carriers to be deployed in the Atlantic. Previously Moore-McCormack Lines' freighter *Mormactern*, she had been stripped of her superstructure and cargo gear, and fitted with a flight deck for fifteen Swordfish aircraft of the Fleet Air Arm. She had a top speed of only 16½ knots, and was lightly armed with three 4-inch and fifteen 20mm guns, but her open-cockpit 'Stringbags', with their low landing speed, were ideal for convoy protection.

The *Elbe* and *Rhein* boats set up a long patrol line across the expected track of both SC 129 and HX 237 and waited, but Bletchley Park intercepted the considerable radio traffic between BdU and the boats and between the boats themselves, with the result that the convoys were diverted to pass south of the U-boat line. By the time this diversion was discovered, HX 237 had already slipped past the ambush and was well out into the Atlantic, while SC 129, which was taking a wider sweep to the south, was in the process of escaping. When BdU realized what was happening, the *Drossel* pack, then on station further to the east, was ordered to deal with HX 237 and *Elbe I* and *II* and *Rhein* were sent south to intercept SC 129.

While they were on their way south, five of the *Elbe* boats dropped out and went in search of the U-tankers to replenish their dwindling supply of diesel, and Fritz Henning's *U-533*, rammed and damaged by the corvette *Sunflower* during the ONS 5 action, was unable to carry on and returned to Biscay for repairs. Some of the *Rhein* boats were then diverted to pursue HX 237, the remainder being absorbed into *Elbe I* and *Elbe II*, giving them a total of twenty-one boats between them. *U-223*, having transferred oil from her leaking tanks to stop the giveaway oil slick, and repaired other minor damage inflicted in her brush with the 1st Support Group, was assigned to *Elbe II*. This pack contained, amongst others, the highly successful Baron Siegfried von Forstner in *U-402*. In the space of just one year, Forstner had been responsible for sinking 92,000 tons of Allied shipping, and had lately been promoted to *Korvettenkapitän* and decorated with the Knight's Cross. He was intent on adding to his total.

Moving south on the surface at all possible speed, the eleven boats of *Elbe II* reached a position some 350 miles to the northwest of the Azores, and there set up a north-south patrol line apart. The line was in position, with each boat twenty miles apart, by the morning of the 11th. It had been expected that SC 129 would appear over the horizon at any moment, but as the day wore on and nothing moved but the restless Atlantic rollers, it began to appear that once again SC 129 had escaped. Then, as the sun was going down, Wilhelm Luis in *U-504*, the southernmost boat of the line, sighted a cluster of masts and funnels on the far horizon. SC 129 was coming.

Luis alerted the other *Elbe II* boats, who came racing southwards, homing in on *U-504*'s signals. Soon, the ether was full of the U-boats' careless chatter as they showed their enthusiasm for the hunt. Captain Macintyre, listening in HMS *Hesperus*, had ample warning of their approach.

In his nine months in command of B 2, Donald Macintyre had not lost a single ship in convoy, and on this occasion he had no intention of spoiling his good record. Despite the adverse weather, the heavily-laden merchant ships of SC 129 were making good progress towards the North Channel, and just a few more days would see them with constant air cover and with the destroyers of Western Approaches Command close at hand. That night, Macintyre dropped *Hesperus* back to cover the vulnerable rear of the convoy, and warned *Whitehall* and the corvettes to be doubly alert.

On the bridge of the British steamer *Antigone*, second ship of SC 129's port outer column, Captain Frederick Williams, not being in Captain Macintyre's confidence regarding the presence of U-boats, was savouring thoughts of a safe conclusion to the voyage. The 4,545-ton *Antigone*, owned by the New Egypt & Levant Shipping Company of Alexandria, far removed from the warm waters of her peacetime voyaging, was bound from St John's, New Brunswick to Avonmouth with 7,800 tons of grain, 255 tons of general cargo and 250 trucks.

The 11 May dawned fine and clear, with only a light north-westerly blowing, although the sea was still rough and confused. After noon sights, something which had not been possible for many days, Captain Williams, for the first time since leaving Halifax, allowed himself the luxury of an afternoon nap on his day-bed. While he was snoozing, *U-402*, having broken through Macintyre's cordon, closed in on SC 129's port outer column. Captain Williams described the events that followed in his report to the Admiralty:

> No-one saw the track of the torpedo, which struck in the after end of No.2 hold on the port side. There was a dull explosion, which I barely heard, as I was sleeping in my room at the time. No flash was seen, but a huge column of water was thrown up on the port side. The port bridge boat was destroyed by the explosion, hatches were blown off Nos 2 and 2a holds, the jumper stay and wireless aerial came down, and the chart room collapsed. No.2 hold flooded immediately, and the ship took a heavy list to port. I could not see any deck damage.
>
> Owing to the damage to the wireless aerial, we were unable to send out a distress message. I ordered 'abandon ship', and the 2nd Engineer stopped the engines by the emergency stop valve on the boat deck.
>
> There was some slight panic amongst my crew, and on hearing

the explosion about seven of them rushed out of their quarters and jumped straight over the side of the ship into the water, resulting in two of them being drowned. One of the ABs released the after fall of the after port lifeboat, causing it to go with a run, and it immediately capsized on becoming waterborne. This AB was pulled over the side with the boat, and was drowned.

It was only necessary to lower the starboard after motor lifeboat, and all the remaining crew abandoned ship in this boat, with the exception of the men who had jumped overboard. This lifeboat was fitted with skates, so we had no difficulty in lowering it, being clear of the ship within ten minutes of the explosion. I did not bother to put the boat's wireless set into the lifeboat, as I knew the rescue ship would be along to pick us up almost immediately. We picked up two of the men from the water, and the other four were picked up by the rescue ship.

Twenty minutes after the explosion, I saw the ship sink. Her back was broken, and she sank with bow and stern rising out of the water.

After about an hour in the lifeboat, we were taken on board the rescue ship Melrose Abbey, which meanwhile had been cruising around looking for survivors in the water before rescuing the men from the lifeboat. A net was put over the side and we had no diffi- culty in climbing on board . . .

Siegfried von Forstner had fired a full salvo of four torpedoes from his bow tubes, one of which sank the *Antigone*, two missed, and the fourth hit the 3,082-ton Norwegian ship *Grado*, which had the misfortune to be abreast the *Antigone* in the adjacent column. Loaded with 1,000 tons of steel and 3,000 tons of lumber, the twenty-five-year-old *Grado* sank very quickly, but not before her master, Captain Theodor Jensen succeeded in getting his thirty-five-man crew away in the boats. Some were picked up by the *Melrose Abbey*, the rest by the escorting corvettes.

So ended a long and chequered career. Built as a wartime replacement ship in 1918 for Morel Limited of Cardiff and named *War Forest*, the *Grado* had been sold to Societié Maritime et Commerciale du Pacifique of Bordeaux in 1920 and renamed *Albergallus*. She became the *Thermidor* of Cie Nationale de Nav of Bordeaux in 1925, a year later being bought by N. Gerakis of

112

Cephalonia and renamed *Andreas Gerakis*. In 1927, she was passed to Union Minière et Maritime of Rouen and took the name *Louis Mercier*, returning to Bordeaux registry in 1930 under the same name. Finally, in 1937 she was bought by Hans Fr. Grann of Oslo, and registered under the Norwegian flag as the *Grado*.

There was swift retribution for *U-402* after the two ships went down. As she tried to creep away from the scene of her victory under water, she was picked up by the probing Asdic beam of the corvette *Gentian*, which smothered her with depth charges. *U-402* was so badly damaged that Forstner was very lucky to get her into La Pallice, where she arrived on 26 May. She did not reappear at sea until September 1943, by which time her run of luck, and the brilliant career of Siegfried Freiherr von Forstner were nearing their end. *U-402* was sunk in mid-Atlantic on 13 October 1943 by aircraft from the escort carrier USS *Card*. Forstner and his crew of forty-nine went to the bottom with her.

At around the time Forstner sank the *Antigone* and *Grado*, Karl Wächter's *U-223* was lying stopped on the surface some twenty miles from the same convoy, but with nothing in sight. Wächter was uncertain as to the exact location of SC 129, but as he searched the horizon with his binoculars, he saw a cloud of smoke rising into the sky to the north-east at a distance he estimated to be between sixteen and eighteen miles.

Wächter waited for dark, which did not come for another three hours, before approaching the convoy. At 20.13, his radio operator picked up a *Kurtzsignale* from *U-402* giving an accurate position for SC 129. Forstner, having escaped the attentions of HMS *Gentian*, was making a last gesture of defiance before heading for Biscay. Wächter adjusted his course accordingly, and increased to full speed. The other *Elbe II* boats followed suit.

It was a black night, with a force 6 westerly blowing and heaping up a nasty sea to add to the heave of the long Atlantic rollers. Heavy rain squalls lashed at the exposed faces of the oil-skinned watch in the conning tower, salt-laden spray crashed down on them, and for much of the time visibility was near zero. The only man in the tiny bridge structure not inconvenienced was Karl Wächter, who welcomed the wind and waves, and the stinging rain, sure in the knowledge that conditions were ideal for a U-boat to creep up on a convoy unseen.

Captain Donald Macintyre did not share Wächter's appreciation of the foul Atlantic weather. Braced against the compass binnacle on *Herperus*'s open bridge head down against the driving rain, he was an angry man. B 2's unblemished record had been broken by Siegfried von Forstner's opportunistic attack, and Macintyre was determined to take his revenge. *Hesperus* was astern of the convoy, and searching with Asdic and radar, and all the 'Mark I Eyeballs' she could muster; searching for those predators Macintyre's experience of convoy work told him would be stealthily moving in to feast on SC 129.

At 21.40, estimating that he must be very near the convoy, Wächter took *U-223* down to periscope depth. Almost immediately strong hydrophone effect was heard ahead and to starboard. The noise was characteristic of an escort vessel. Wächter surfaced again and approached cautiously along the bearing obtained. There was nothing there. Another two hours passed, with *U-223* on minimum revolutions groping her way through the rain, but there was nothing to be seen except the luminous tops of the waves as they surged past on their unending journey across the wide ocean. Wächter dived briefly to confirm the hydrophone effect. It was still there, on the same bearing and growing stronger. He went back to the surface, confident that he would soon have the convoy in sight. His confidence was justified a few minutes later when, in a break in the rain, a dark shadow was sighted to port. It appeared to be a destroyer or corvette and it was running across *U-223*'s bows. Wächter altered course to get in astern of the escort, hoping she would lead him to the convoy.

On the bridge of HMS *Hesperus*, it was near to the change of the watch, and steaming mugs of hot cocoa were being passed up from the galley. The long hours of searching for the enemy without result were beginning to tell, and there was an air of tired frustration hanging over the bridge. This vanished instantly when, on the stroke of midnight, a report was passed from the radar office of a small blip on the screen some five miles astern. 'U-boat!' Macintyre shouted, and threw the destroyer round in a tight, high-speed turn that put her port rails under and sent cocoa mugs crashing to the deck. The strident alarm gongs were still ringing as *Hesperus* straightened out and ran at full speed down the radar bearing.

Intent on shadowing the unidentified escort, Karl Wächter was caught unawares. He swung around at the urgent shout of the port lookout to see *Hesperus*, bow-wave creaming, charging at him out of the rain. For a brief moment, he considered a getaway on the surface, but it was obviously too late for that. He punched the klaxon and followed the watch down the conning tower hatch, slamming it shut as he screamed, *Dive! Dive! Dive!*.

The first sighting of the U-boat through Macintyre's night glasses was her phosphorescent wake, and it was fast disappearing as she dived. Now that his prey was in sight, he was icy calm. He altered course, hoping to cut the U-boat off before she went down, but she was too quick, her vents erupting spray as she flooded her tanks and slid beneath the waves.

Karl Wächter, in the mistaken belief that *Hesperus* had not yet seen him – he was not aware of the full capability of British shipborne radar – had left his dive very late. Macintyre's first pattern of depth charges followed him down and inflicted severe damage on the boat. The gauge glasses shattered as always, but it was far worse than that as they fought to gain depth. Water spurted from valves blown open, and there was a strong smell of chlorine gas coming from the battery room, indicating cracked cells. As the electric motors whirred into life, heavy vibrations from the after part of the boat were a sign that a propeller shaft was damaged. To make an already bad situation worse, the rudder refused to answer to the helm.

Wächter took the boat deep, and for the next hour *U-223* and her crew were subjected to a massive pounding by *Hesperus*' depth charges. The War Diary gives a bare outline of the ordeal:

0345	11 heavy depth charges. The destroyer comes after me, but I cannot hear her asdic. My hydrophones are not working.
	Between each depth charge there is a double bang and three double concussions, one of which is very heavy.
0415	14 heavy depth charges.

0430	9 heavy depth charges. Throughout the depth charging the boat remains on silent routine.
0445	8 heavy depth charges. They are right over us and to one side. Very heavy shock waves. I fear that we cannot get away. Main and emergency lighting has gone. We are in complete darkness. Most valves are jammed and the needle of the depth meter is stuck.
	Water flooding into bow torpedo room. Assume outer doors of tubes are cracked. Bridge voicepipe broken. Inner hatch jammed. Unable to close upper vent.
	Bunker and fresh water tank valves leaking. Some pipes split.
	Most inboard valves have lifted. Main steering jammed. Torpedo room flooding through vents.
	Reports of state of boat reaching control room:
	1.) Water in bow space.
	2.) Starboard electric motor burnt out. Insulation on fire.
	3.) Water spraying onto both diesels and electric motors.

Captain Donald Macintyre later recorded his version of the attack:

As the depth charges exploded, the tall columns of gleaming phosphorescent water soared up to stand momentarily like pillars of light before tumbling back into the sea in a torrent of foam.

I knew we could not have missed him by much and that he must be severely shaken at least. Now was the time to hammer him, to keep at him so as to give him no respite to repair damage. Reducing to a more moderate speed to give the asdics a chance we quickly picked up contact. As we expected, he had gone deep, so this was not a suitable target for the Hedgehog. Putting deep settings on the depth charges, we ran in and gave him another full pattern. Once more we ran in and this time for good measure we added a one-ton depth charge.

U-223 had taken a very severe hammering at Macintyre's hand, but with the emergency lighting restored and in hand steering, she was still capable of attempting her escape on one motor, but she was taking in too much water. The bilges were full, the forward torpedo room flooding, and the engine space awash. Karl Wächter decided that their only hope lay on the surface. Hatches were cleared, lifejackets broken out, and with a thunderous roar of compressed air into the main ballast tanks, *U-223* shot to the surface. Much to Wächter's relief, both diesels started at once, sucking in clean air through the open conning tower hatch in great gulps. Followed by his 1st Watch Officer, Wächter heaved himself up through the hatch onto the bridge. The destroyer was still there, less than 300 metres away, and waiting to pounce like a predatory animal. He went ahead on both engines, and with the helm hard over brought the boat short round to port to put the enemy astern. His only chance was to run for the cover of the nearest rain squall.

The U-boat breaking surface in a welter of foam so close to *Hesperus* took Macintyre by surprise. The range was too short for the destroyer's 4.7s to be brought to bear, but her 20mm Oerlikons opened up, spraying *U-223*'s conning tower and casings. Macintyre then ran alongside her, scattering depth charges set to explode at fifty feet. But Wächter, driven by desperation, was one move ahead of him. By now his diesels had worked up to full speed, and he turned inside *Hesperus*, letting fly with a torpedo from his stern tube as he fled. The torpedo missed its target, but the sight of its feathered wake streaking past within a few feet of the destroyer was enough to make Macintyre hold back. He resorted to using his searchlight and opening fire with his main armament as soon as the guns would bear.

The chase went on for half an hour, Macintyre all the time keeping a respectable distance from the fleeing U-boat while his guns continued to fire at her. *Hesperus* was rolling heavily in the big swell, and her gunners had great difficulty in keeping the U-boat, with little more than her conning tower above water, in their sights. Most of their shells were going wide, but the occasional shot went home on the U-boat's casing. The weather was very definitely in Wächter's favour, and this was just as well. In hand steering, *U-223* was painfully slow to manoeuvre, and any attempt to dodge the enemy's shot was out of the question. There was only one other option, and Wächter used it. Throughout the chase, *U-223*'s torpedomen, working up to their waists in water, had been struggling to clear the bow tubes. This was finally done, and when he saw the opportunity, Wächter turned the boat about and fired all four torpedoes at *Hesperus*.

The attack went unnoticed aboard the destroyer, for *U-223*'s torpedoes, set too deep in the confusion reigning in her bow section, all passed underneath *Hesperus*. Macintyre, unaware of his narrow escape, began to circle the U-boat, which was stopped and wallowing sluggishly in the swell. He was tempted to bring a swift end to the confrontation by ramming, but he was haunted by the last occasion on which *Hesperus* had rammed a U-boat. The U-boat was duly sunk, but the destroyer ended up with her bows bent and open to the sea, her forward compartments flooded, and her Asdic dome smashed. The convoy still being in danger from other U-boats – there might well be another dozen lurking in the shadows – Macintyre could not afford to put *Hesperus* out of action.

It was time for a compromise. Macintyre rang for full speed and took a run at *U-223*, altering course at the last moment, so that the destroyer slid along the U-boat's port side, rolling her over to starboard. It was a clever move, resulting in *Hesperus* suffering no more than scratched paintwork; for *U-223* it was almost a death blow. Pushed over on her beam ends, she righted herself again, but she was now very low in the water and completely stopped. Macintyre judged that the end of the U-boat must be very near, and pulled back to allow his guns to finish her off. This was a bad mistake, which could have ended in disaster for the destroyer. Wächter's men had not been idle. *U-223*'s stern tube was full again and, as *Hesperus* withdrew, a trail of phosphorescence raced towards her. The torpedo narrowly missed its target, causing Donald Macintyre to marvel at the persistence and courage of his German opponent.

The torpedo was Wächter's final gesture of defiance. His boat was in a sinking condition, and two of his men, the 2nd Watch Officer and the Senior Boatswain, had been injured by gunfire. The 2nd WO was only slightly wounded, with splinters in both thighs and left arm. Nevertheless, he was out of action for some time. Boatswain Rutz, was in a much more serious condition, with splinters in his head. It was time for Wächter to think of saving the rest of his men. He ordered everyone up from below onto the casing, where they stood, huddled around the conning tower, resigned to their fate as the waves smashing against the casing drenched them with icy spray. One of their number, Able Seaman Heinz Hoog, lost his grip and was washed overboard. Petty Officer Sieger went over after him, a brave but futile gesture. Both men drifted away, their cries for help fading. There was nothing anyone could do for them.

At this point Macintyre ordered *Hesperus*'s searchlight to be switched on. *U-223*, caught in its brilliant beam, was a sorry sight, listing heavily, low in the water, and her crew on deck waiting to abandon ship. In Macintyre's opinion, she could do no more harm, and mindful that SC 129 must now be at least thirty miles ahead, he decided he must leave the U-boat to her fate. With one final salvo of shells directed at her beaten enemy, *Hesperus* turned under full helm, and raced away to rejoin the convoy.

Fully expecting the enemy destroyer would come in for the kill, Karl Wächter was astonished when he saw her steaming away. However, he was not one to be slow in taking advantage of an opportunity. Abandoning all thoughts of leaving the boat, he sent his engineer below to survey the damage. The engineer reported back that the situation below was not good. The bilges were full of paint and broken glass, the pumps were out of action and there were ten tons of water in the after part. On the other hand, the boat did not appear to be in imminent danger of sinking, and while the main steering was out, they still had the hand gear, both diesels were working, and the damaged electric motor could be repaired on board. This was enough for Wächter. Sending his crew below again, he got under way and headed south, anxious to put as much distance between himself and SC 129 as possible before the escorts came looking for him.

Captain Donald Macintyre's B 2 Group was by then far too busy to chase *U-223*. U-boats were popping up all around the convoy, and with a speed of 17 knots on the surface they were able to run rings around the Flower-class corvettes, who could only manage 15 knots. Over the next twenty-four hours, while the weather began to moderate, the battle around SC 129 raged furiously. Thanks to a truly magnificent defensive action fought by the B 2 ships, no more merchantmen were sunk. *Hesperus* sent Siegfried Hesemann's *U-186* to the bottom when she found her at periscope depth ten miles out from the convoy. Hesemann and his crew of fifty-two were all lost. A number of other boats received serious damage before BdU called off the attack on the 14th. Macintyre's escorts were by this time running low on fuel and down to their last few depth charges, but help was at hand. HX 237 was by now under the protection of land-based aircraft, leaving the E 5 Support Group, with the carrier *Biter* and her destroyers to come to Macintyre's aid.

Chapter Nine

Some New Weapons

SC 129's faster neighbour, HX 237, had not escaped unmolested. The newly-formed *Drossel* pack, comprising eleven boats, had been searching for this convoy for some days, but without success, largely due to the poor visibility. Then, the German intelligence agency, *B-Dienst*, decrypted a signal giving a rendezvous position for stragglers from HX 237 on 11 May, and the pack closed in. The first sighting was made at 06.15 on the 12th by Paul Siegmann's *U-230*. Siegmann reported to BdU, and then approached the convoy, diving to attack before his presence became known to the escorts. The view through *U-230*'s periscope caused her 1st Watch Officer, Herbert Werner to go into raptures: 'I saw an amazing panorama. The entire horizon, as far and wide as I could see, was covered with vessels, their funnels and masts as thick as a forest. At least a dozen fast destroyers cut the choppy sea with elegance. As many as two dozen corvettes flitted around the edges of the convoy.'

Herbert Werner's exuberance must have led him to exaggerate the composition of HX 237 somewhat. By mid-1943 standards it was not a big convoy, only forty-one merchant ships, but its escort was formidable, although certainly not running into dozens. In addition to Lieutenant Commander Chevasse's C 2 Group, comprising the destroyer *Broadway* (S.O.E.), the frigate *Lagan* and the four corvettes *Primrose*, *Chambly*, *Drumheller* and *Morden*, the escort carrier *Biter* and her three destroyers *Obdurate*, *Opportune* and *Pathfinder* were in attendance. *Biter*'s Swordfish were flying continuous patrols over the convoy, and no matter how hard they tried, the *Drossel* boats were unable to get close to HX 237. However, they would not go empty-handed.

121

The 7,138-ton British ship *Fort Concord*, a wartime replacement belonging to the Ministry of War Transport and managed by the Larrinaga Steamship Company of Liverpool, was commanded by Captain Francis P. Ryan. She sailed from Halifax with HX 237 on 3 May carrying 8,500 tons of grain and 700 tons of military stores, including four aircraft. Chief Officer J.B. Tunbridge related events in a report submitted to the Admiralty on 21 May:

> During the night of 4/5th May we ran into dense fog which continued throughout the day and following night, and during the first watch on 6th May we lost contact with the convoy. We endeavoured to make the rendezvous for the 7th May using dead reckoning as the visibility was too bad and we were unable to obtain sights. At 1200 on the 7th we sighted a destroyer who gave us the bearing and distance from the convoy, but I think the officer responsible reversed the bearing, because, instead of dropping astern to where the convoy was, we proceeded on a bearing which took us well ahead of it, and consequently failed to contact the convoy. On the 8th May we received a signal from the Admiralty giving us rendezvous for the 8th, 9th, 10th and 11th May. The fog lifted during the night of 8/9th May, so on the morning of the 9th we were able to take sights and succeeded in making the rendezvous for 10th May. We found only four other merchant ships at the rendezvous, but there was no sign of the main part of the convoy or any escort vessels.
>
> We continued in company with these four other vessels, making the rendezvous for the 11th May. The convoy was still not in sight and as we did not see any escort vessels or aircraft, we opened up our sealed orders and proceeded independently at full speed. During the day we intercepted distress messages from two ships astern of us. We did not know submarines were in our immediate vicinity and received no diversionary signals.

The distress calls the *Fort Concord*'s radio room intercepted were from the SC 129 ships *Antigone* and *Grado*, then 750 miles to the west, and victims of Baron Siegfried von Forstner's torpedoes. The *Fort Concord* was at that point 500 miles south-west of Ireland, and at her top speed of 10½ knots would expect to be in the Western Approaches within thirty-six hours. This was of some comfort to Captain Ryan, who had already lost one ship to the U-boats in this war. Unfortunately for Ryan, Max-Martin Teichert in *U-456*, having failed to break through the tight escort screen around HX 237, was hunting for stragglers – or rompers, as the case may be. Chief Officer Tunbridge takes up the story again:

On the 12th May at 0240 in position 46°05' N 25°20' W, steaming at 10¼ knots on a course of 037°, we were struck by a torpedo. The weather was fine and clear, visibility good; with a moderate sea and heavy swell, wind south-west force 5.

At the time of the torpedoing there were no other ships in sight. I do not know if the track of the torpedo was seen as none of the lookouts are among the survivors, but certainly the ship did not alter course before the explosion. The torpedo struck the after part of the engine-room on the port side with a very heavy explosion. I was in my cabin at the time and heard no mention of any flash or water being thrown up. The port after lifeboat was blown away and there was a split in the boat deck on the port side. All accommodation on both sides collapsed. The ship did not list but settled rapidly on an even keel.

I rushed up to the bridge and heard the Captain ordering the crew to boat stations. I made my way to the after port motor boat, but found this boat had disappeared, so I rushed across to the starboard after lifeboat, the boat deck was awash before this boat got away. We were clear of the ship in this boat by 0243. The Captain was still forward lowering the other starboard boat when at 0244 the ship sagged amidships, broke her back, and sank with her bow and stern in the air.

There were 15 men in my lifeboat, which was full of water, two of the crew, thinking the boat was sinking, clambered out of it onto a raft. We succeeded in picking up two more men from the water, and could hear several others shouting and blowing their whistles but were unable to pick them up as we could not see them owing to the large amount of wreckage which was floating about on the water, also the boat was full of water and it was practically unmanageable. Two apprentices and the 4th Engineer, who were in my boat, told me that their accommodation had collapsed on the starboard side and that probably many of the crew were trapped. One of the sailors said that the A.N.D nets were blown inboard onto the deck, this man had apparently become entangled in them, and was certain that a number of the crew were also trapped in those nets, being unable to extricate themselves before the ship sank. The

Chief Engineer thought he saw the Captain's boat in the water after the ship sank, but no one else saw it and I think it is extremely doubtful that this boat got away. The Wireless Operator was in his room at the time of the explosion but I do not know if any message was sent out.

At 0315 the submarine surfaced, so I told the crew to lie down in the lifeboat, which was very low in the water owing to the amount of water still in it. The submarine apparently thinking it had been abandoned steamed over to the raft, I could hear them speaking to the two men on the raft but was not able to hear what was said. The submarine only remained with them for a few minutes, then after steaming round the wreckage went off on the surface. At 0300 we experienced a heavy rain and hail storm during which it was very cold but the weather soon cleared and we set to work bailing out the water, using the hand pump, but I found it more practicable to use the buckets. By daylight the boat was dry so I hoisted the sails and set a course to the North East.

We had all the usual food in the lifeboat, including tins of condensed milk. I do not think we had hand rockets, only smoke floats and ordinary red flares. At 1330 a Swordfish aircraft came along. I think this plane must have sighted our boat before we saw it, because it flew straight over to us, circled and flew off. At 1500 we sighted the smoke of a ship on the horizon, and HMCS Drumheller steamed over and rescued all survivors. We remained on board HMCS Drumheller, arriving at Londonderry on the 16th May.

Although there was an aircraft carrier with the convoy, no aircraft were seen at the rendezvous to instruct ships where the convoy was. We were at the rendezvous for two days with four other ships and had an aircraft been there to instruct us there is a probability that neither my ship nor Norwegian who was torpedoed would have been lost.

Of the *Fort Concord*'s crew of fifty-five, twenty-eight were lost with her, including Captain Francis Ryan and the ship's eight DEMS gunners, many of whom, as suggested by Chief Officer Tunbridge, were trapped in the heavy steel anti-torpedo nets which had fallen on deck. Their end will not have been easy. Two others, probably those on the liferaft, were picked up after forty-seven days adrift on their raft. Two more men were said to have been taken prisoner by *U-456*. They must have perished with

Max-Martin Teichert and his crew when the U-boat was sunk later on the 12th.

Surprised on the surface by a patrolling Liberator, *U-456* was damaged by a *Fido* homing torpedo. The Liberator called up one of E 5's destroyers, HMS *Opportune*, which came racing to the scene to find the U-boat still on the surface. With his boat so severely damaged that she seemed in imminent danger of sinking, Teichert was trapped between two enemies, one in the air and the other on the sea. Surrender seemed the only feasible option, but as *Opportune* opened fire, Teichert decided to risk diving. No one knows what happened to *U-456* after she dropped below the surface, but she was never seen again. It seems likely that her pressure hull must have been breached, and when she dived she just carried on going to the bottom, taking all on board with her.

In addition to the *Fort Concord*, HX 237 lost two other ships, the 4819-ton Norwegian motor ship *Brand*, and another Norwegian, the 9,432-ton tanker *Sandanger*, both of which had romped ahead and were at one time in company with the British ship. The *Drossel* pack was withdrawn on the 13th, having lost four of their number to the British, namely *U-89* (Dietrich Lohmann), *U-447* (Friedrich Bothe), *U-456* (Max-Martin Teichert) and *U-753* (Alfred Manhardt von Mannstein). This proportionately heavy loss drew a grudging admission from BdU that the North Atlantic was becoming a very dangerous sphere of operations for the U-boats, right from the first day carrier-borne aircraft were sighted, and later on the carrier herself. These and other land-based aircraft greatly hampered operations, which finally had to be broken off because the air support was too powerful.

Far astern of the shifting battleground for HX 237, the battered and bruised *U-223* limped slowly eastwards. Listing awkwardly, and on one engine to conserve her dwindling supply of fuel, she steered an untidy course under her emergency hand steering. During the night of the 13th, Karl Wächter was faced with the sad task of committing to the deep the body of Boatswain Rutz, who had died of his wounds.

Pausing only to reflect that the North Atlantic made a cold and lonely grave for Rutz, Wächter continued on his way. With over 1,200 miles to go to St Nazaire, the passage ahead promised to be long and filled with known and unknown dangers. Navigation would be a hit and miss business, for both *U-223*'s delicate chronometers had been smashed in the depth charging, and without them they had no means of fixing longitude. To add to that, Wächter was unable to reload his bow tubes, and would have to rely on his single stern tube should he meet up with an enemy warship. But the greatest challenge must come when they neared the Bay of Biscay. Rumour had it that the skies over Biscay were dark with U-boat-hunting aircraft of RAF Coastal Command, which now had over thirty squadrons of radar-equipped planes at its disposal. They would need to tread carefully when nearing the Bay, running submerged by day, and on the surface at night only if no aircraft were around.

The realization of how dire his situation was prompted Wächter to send out a radio call for help, which was answered by *U-359*, commanded by *Oberleutnant* Heinz Förster. The two boats met up north of the Azores before dawn on the 14th, when to the astonishment of all on board *U-223*, the missing Leading Seaman Heinz Hoog was returned to them with a remarkable tale to tell. After being washed overboard when *U-223* was rammed by HMS *Hesperus*, Hoog had drifted around for some hours in the dark, convinced that he was going to die a lonely death in this cold ocean. Then, by some quirk of fate – or perhaps Hoog's prayers were answered – there was a loud hissing sound, and *U-359* broke the surface within a few metres of him. He was pulled from the water, numb with exposure and near to delirium, but the luckiest man alive.

On orders from BdU, Heinz Förster abandoned his patrol, and the two boats proceeded in company towards St Nazaire, miraculously escaping the attentions of Coastal Command on the way. They arrived off the port on the night of 24 May.

U-223's second war patrol, lasting seventy-nine days, had not left any lasting impression on the enemy, except perhaps for some superficial damage to one destroyer, but in bringing his damaged boat home safely Karl Wächter had shown commendable seamanship and courage. His achievement did not go unrecognized. On 1 June 1943, Grand Admiral Dönitz promoted Wächter to *Kapitänleutnant*.

In April 1943, the German Minister of Propaganda, Joseph

Goebbels, assured the German people that: 'In the U-boat war we have England by the throat.' An increasingly beleaguered nation, ready to clutch at any straw offered, might have believed the Reich Minister, but Karl Dönitz knew better. The Atlantic convoys, bigger and crossing at more frequent intervals, were getting through often with insignificant losses. At the same time, the U-boats were being severely mauled at the hands of the aggressive Allied surface escorts and aircraft. German casualties for the first four months of 1943 made grim reading; six boats being lost in January, nineteen in February, sixteen in March, fifteen in April – and then came May, with no less than forty-two boats destroyed. And with those forty-two boats had gone 2,000 men, among them Grand Admiral Dönitz's son, twenty-one-year-old *Oberleutnant* Peter Dönitz, 2nd Watch Officer of *U-954*. His boat had been sunk with the loss of all hands on 19 May while attacking Convoy SC 130.

For the first time since the war began, the number of U-boats being sunk – most of them on the North Atlantic convoy routes – exceeded the monthly production of the German shipyards. And for Dönitz, stricken with grief by the loss of his son, there were more ominous signs. The U-boat crews, harassed by a superior enemy day and night at sea, and subjected to heavy bombing while they were in port, were beginning to lose heart.

SC 130, the convoy which cost him his son, proved to be the decision maker for Dönitz. Four wolf packs were sent in to attack this convoy, and while they failed to sink one Allied ship, five of their number were lost. This was a fight that had become too one-sided, and by the end of the month Dönitz began to withdraw the U-boats from the Atlantic convoy routes, leaving only a small number operating off the coast of Brazil and in the Freetown area.

For the next three and a half months, an unnatural calm settled over the broad reaches of the North Atlantic, a calm they had not known in four years of bloody war. Then, in mid-August, the U-boats began to emerge from the Biscay ports again. They were not in great numbers, but their teeth had been sharpened. All were fitted with extra guns against air attack, and a number were equipped with the new *Hagenuk* receiver and *Zaunkönig*, or T5, acoustic torpedoes. The *Hagenuk* was an improvement on the old Metox receiver, in that it was able to detect radar transmissions without radiating detectable signals of its own. The *Zaunkönig*, known to the Allies as the GNAT (German Naval Acoustic Torpedo), was designed to home in automatically on to propeller noise, and had only to be aimed in the general direction of the convoy, and left to find its own target.

As a curtain raiser for the return of the U-boats to the North Atlantic, it was decided to target a slow westbound convoy which *B-Dienst* advised would be sailing from British waters in late September. The exact route of the convoy was unknown, but it was assumed it would be going north along the great circle route, the shortest distance between Britain and America. A pack of twenty-one U-boats, code named *Leuthen*, was formed and ordered to set up a 350 mile long patrol line straddling the great circle route in longitude 25° West by 20 September. Nine of the *Leuthen* boats were equipped with the *Hagenuk* search receiver and *Zaunkönig* torpedoes. The T5s, fired through the stern tube, were to be used exclusively against convoy escorts, while the bow tubes would be loaded with standard torpedoes for use against merchant ships. Hopes were high in Berlin that this wolf pack, with its new weapons, would deal a hammer blow to Allied shipping.

BdU would have been even more confident of a stunning victory had it been known that not one convoy, but two, were about to sail into *Leuthen*'s net. The slow convoy ONS 18, with twenty-seven merchantmen, cleared the North Channel on the 13th, to be followed three days later by the fast convoy ON 202 with thirty-eight ships. ONS 18 was escorted by B 3 Group under the command of Commander M.J. Evans RN, in the destroyer HMS *Keppel*. With him was a second destroyer HMS *Escapade*, the British corvettes *Narcissus* and *Orchis*, the Free French corvettes *Lobelia*, *Renoncule* and *Roselys*, the trawler HMS *Northern Foam*, and a new innovation, the merchant aircraft carrier *Empire MacAlpine*, which was, in effect, a bulk carrier fitted with a small flight deck from which the three Swordfish biplanes she carried could take off and land. She was manned by a merchant crew, and her like were regarded by many as a poor substitute for an escort carrier, but she was the sting in the tail of B 3 the U-boats would not be expecting. Working with the group was the rescue ship *Rathlin*. The other convoy, ON 202, was under the protection of Escort Group C 2, whose Senior Officer, Commander P.W. Burnett RN, sailed in the Canadian destroyer *Gatineau* with three other British ships, the destroyer *Icarus*, the frigate *Lagan* and the corvette *Polyanthus*, and the Canadian corvettes *Drumheller* and *Kamloops*. Air cover for both convoys was to be provided by very long range Liberators of 120 Squadron from Iceland.

The first part of the crossing was made in fine, settled weather, with the faster ON 202 slowly overhauling ONS 18. It was known that the U-boats were gathering, but their position was unknown until, early on the 19th, a Liberator of 10 Squadron RAF, on its return flight from Iceland to Gander, surprised *U-341* on the surface. *U-341*, commanded by *Oberleutnant* Dietrich Epp, was the northernmost marker of the *Leuthen* patrol line in 25° West. Epp made the decision to stay on the surface and fight it out with his new improved anti-aircraft batteries, but this proved to be a mistake. *U-341* went down under a hail of bombs and cannon fire, taking Dietrich Epp and his crew of forty-nine with her.

At noon that day, ONS 18 was in latitude 57° North, about 475 miles west of Rockall, with ON 202 some sixty miles astern. It had now been decided that the two convoys would merge during the next twenty-four hours and become one. To assist in their defence, the 9th Support Group was to join B 3 and C 2. This was made up of the frigate HMS *Itchen* (S.O.E.), the Canadian destroyers *St Croix* and *St Francis*, and the corvettes *Chambly*, *Morden* and *Sackville*, also Canadian.

During the day, as the two convoys moved closer together, it became evident from increased radio activity that a number of U-boats were gathering around them. These began probing the defences of ONS 18 that night from about 22.30, and continued to do so throughout the night. They were successfully repulsed by the escorts, but during one of their attacks B 3 suffered the first casualty. HMS *Escapade*'s Hedgehog exploded prematurely, causing major damage to the destroyer, and she withdrew from the convoy and returned to port for repairs. Thus, *U-341* was avenged without the *Leuthen* boats firing a shot.

ON 202 came under attack in the early hours of the 20th, but once again the U-boats were beaten off. Then, at around 04.00, the frigate *Lagan* obtained an HF/DF bearing, then a radar contact on Paul-Friedrich Otto's *U-270* and gave chase. The radar echo faded at 3,000 yards, indicating that Otto must have dived, but when *Lagan* was within about 1,200 yards of his estimated diving position and moved in to drop depth charges, the frigate's stern was blown off by a torpedo. She had become the victim of a T5 accoustic torpedo. *Lagan* did not sink, but with her rudder and propellers smashed and twenty-nine of her crew dead, she was out of the fight for good. She was eventually towed into port, but proved to be beyond repair, and was scrapped.

Hubertus Purkhold in *U-260* also made an underwater attack on ON 202 while all attention was focused on HMS *Lagan*, but all three torpedoes, aimed at merchant ships, missed their target, and Purkhold was forced to retire in a hurry when the escorts came after him. Another boat, Horst Hepp's *U-238*, was also in the vicinity of ON 202, but was at first driven off by the corvette *Polyanthus*. Hepp came back a little later and began shadowing, waiting for an opportunity to strike. Around 08.00, with the sun well up, he saw a gap in the escort ring and broke through to torpedo simultaneously two 7,000-ton US-flag Liberty ships, the *Theodore Dwight Weld* and the *Frederick Douglas*. The *Weld* sank at once, but the other ship remained afloat for another twelve hours, before being sent to the bottom by Otto Ferro in *U-645*.

After the torpedoing of the two American ships, the visibility deteriorated, and the U-boats lost touch. While they were out of sight, ONS 18 and ON 202 merged to form one single convoy of sixty-three ships. The 9th Support Group had also arrived on the scene, with the result that Convoy ONS 18/ON 202's combined escort force, with Commander M. J. Evans as Senior Officer Escort, now totalled five destroyers, one frigate, eleven corvettes, one merchant aircraft carrier, and one armed trawler, while Liberators of 120 Squadron were overhead. This was not a convoy to be trifled with.

The *Leuthen* boats were obviously unaware of the odds against them, and were not about to go away. Fritz Albrecht in *U-386* regained contact late that afternoon, but unfortunately for Albrecht his radioed sighting report was intercepted, and he was immediately pounced on by the destroyer *Keppel* and the corvette

Roselys, who chased him off. Several other boats tried to break through the ring of escorts, but failed miserably. BdU now decided that more might be gained by allowing the *Zaunkönig*-equipped boats to mount an attack on the escorts.

The ex-US Navy *four-stacker St Croix* was the first victim. Just after dusk, she was away from the convoy investigating a contact when she was sighted by Rudolf Bahr in *U-305*. Bahr turned stern-on to her and fired a T5, which went home with devastating results. The explosion completely crippled the Canadian destroyer, leaving her drifting helplessly. The frigate *Itchen* went to her rescue, but in doing so put herself in the line of fire of another of Bahr's torpedoes, but luckily this exploded in her wash and did little damage to the frigate.

Bahr now turned his attention back to the crippled *St Croix*, putting two more torpedoes into her from his bow tubes. The destroyer sank in a few minutes, leaving most of her crew clinging to rafts or struggling in the near-freezing water. And there they would stay for the next twelve hours. *Polyanthus* was sent to pick them up, but she too fell to a T5, this time fired from the stern tube of Oskar Curio's *U-952*. The torpedo literally blew the little corvette out of the water, killing all but one of her crew. The lone survivor, along with eighty-five survivors from the *St Croix*, were pulled from the water by HMS *Itchen* next morning.

Other U-boats, including Robert Schetelig's *U-229* and Horst Rendtel's *U-641*, made determined attacks on the convoy during the night, but they were all repulsed by counter-attacks mounted by HMS *Keppel*, supported by *Itchen* and the corvette *Narcissus*. In the general mêlée, it was thought that at least one U-boat was damaged.

Early on the 21st, the convoy was re-routed to the south in order to come within range of aircraft based in Newfoundland, as the Liberators from Iceland were operating near to their extreme range. The move proved to be counter-productive, for during the day the convoy ran into dense fog and air cover was out of the question. On the other hand, the fog proved to be an equal handicap to the U-boats, and for the next twenty-four hours the convoy and its attackers sailed on through the fog, invisible to each other, and impotent in attack or defence.

The fog became patchy at first light on the 22nd, and then

began to clear. Within the hour, at least seven *Leuthen* boats had made contact with the convoy, but by this time Liberators of the RCAF from Newfoundland were overhead. The hunters soon became the hunted. But the U-boats threw caution to the winds and, using their quadruple 20-mm guns to good effect, fought back on the surface, and for the most part succeeded in spoiling the Liberators' aim. Two of their number, however, paid the price of their defiance. Paul-Friedrich Otto's *U-270*, responsible for crippling HMS *Lagan*, was badly damaged, and followed her victim on the long road back to the repair yards. Likewise, *U-377*, damaged and with her commander Gerhard Kluth wounded, withdrew from the fray and made for home.

During the day, as more *Leuthen* boats joined the attack on the convoy, their numbers began to tell, and Commander Evans' combined escort force was sorely tested. *U-584* (Joachim Deecke), in attempting to hit *Chambly* with a T5, was damaged by the corvette's gunfire, while *U-952*, responsible for sinking *Polyanthus*, was rammed and severely damaged by the trawler *Northern Foam*. Evans also had the satisfaction of spearing Robert Schetelig's *U-229* with *Keppel*'s sharp bows. She went to the bottom. The battle raged fast and furious, with even a 'Stringbag' flown off from the *Empire MacAlpine* joining in. When the sun went down, the honours were in favour of the combined British, French and Canadian escort force. The *Leuthen* boats pulled back to lick their wounds, but they would be back again after dark.

The night attack was led by Herbert Engel in *U-666*, who made his approach at 23.00 and loosed off two T5s in the general direction of the escorts. One torpedo exploded in the wake of the corvette *Morden* without doing any damage, but the other streaked towards HMS *Itchen* and exploded at her stern with a deafening roar. The explosion was so devastating that it demolished much of the after part of the frigate, some of the debris being later found on *U-666*'s casing. *Itchen* went down within minutes, taking with her not only her crew but the survivors she had on board. Of more than 200 men, only three were picked up alive, one from the frigate, one from *St Croix* and the lone survivor from *Polyanthus*, who must have been endowed with extraordinary good luck.

Encouraged by Engel's success, Horst Hepp brought *U-238* in soon after midnight and fired five torpedoes, three of which were *Zaunkönigs*. Hepp reaped a rich reward, his five torpedoes sinking three merchantmen, two of them Norwegians, the 3,642-ton motor ship *Oregon Express* and the 5,096-ton steamer *Skjelbred*, and the 7,134-ton British steamer *Fort Jemseg*. The *Fort Jemseg*'s story, as recorded by her master, Captain L. J. White, is worth relating.

. . . At midnight 22/23rd September things quietened down, so I decided to take the opportunity to get some sleep. I had only been in my cabin for about 10 minutes, when, at 0010 0n the 23rd September, in position 53°18' N 40°24' W, steering 230° (T) at 7 knots, the ship was struck by two torpedoes in quick succession from a U-boat. There was a moderate swell, with a SW'ly wind force 3/4, weather being fine and visibility good, but dark . . .

. . . The two torpedoes hit my ship within half a minute of each other. Immediately after the first torpedo struck I jumped out of bed, went to the bridge and rang the engine-room telegraph to 'stop'. I was about to help the 2nd Officer to fire the rockets, when the second torpedo hit the ship. The first torpedo exploded on the port quarter, blowing the propeller off, damaging the rudder and causing the ship to shudder. No flash was seen, nor did anybody report seeing a column of water thrown up. The second torpedo exploded just as violently as the first and I saw a big flash from it on the port side (I was on the bridge by this time). From the position of the flash I think this torpedo exploded immediately on hitting the ship's side. I did not see any water thrown up and nothing came down on the bridge. The gunner in charge of the after gun reported that he heard the first torpedo as it approached from the port side, but no one saw the tracks of either torpedo. The second explosion blew No. 5 hatches, beams and derricks into the air. It also shook the main throttle valve open, which started the main engines turning, and they continued to do so for about an hour and a half, but as the propeller was missing, it made no difference to the ship.

I switched on the red light and fired the 'Roman Candles', which were supplied instead of rockets. They worked well, throwing bright lights. After the wireless operators had transmitted a distress message I ordered 'Abandon Ship'. There were four lifeboats, none of which was damaged, but it was only necessary to lower one from each side; the other two were left on board. They were under ordinary radial davits and were lowered successfully, the ship being abandoned 7 or 8 minutes after the first explosion. All the crew abandoned in an orderly manner. The accommodation bulkhead collapsed and several of the crew had great difficulty in getting out. I was afraid some of them had been left behind, as the Chief Officer, in charge of the other boat, had pushed off before all his crew had time to reach it. He shouted for them to jump overboard, but as they were able to get into my boat, they did not do so . . .

After clearing the ship we had to dodge the ships of the slow convoy (ONS 18) coming up astern. The S.O. ordered HM Trawler *Northern Foam*, an escort vessel, to pick up survivors. This vessel arrived and within an hour had picked up my boat, with 32 men. I did not learn until 10 days later that the Chief Officer's boat, with 22 men, was picked up by the ss *Romulus*, a vessel in the slow convoy.

HM Trawler *Northern Foam* also received orders to take the crew off the torpedoed Norwegian ship, but they did not want to leave her as only the steering gear was damaged. This vessel was making water slowly in one of her after holds; they considered that this could be kept under control easily with their pumps and if they could repair the steering gear the ship could proceed with the convoy. The Master tried to get the ship under way, but as the rudder was damaged, she went round in circles. The S.O. was unable to wait for the necessary repairs to be carried out, so the crew were obliged to abandon ship.

After remaining on board HMT *Northern Foam* for about half an hour, I decided to return to my ship to make sure nobody was still on board. A lifeboat was launched in charge of an RN lieutenant from the *Northern Foam* and manned by a naval crew. I stayed on board for about 10 minutes. Although it was still dark, I made a thorough search and found one seriously injured man lying on deck. He was unconscious and delirious; both his legs were broken, he also had internal injuries and was bleeding from the nose and mouth. I think he must have been blown into the air when the torpedoes exploded. I gave him an injection of morphia and put him in the boat, but he did not regain consciousness, and died at 0700 aboard *Northern Foam*, being buried at sea at 1600 the same day.

I saw that the ship was slowly sinking. The decks were badly buckled along the port side, although there were no cracks and no visible holes in the sides. No. 5 hold was flooded to the hatch coam-

ings and the after decks awash. Some of No.4 hatch covers were
blown off, but the tarpaulin still held a few in place. I listened at
the ventilator of No. 4 hold, but could not hear any water rushing
in, but I think it was possible that it was seeping through slowly.
The Chief Engineer had told me that as soon as the auxilliaries
stopped, water percolated into the engine-room. There was no
damage on the starboard side, as far as I could see. After making
sure that there were no further survivors on board, I returned to
HMT *Northern Foam*. The last thing I saw of my ship was at 0200,
when her bow was well out of the water, and the poop awash . . .

Captain White added a footnote to his report which paints a
stark picture of life at sea for many British merchant seamen of
the day:

This is my fourth experience. In November 1940 I was serving in
the ss *Behar* when she was sunk by one of the first acoustic mines.
In July 1941 whilst proceeding independently in the Atlantic on
board ss *Bangalore*, she collided with the *Richmond Castle* and
was sunk. Both ships were steaming without lights at 16 knots. In
March 1943 I was torpedoed in ss *Empire Bowman* whilst homeward bound from the Middle East. This vessel also sank.

The *Leuthen* boats last sally against ONS 18/ON 202 was made
just on sunrise of the 23rd, when Oskar Curio in *U-952* sank the
American steamer *Steel Voyager*. Curio hit another American
Liberty, the *James Gordon Bennett*, but his torpedo failed to
explode, doing no more damage than putting a significant dent
in the American's hull plating.

During the morning, dense fog again came to the rescue of the
harassed convoy, and the U-boats, exhausted by their long
struggle, were called off. They were justified in claiming a victory
of sorts, but not on the scale of that claimed by U-boat Command:

From the boats' radio messages, the result of this four-day battle
appeared to be twelve destroyers definitely and three probably
sunk by T5 (*Zaunkönig*) torpedoes, and nine merchant ships sunk
by ordinary torpedoes, for the loss of two U-boats. This was
undoubtedly a splendid achievement and even better results might
have been attained had not fog impeded the second day of the
operation . . .

In reality, the convoy lost six merchant ships of 36,000 tons, while the escort force suffered a destroyer, a frigate and a corvette sunk, with one other frigate severely damaged. Nevertheless, the operation had proved the deadly effectiveness of the *Zaunkönig* torpedo. *Leuthen* lost three boats, *U-229* to HMS *Keppel*, and *U-338* and *U-341* to the Liberators. Three others, *U-270*, *U-377* and *U-952* were so badly damaged that they were forced to make for home. The U-boats failed to regain even a vestige of their former dominance over the North Atlantic convoy routes. Nor would they ever do so again.

Chapter Ten

Fresh Pastures

For *Kapitänleutnant* Karl-Jurgen Wächter and his crew, the long summer months of 1943 with *U-223* under repair in St Nazaire passed in an idyllic blur of good living. The constant bombing as the British tried in vain to smash their way into the U-boat pens was unnerving at times, but cocooned in this little corner of Brittany, quartered ashore in comparative comfort, the horrors they had experienced in the Atlantic battles faded into the background. But, as the time to return to sea came ever nearer, the reality of Germany's impending defeat could not be ignored.

Out in the Atlantic, the scales had tipped heavily in the favour of the Allies. Harassed from the air and mercilessly pursued by the Royal Navy's new hunter-killer groups, the U-boats were fighting a desperate rearguard action, with as many as twenty of their number being lost every month. And, whereas in the heydays of 1942 they were consistently sending over 100 enemy merchant ships to the bottom month on month, they were now hard-pressed to bring their monthly score up to double figures. At the same time, with the new 7,000-ton Liberty ships sliding down the slipways of the American yards at the rate of two a day, Allied ship production had at last caught up with, and was now exceeding, the losses inflicted by the U-boats.

On land, in Soviet Russia, there was a summer stalemate, with greatly depleted and demoralized German forces holding a line from Lenigrad in the north to the River Donetz in the south, but the massed battalions of the Red Army were poised for a break-through. In the Mediterranean, General Erwin Rommel's once unstoppable drive for the Suez Canal had ended in a hasty evacu-ation from Cape Bon, Sicily had fallen to the Allies without significant resistance and, at dawn on 3 September, British and Canadian troops of the 8th Army crossed the narrow Straits of Messina and stormed ashore on the Italian Mainland north of Reggio. The soft underbelly of Hitler's Europe had been pierced.

The news from home was every bit as bad. German cities and ports were being pounded day and night by British and American bombers in a campaign designed to break the morale of the German people and disrupt industrial production. On 19 August, following a tour of the northern port of Hamburg, Grand Admiral Dönitz had reported to Hitler:

> The general feeling of the people is one of depression in spite of their willingness to work. Everybody sees only the many reverses of Germany. In view of the impressions I gained from my visit to Hamburg and on the basis of many reports and intelligence I believe it is urgent that the Fuehrer should speak to the people very soon. I consider this to be absolutely necessary in view of the current difficulties and the war situation; the entire German nation longs for it.

Unlike Winston Churchill, who in the dark days of 1940 had no hesitation of informing the British people that they faced 'blood, sweat, toil and tears', Hitler remained silent, perhaps refusing to believe what was patently true. Germany, on the verge of defeat at sea, fighting on two fronts on land, and in retreat on both, was looking at a bleak future.

Such were the failing fortunes of the Third Reich when, on 14 September 1943, Karl Wächter took *U-223* out of the locks at St Nazaire with orders to join a small force of U-boats already inside the Mediterranean. The object was to inflict maximum damage on Allied troop supply convoys, but first there was a very dangerous road to travel.

The crossing of the Bay of Biscay had long been a hazard for the U-boats, but for some months now this broad expanse of troubled water had become a veritable death trap. British and American aircraft, equipped with high-performance radar and the extremely effective Leigh Light, swarmed overhead, while on the surface the Royal Navy's hunter-killer groups of destroyers and sloops roamed at will. In one month, from 3 July to 2 August, a total of twenty-one boats were sunk in the Bay and off the west coasts of Spain and Portugal with terrible loss of life. As a result of this, tactics had recently been changed by U-boat Command. Hitherto, standing orders were for U-boats, now heavily armed against air attack, should stay on the surface and shoot it out with with enemy planes. In many cases this had worked well, RAF Coastal Command in particular, incurring heavy losses in these sea-to-air fights, but now the superiority was with the air. Boats were ordered to stay below at all times while crossing the Bay, surfacing only at night to recharge batteries and air the boat, and then to keep a sharp lookout for the hunter-killer groups and Leigh Light-carrying planes. In reality, there was no hiding place for the U-boats, above or below the surface.

Assuming that *U-223* was successful in breaking out of the Bay of Biscay and gained the shelter of Spanish and Portuguese waters, she still had to run the gauntlet of the Straits of Gibraltar, and in the summer of 1943 this was no mean challenge. Firmly established on the Rock of Gibraltar since 1704, the British Navy held complete sway over the ten-mile-wide stretch of water separating Spain from North Africa. A complete blockade was in force, with destroyers and anti-submarine trawlers patrolling the straits day and night, again backed up by aircraft equipped with radar and Leigh Lights flying low overhead at all times. Only the small fleets of Spanish and Moroccan fishermen, to whom the war was an irritating but minor inconvenience to their business in deep waters, were free to come and go, although they were kept under close surveillance. Any hostile submarines attempting to penetrate the strait were in for a very rough time, although the weather and currents of the area were in their favour. As a result of the differing densities of the Atlantic and Mediterranean, a constant current flows easterly between 2 and 3 knots, thus ensuring a fast inward transit of the strait. Mist and fog were frequent, and marked differences in water temperature and salinity affected the enemy's Asdic beams, sometimes allowing a submerged U-boat to pass undetected.

For those U-boats already inside the Mediterranean, life had always been difficult, but ever since the defeat of Rommel in North Africa and the collapse of Italy, their offensive against Allied shipping had turned into a fight for their own survival.

Since the middle of July 1943, five boats, *U-375*, *U-409*, *U-458*, *U-504* and *U-561* had been sunk with the loss of 160 lives. The fate of the sixth casualty of the eighteen-strong flotilla, *U-617*, provides an insight into the odds faced by the U-boats in the Mediterranean at that time. *U-617*, commanded by Albrecht Brandi, entered the Mediterranean on 8 November 1942, and had a moderately successful career, sinking six Allied ships, including the fast minelayer HMS *Welshman* of 2,650 tons and the escort destroyer HMS *Puckeridge*. On the night of 10 September, Brandi was caught on the surface off the coast of Spanish Morocco by a Wellington of 179 Squadron RAF, which immediately dived to attack, dropping six depth charges, which disabled *U-617*. Another Wellington was called in, and more charges were dropped.

Unable to dive, Brandi ran his boat ashore in shallow water and abandoned her. He and his crew reached the shore in dinghies. With the coming of daylight, the wreck of *U-617* became the target of every Allied aircraft and ship in the area. Hudsons of three British squadrons based at Gibraltar attacked with bombs and rockets, while the corvette HMS *Hyacinth*, the armed trawler *Haarlam* and the Australian minesweeper *Woollongong* got in some useful target practice for their 4-inch guns' crews. The battered hulk of what was once one of Karl Dönitz's proud Type VIICs was finished off by a couple of Swordfish from 886 Squadron Fleet Air Arm, who were unable to resist joining in the turkey shoot. Albrecht Brandi and his men all escaped with their lives, and were arrested by Spanish troops when they waded ashore, but were soon released to return to their base in Toulon.

The prompt dispatch of *U-617* by an overwhelming force left only thirteen U-boats operating in the Mediterranean. This, combined with the surrender of the Italian fleet, which included thirty-four submarines, gave the Allies the upper hand over the sea routes supplying their armies ashore. Seeing the control of the land-locked sea slipping from his hands, Hitler ordered Dönitz to reinforce his flotilla in the Mediterranean at once, and at all costs. The Grand Admiral was loathe to risk any more of his rapidly shrinking underwater fleet, and it was with great reluctance that he ordered five more boats south. *U-223* was the first to leave.

Wächter's orders were clear. Although *U-223* was equipped

with the usual formidable array of anti-aircraft guns, he was not to try to fight it out on the surface under any circumstances. So many Allied aircraft were quartering the skies over Biscay that he was strongly advised to dive after clearing St Nazaire, and stay down, except for a very limited time at night, until he was certain he was out of the danger area. Wächter had his reservations on this.

U-223's escorting ship left her 130 miles out into the Bay on 15 September, and with a clattering of signal lamps set course for home. The weather was then fair, with a light south-westerly wind, a flat sea, and half cloud cover. With his guns manned and extra lookouts posted, Wächter decided to remain on the surface for another three hours, putting as much distance behind him as possible. Half an hour after noon, with the sun high in the sky, he judged it would be unwise to tempt fate any longer and dived to periscope depth, not surfacing again until midnight. He then remained on the surface, driving southwards on both diesels until the first flush of dawn showed in the east. This was the pattern he followed from then on, with *U-223* logging between seventy and eighty miles in every twenty-four hours. This was slow progress, but it was at least safe. By noon on the 18th, they were twelve miles off the rocky promontory of Cape Ortegal, and at last leaving the exposed waters of the Bay of Biscay. From then on, Wächter proposed to hug the coast, keeping as far as possible inside the neutral waters of Spain and Portugal, where he hoped to escape the attentions of the Sunderlands and Catalinas circling on the horizon.

While Karl Wächter studied the stark outlines of Cape Ortegal through his periscope, some 900 miles to the north-north-west, as the gulls fly, there was movement in the anchorage off the Scottish port of Oban, where Convoy KMS 27 had assembled to begin its passage to the Mediterranean. Comprising only eight ships, KMS 27 was nevertheless of vital importance, carrying more than 50,000 tons of arms, equipment and stores for the advancing British armies in Italy.

One of the ships bringing home her anchor on that cold, clear Scottish morning was the London-registered *Stanmore*, owned by the Stanhope Steamship company. Stanhope had a long association with the Mediterranean and the transport of military stores, having been heavily involved in the Spanish Civil War during 1937–38, in carrying cargoes for the doomed Spanish Republican Government. The company had prospered from that war, ending up with a fleet of twenty-three ships trading worldwide.

Commanded by Captain Howard Phillips, the 4,970-ton *Stanmore* carried a crew of forty-eight, which included seven DEMS gunners. She had sailed from Middlesbrough a few days earlier, taking the northabout route, and braving the fast-running tides of the Pentland Firth to join the convoy off Oban. In her holds were 2,500 tons of what were manifested as 'government stores'; an assortment of vehicle spares, boots, clothing, field rations, bags of mail, guns, and a large quantity of highly explosive ammunition. She was to call first at Malta, and then go on to an, as yet unnamed, port in Sicily. Captain Phillips was not anticipating a difficult passage; the weather was set fair and, if he were to believe all reports, the U-boats that had blighted his life for four long years were a spent force. However, the three-year-old *Stanmore* would be required to go at the pace of the slowest ship of the convoy, and that was no more than 7 knots. At least fifteen days would pass before Malta hove in sight.

Anchors home and washed down, the eight ships of KMS 27 moved off in line astern, and soon the heather-covered hills of the Western Highlands were fading out of sight. The shores of the brooding Isle of Mull slipped past, and with the holy island of Iona to starboard, they set course to the south-west. Ten hours later, KMS 27 rendezvoused with its small escort force off Rathlin Island, on the north-east coast of Ireland. The long haul to Gibraltar and the Mediterranean had begun.

By this time, *U-223* had rounded Cape Finisterre, on the north-west tip of Spain, with the weather holding fine and calm. Only the occasional breaking wavelet disturbed the sea, and the horizon was as sharp as a whetted knife. Wächter felt dangerously exposed, and longed for the stormy waters of the North Atlantic, where the tumbling waves, the mist, the fog and the driving rain provided a hiding place for a U-boat. There was no cover at night, either, for a brilliant full moon shone down out of an almost cloudless sky, and the curse of phosphorescence was on the surface of the sea. *U-223*'s bow wave and wake glowed and frothed with tiny points of blue light created by plankton in the water, a trail that no patrolling aircraft could fail to miss. The net result was that Wächter was forced to spend much more time below the surface than above. The run down to the Straits of Gibraltar, which should have been a leisurely cruise, was assuming marathon proportions.

Cape St Vincent, the south-west corner of Portugal, was rounded on the afternoon of 23 September, and Wächter set course across the Gulf of Cadiz towards the narrow gateway to the Mediterranean. By now, the skies were clear of avenging aircraft, and only the occasional sardine fisherman came in sight, but Wächter had been well briefed as to what to expect when they approached the waters where the British Navy had held sway for centuries. He approached with caution, if not a little trepidation.

Wächter's caution proved to be well justified. Before dawn on the 25th, U-223 had reached a point thirty miles west of Cape Espartel, the north-western extremity of Africa. Following the advice he had been given, Wächter intended to keep to the southern side of the Straits of Gibraltar, hugging the Moroccan coast. At 04.30, while it was still dark, he decided to surface to take a look around. This almost proved to be one risk too many, for no sooner had he climbed through the conning tower hatch than the boat was caught in the blinding beam of a searchlight. Not waiting to see where the light came from, Wächter hit the diving alarm, dropped back through the hatch, and slammed it shut after him. Blowing all main ballast, he went deep and waited for the inevitable depth charges to come tumbling down after them.

Nothing happened, and an hour later Wächter went back to periscope depth. A quick look around the horizon showed the sky astern to be lit up by brilliant blue flares. They were looking for him. Minutes later, U-223's hydrophone operator picked up the beat of fast revving propellers, which he identified as a destroyer, less than three miles off, and heading directly towards them.

Fearing that his attempt to go through the enemy's front door was over before it had begun, Wächter went deep again and onto silent routine. Once again, the frightening ordeal they had prepared themselves for, the threshing propellers overhead followed by the crash of exploding depth charges, failed to materialize. The destroyer came very close, and her Asdic beam

143

could be heard sweeping the boat from end to end, but that was all. For some reason the destroyer had failed to detect them, and soon moved away.

This was *U-223*'s first brush with the enemy since leaving St Nazaire eleven days earlier, and the sigh of relief that went through the boat when the beat of the destroyer's propellers faded was like an amen to a fervent prayer. Having escaped this time, Wächter took no further risks that day. He closed the African coast until the lighthouse on Cape Espartel was clearly visible, and at 10.37 stopped and settled the boat gently on the sandy bottom. He would attempt a transit of the Straits when darkness came again that night.

It seemed a long wait, the hours dragging by with excruciating slowness. In order to eke out the air in the boat, Wächter reduced all activity to an absolute minimum. Men talked in whispers, moved only when necessary, and then slowly and deliberately. Some tried to sleep, but the ordeal they knew they must soon face kept them awake. They could only cat-nap, nodding off, only to come bolt upright after a few minutes with their nerves jangling. *U-223* was a boat waiting on the passage of events.

At 16.40, an hour before sunset, Wächter broke the tension at last, and gave the order to blow tanks and go to periscope depth. He set a north-easterly course to give Cape Espartel a wide berth and headed in towards the Straits of Gibraltar. At 22.00, with the flashing light on Cape Espartel showing abeam, he came to the surface to find the weather in *U-223*'s favour. The wind was light south-westerly and the sea flat, but it was a very dark night, overcast and with a light drizzle restricting visibility enough to give good cover for the boat. Conditions were ideal for a quick dash through the Straits on the surface; at full speed, *U-223* could be through the narrows in just over two hours. With all torpedo tubes and guns manned and both diesels on full throttle, Karl Wächter prepared to break into the Mediterranean.

The high hopes for a quick passage were dashed when, after only ten minutes under way, the rain stopped and the horizon cleared. And whereas she had been in complete darkness before, *U-223* was running into the glow of the lights of the port of Tangier, which silhouetted her against the shoreline. Wächter kept going, but a few miles further on he found himself in the middle of a fleet of Moroccan sardine fishermen, who were illuminating their nets with acetylene flares, which at the same time bathed the stealthily advancing U-boat in their brilliant white light. Knowing they must be clearly visible for miles around, Wächter was sorely tempted to dive, but the boat was now feeling the pull of the strong in-going tide, and he resisted the temptation.

Moving closer inshore to avoid the glare of the fishermen's lights, Wächter estimated they were making in excess of 18 knots with the help of the tide and was determined to press on. Then he heard the roar of engines overhead, and saw the navigation lights of an aircraft heading in their direction. It could be friend or foe, but he was not prepared to wait to find out, diving immediately. As soon as they were below the surface, hydrophone effect from a destroyer was picked up. Cautiously, Wächter came to the surface again, only to find a destroyer some distance ahead, apparently stopped, and lying beam on to *U-223*. The temptation was to try a quick torpedo – a stern shot would be best – but as Wächter weighed up the pros and cons of an attack there was a flurry of white water at the destroyer's stern, and she moved away.

Wächter now abandoned all thoughts of attempting to go through the Straits on the surface, and returned to periscope depth, where he stayed. The east-flowing tidal stream had *U-223* firmly in its grip, and she made good speed underwater, finally emerging from the eastern end of the Straits into the Mediterranean at 08.00 on the 26th. Apart from the inconvenience of the fishing fleet, the near-brush with an aircraft, and a good deal of hydrophone effect heard, the transit had not been too stressful. Wächter made the following entry in his log:

In reality this passage was not difficult, and I fail to understand why so much is made of it. Most of the passage was made underwater, surfacing only to look around. The course taken appears to be the right one, and at no time when submerged were we detected by Asdic.

There were only three places where, because of the tide, the patrol boats could have caught me. The depth and navigation presented no difficulties. Tidal streams running at 2 knots were calculated and allowed for from Tarifa onwards.

Navigation on the surface is difficult because of the many lights on shore. It is best to keep in the shadow of the coast and behind the fishing fleets. The patrol boats are not very alert, and even though they were using Asdic both in the bow and stern, they did not detect me.

Once clear of Ceuta, dominated by the 2,750ft high Sidi Musa which with Gibraltar formed the Pillars of Hercules of the ancients, Wächter set a course of 080° and resumed his cautious routine of sailing submerged by day and on the surface at night. The weather continued in his favour, with light winds, a slight sea and frequent spells of drizzle providing a convenient cloak. There still appeared to be very little enemy activity, and the only thing that marred what was really an easy passage was the heat. The air temperature during the day was in excess of 28° C, and the sea was at a constant 23° C, with the result that the temperature in the boat while she was submerged became unbearable. Under these conditions, with fifty men battened down in the hull for twelve hours at a time, mind and body were stretched to their absolute limits, but there could be no going back.

At 01.30 on 1 October, when south of the Balearics, Wächter received the news they had all been waiting for; a small enemy convoy had passed through the Straits of Gibraltar early on 30 September and was heading their way. As instructed, Wächter moved south to a position off Cape Tenez, a prominent headland midway between Oran and Algiers and on the known Allied convoy route. Keeping between twenty and forty miles off the coast, he took up a north-south patrol line and waited.

KMS 27, after an uneventful passage south from British waters with not even one U-boat alert to disturb its slow progress, passed through the Straits of Gibraltar at 03.00 on 30 September, duly observed by Spanish watchers at Algeciras, who then informed the German consul in the port. At eight ships strong, this would not have been regarded by the enemy as a significant convoy, but thirty hours later, when off Oran and out of sight of the Spanish observers, KMS 27 was joined by thirty American merchant ships, who had been waiting outside the port. The convoy, now thirty-eight strong, formed up into seven columns abreast, and set course for Sicily under heavy escort. The *Stanmore* found herself sailing in the middle of the convoy, a position much to Captain Phillips' liking, for it offered good protection. However, when that afternoon the Convoy Commodore ordered all ships to steer a zig-zag pattern at 5 knots, Phillips realized his inside position was not all to his advantage. Attempting to zig-zag when hemmed in by nearly forty other ships, some of which were not very adept at manoeuvring, was far from easy. He was much relieved when the convoy resumed a steady course at 7 knots after dark.

The night was fine, the visibility fair but deteriorating, and a fresh easterly breeze was heaping up a rough sea when Karl Wächter brought *U-223* to the surface just after 21.00. Calculating he was then forty miles north of Cape Tenez, he came round onto a southerly course, and using the loom of the light as a marker, headed back towards the coast at slow speed on one diesel only. When the flash of the light lifted above the horizon, indicating he was within twenty miles, he would turn back to the north again. This had been *U-223*'s monotonous routine for the past twenty hours, twenty miles out and twenty miles back, with nothing on the horizon to relieve the boredom. Wächter was in the conning tower when, at 00.53 on 2 October, the waiting game came to an end. His War Diary records what followed:

0053   Several shadows bearing 210 degrees. This must be the expected convoy.

Because of the poor visibility we did not sight them until they were nearly on top of us. I re-engage both engines. This is a stroke of luck. We are in exactly the right position. All I have to do is press the button.

Four shadows are now visible and there are more behind them. The first ship is a medium-sized steamer, and astern of him is a big one. He is nearly twice as big and I will go for him. Looking through the telescope I can only see his hull, no upperworks. There is a mist, almost a fog. Ahead of the steamer is a destroyer.

0101	Because of the position of this ship I will need to use three tubes.
	Depth 7 metres, range 4000 metres.
	Fired No.1 tube. Running well and true.
	Next ship to starboard. Fired No.2 tube.
	Depth 4 metres, range 3,500 metres. Overran.
	After that I turn hard to starboard and stop engines. Behind is the small shadow of a destroyer, type not known. Luckily, he has not seen us.
	Fire No.4 tube.
	Depth 4 metres, range 2000 metres.
0105	Near miss. I disengage engines for 30 seconds, then re-engage them and turn slowly onto 000 degrees.
	Two heavy detonations heard after 4 minutes 15 seconds (3,600 metres) in quick succession. Very loud, even on the bridge. That must be my first target. No flash or water spout seen. Because I am so low down on the water I cannot get a better view.
	A third hit after 4 minutes 40 seconds. Must have been on the second ship.
	Loud detonation and small fireball rising to 10 metres seen.
	As I was unable to see much of the ships' masts and upperworks I can only judge tonnage by silhouette seen through the periscope.
	1.) Ship of 10,000 BRT to 12,000 BRT.
	2.) Ship of 8000 BRT to 9000 BRT.
	3.) Hit after 3 minutes 15 seconds on destroyer. Short bright flash seen and detonation heard.

Wächter's claim to have made every one of his torpedoes count was sincere but far removed from reality. As he reported in his War Diary, the visibility was not good, and confronted by so many ships the impression that he could not miss must have been very strong. In fact, Wächter's only victim that night was the rather small and insignificant British steamer *Stanmore*.

Captain Howard Phillips was on the bridge of the *Stanmore* at midnight on the night of 2–3rd October, haunting the starboard wing while Third Officer Coles handed over the watch to Second Officer Boyes. The night was quiet, and no warning had been received of U-boats operating in the area. As soon as the new watch was settled in, Phillips intended to go below and take a well-earned rest. He was about to go through into the chartroom to check the ship's position, when he was pulled up short by two muffled explosions, which he thought could be depth charges. Looking around the horizon, he could see no signs of unusual activity, then, as he was checking the ships astern, a sheet of flame shot up from the *Stanmore*'s starboard quarter, followed by another muffled explosion.

The *Stanmore* staggered, and her head swung sharply to starboard, confirming to Phillips that she had been hit. He immediately rang the engine-room telegraph to stop, but he received no reply, nor did the watch below answer when he used the bridge/engine-room telephone. It was only when Chief Engineer Sykes arrived breathless on the bridge that he learned the full extent of the damage to his ship. Wächter's torpedo had dealt the *Stanmore* a crippling blow in her stern, ripping open her after peak tank and No. 4 hold. The hold had flooded quickly, leading to the collapse of the bulkhead between it and No. 3 hold, which in turn flooded. The explosion had also breached the propeller shaft tunnel, which ran through these holds. Unfortunately, being on the change of the watch, the watertight door between the engine-room and the shaft tunnel had been open for routine inspection, and consequently the sea rushed into the engine-room. Within the space of no more than ten minutes, the whole of the after part of the *Stanmore*'s hull was flooded.

It was fortunate that the *Stanmore*'s after hold contained a consignment of steel pontoons, and these kept her stern afloat.

However, conscious of the fact that he had a large quantity of explosives on board, and expecting another torpedo to strike any minute, Phillips ordered his men to abandon ship. This was accomplished in two lifeboats quietly and in an orderly manner. The boats hit the water, dropped astern, and half an hour later Phillips and his men were picked up by the armed trawler HMS *Filla*. Only three of the *Stanmore*'s crew of forty-nine had been slightly injured when she was torpedoed.

Howard Phillips had no intention of abandoning his ship altogether, for when he left her she was still well afloat, although noticeably down by the stern. When daylight came, around four hours later, and she remained afloat, Phillips persuaded the commander of HMS *Filla*, Lieutenant J.B. Hornby, RNVR, to put him back aboard his ship. With him went Chief Officer Williams, Second Officer Boyes, Third Officer Coles, Chief Engineer Sykes, Third Engineer Garner, Boatswain Rankin, Carpenter Buzzard and Able Seamen Maine and McMahon.

Although the *Stanmore*'s engine-room was under water and there was no prospect of raising steam, Phillips judged the ship to be in no immediate danger of sinking, and suggested to Lieutenant Hornby that *Filla* take her in tow. Algiers was less than 100 miles to the east, and once there at least the *Stanmore*'s cargo could be salvaged. Hornby agreed, and a towrope was connected, but it soon became clear that the trawler did not have sufficient power, and little forward progress was made. Later that day, the powerful fleet tug *Charon* arrived, and the *Stanmore*, which had by then become unmanageable, was towed into Tenez Bay, and anchored in nine fathoms just as darkness was setting in. The rest of her story is best told in Captain Phillips' words:

> The captain of the tug *Charon* estimated that he could pump about 800 tons of water an hour and started pumping at 2000. The pumps broke down 45 minutes later and it took the remainder of the night to effect repairs, with my Chief Engineer helping them. Whilst the pumps were working they were able to make a substantial effect on the water in the ship, but directly they stopped the water increased.
>
> At dawn the next day (3rd October), the poop was under water,

so I decided to beach the ship. I let go the starboard anchor and towed towards the beach until she touched bottom about 0810. I decided to get the ship on the beach as far as possible, so kept towing until about 1030, when we towed her head into the wind and let go the port anchor. At 1300 the tug *Charon* again started pumping, but by this time the water had increased so much that they had to give it up and reported the position to the C-in-C Algiers.

At 1100 the next morning (4th) the rescue tug *Salvina* arrived to assist with the pumping, but she had to give up after two hours. By this time I had sent the rest of my crew to the US Naval Base ashore.

There was an air raid during the night on a convoy off Tenez, which was attacked by about 30 planes. There was a terrific anti-aircraft barrage put up, but two ships were sunk and I believe six were damaged. As a result, the two rescue tugs left us, after sending a message to the C-in-C; there was nothing for us to do but to re-board, although I was afraid she would break in half. The ship was now drawing 6ft of water forward, with water up to the after mast-house. At 0300 a Salvage Officer, Lieutenant Commander Wilson, RNR, from Algiers boarded the ship. After making an examination at dawn, he said that he would send the salvage ship *Salvestor* to carry out the pumping operations.

This salvage vessel arrived two or three days later, by which time the weather had deteriorated and for a time she could not get alongside, but eventually did so. By this time it was apparent that it was too late to save the ship. I understand this salvage vessel had been lying at Algiers for three days, in which I can see no reason why she could not have been sent to my assistance earlier. The salvage crew behaved in a disgusting manner, stealing everything they came across, causing much trouble and wasting so much time, that I do not know exactly when we eventually started discharging the cargo. I have already made a full report on this matter. The Captain appeared to have no control whatsoever over his crew. I understand he was master of a 500-ton coaster before the war and I do not think he was sufficiently experienced to be put in charge of salvage operations. The Police, who were on board the whole time, had to put armed guards on the gangways during the night, with instructions to shoot if anybody went on board. This looting made it impossible to continue discharging during darkness, and the ship had to be completely evacuated. On their subsequent arrival at Algiers, 29 members of the salvage vessel's crew were found by the Police to be in possession of stolen property. Full particulars were taken, but beyond taking the stolen goods away from them, nothing was done.

The whole position at Tenez was most unsatisfactory. I was responsible to the STO, Captain Johnson, who had come from Algiers, for the safety of the cargo, but the CO of the *Salvestor* phoned Algiers for authority to take full charge of everything. We had several arguments about this and I was told not to interfere, but in my opinion I had very definite cause to do so. On one occasion 70 cases of beer were landed and locked in a shed. Two mornings later, 60 cases had disappeared and nobody knew where they had gone. Together with the STO I examined the remaining ten cases, and found them all to be empty except one. Whoever stole the cases of beer must have done so during the night time, using a lorry to take them away. However, as the Salvage Officer was in charge, there did not seem to be anything I could do about it.

The Diver's survey was not completed until 23 days after the ship was beached, by which time the ship was nearly buried aft, with the water well up in No. 2A hold. As far as the diver could see there was no hole on the starboard side, but the shell plating was corrugated 30ft along the bottom, forward of the stern post on the port side. There was a bulge in the shelter deck plating over the engine-room on the starboard side, 150ft from where the explosion occurred. So much of our attention was diverted to the plundering of the cargo, etc. that the survey was somewhat neglected. After 23 days at Tenez I returned home and I do not know how I stand, as the ship was never officially abandoned.

All my crew behaved well and the following officers and men re-boarded with me voluntarily:

> Chief Engineer Sykes, who already has the OBE.
> 3rd Engineer Garner
> Chief Officer Williams
> 2nd Officer Boyes
> 3rd Officer Coles
> Carpenter Buzzard
> Bo'sun Rankin
> Able Seamen Maine and McMahon.

Having survived the loss of their ship at the hands of the enemy, Captain Howard Phillips and his crew, mainly by their own efforts, had beached her with the object of saving the cargo. They had then suffered the humiliation of that cargo being plundered, and this apparently without interference by the authorities ashore who had it in their power to stop the theft. In the end, it seems that the last voyage of the *Stanmore* had been in vain.

Chapter Eleven

The Waiting Game

Having shattered the peace of the midnight hour by torpedoing the *Stanmore*, Karl-Jurgen Wächter broke off his lone attack on KMS 27 and, taking advantage of the poor visibility, slipped away to the north before the convoy's escorts came looking for him. He then spent four hours submerged while he reloaded his torpedo tubes, surfacing briefly before dawn to recharge batteries. He would have preferred to remain on the surface to put as much distance as possible between himself and the scene of his recent success, but the drone of aircraft engines overhead warned him it was time to go below again. Allied aircraft, now based on both shores of the Mediterranean, were constantly patrolling the skies, sometimes singly, more often in flights of up to ten planes. Their main object was to protect the supply convoys from predators like *U-223*, and everything seemed to be in their favour. By day, predominantly calm seas and the exceptionally clear water made it easy for an aircraft to spot a U-boat running at periscope depth, and by night a boat on the surface was often betrayed by its phosphorescent wake. Then the powerful search-lights carried by the planes turned night into day, usually with disastrous results for the unwary U-boat commander.

The next two weeks proved to be difficult ones for *U-223*. Instructed to move further east to the Algiers area, Wächter waited in vain for an expected convoy that failed to appear. Hampered by poor visibility – much of the time below 1,000 metres, and not improved by sheet lightning at night – and unable to stay on the surface long because of patrolling aircraft overhead, he achieved nothing. On the night of the 6th, when twenty-five miles off the coast near Bougie, *U-223* fell foul of two destroyers,

154

probably part of a hunter-killer group, and only narrowly escaped unscathed. And still no convoy put in an appearance.

Wächter used his own initiative and moved further east, taking up station off the western entrance to the Galita Channel, which runs between Île de la Galita and its attendant group of rocks and the bulge of Africa nearest to Sicily, a well-used through route for shipping. But the channel seemed deserted, the only sight of the enemy being a large, brilliantly lit hospital ship, seen on two separate occasions on the 7th and 8th. It was a tempting target, but taboo under the international rules of warfare, and Karl Wächter was not a man to indulge in deliberate atrocities. He satisfied himself with watching the big, two-funnel ship as she came and went.

The dearth of convoys continued, and *U-223*'s incessant patrolling became a wearisome routine. There were constant alarms, for aircraft cruising overhead or destroyers appearing over the horizon, all of whom seemed to be searching for them. *U-223*, once the hunter, was now the hunted, and it was with some relief that, on the night of the 11th, Wächter received orders to proceed to Toulon, which would be *U-223*'s base while she was attached to the 29th U-boat Flotilla in the Mediterranean.

It was a straight run north to Toulon, across 360 miles of open water, but the dangers were no less. Allied aircraft seemed to be everywhere, having complete control of the skies. Wächter spent much of the day and a good part of the night at periscope depth, surfacing only when necessary, with the result that the boat was averaging little more than seventy miles in a day. It was the morning of the 16th before they made a rendezvous with a German patrol boat in the Gulf of Lyons and were escorted into Toulon. The port, once the major French naval base in the Mediterranean, had been in the hands of the Italians, but seized by German forces on the collapse of their erstwhile allies in August. The naval dockyard was still intact, but there were no concrete pens in which to hide a U-boat from the attentions of British and American bombers. Wächter hoped their stay in Toulon would be a short one.

U-223's demands on the Toulon dockyard were not great; a few essential repairs, compasses and other instruments to be re-calibrated, and fuel, stores and water to be taken on board.

Nevertheless, it was 20 November before she set off on her next patrol. This was to be Wächter's last voyage in *U-223* for, while in Toulon, he had been appointed to take command of the 29th Flotilla, leaving the boat when his replacement arrived.

Under orders to operate against Allied convoys off the North African coast between Algiers and Bougie, Wächter was aware that he would be fighting the battle in increasing isolation, as the Mediterranean flotilla, never great in numbers, was slowly being whittled down. Attempts had been made to bring in reinforcements, of which *U-223* was one, but only two other boats, Kurt Böhme's *U-450* and Herbert Brunning's *U-642*, had succeeded in breaking through the heavily defended Gibraltar Strait. Others had tried and failed. *U-431* (Dietrich Schöneboom) spotted by a Leigh Light-equipped Wellington of 179 Squadron on 22 October, put up a stiff fight, but was destroyed by a stick of six depth bombs along with all her crew. She was followed two days later by *U-566* (Hans Hornkohl) which had not even reached the Straits, bombed and sunk by the same Wellington off Vigo on the 24th. *U-732* (Claus-Peter Carlsen) fell to the depth charges of a Gibraltar sea patrol consisting of the destroyer *Douglas*, the frigate *Loch Osaig* and the anti-submarine trawler *Imperialist* on the 31st. Next day, a combined operation by the destroyers *Active* and *Witherington* with the sloop *Fleetwood* and aircraft of 179 Squadron put an end to *U-340* in the Straits. Then, four days after he sailed from Toulon, Wächter received news of a heavy air raid on the base in which five other boats were severely damaged. If losses continued at this rate, the newly-promoted Wächter would have no flotilla to command.

By 23 November, *U-223* was to the east of the island of Minorca, and heading south into nasty weather. Contrary to the often repeated myths, the Mediterranean is not always benign, with cloudless blue skies and calm seas. Winter comes here as sure as it does in the open Atlantic, often bringing grey skies, gale-force winds and short, steep seas. Mediterranean depressions are fortunately short-lived, but when they pass through there is no comfort in a small ship, much less in the conning tower of a surfaced U-boat, only a few feet above the sea. Safety harnesses were an essential for the watch in *U-223*'s conning tower as she ploughed south through heavy seas. The harnesses prevented the men being washed overboard as the waves climbed the fore casing and smashed against the tower, but they could not prevent them enduring a demoralizing and continuous soaking. Nor was there much comfort to be had below the surface. The shallow waters prevented the boat from going deep, and her motion was severe.

The weather relented on the 27th, by which time *U-223* was again on station in the western approaches to the Galita Channel, and continuing her vigil on the Allied convoy route. As before, the visibility was mainly poor, but there was also excessive phosphorescence in the water, making it dangerous for Wächter to stay on the surface at night, and enemy sea and air activity had not diminished. Just before noon on the 28th, Wächter was at periscope depth when a destroyer, which he identified as a 'G'-class, came within 4,000 metres, but failed to detect the U-boat with her Asdic. Wächter was tempted to try a long shot, but as he lined the enemy ship up in his sights, she suddenly made off to the north.

Surfacing at around 02.30 next morning, *U-223* came near to meeting her end when an aircraft suddenly appeared out of the night sky, and roared overhead no more than sixty metres above the water, filling the boat with the awesome roar of its engines. It seemed that they had not been seen by the plane until the last minute, for tracers were hitting the water more than 500 metres astern of the boat. Possibly, the pilot, flying low, saw the U-boat's tell-tale phosphorescent wake only at the last minute, and was as surprised as they were. The aircraft banked sharply, and began another run, but Wächter already had the hatches battened down, and *U-223* was sinking out of sight. There were anxious moments as they waited for the depth charges to come hurtling down, for the deafening multiple bangs and the shock waves slamming into the pressure hull. But after several stomach-churning minutes with only the whine of the electric motors to be heard, they slowly realized that they had once again escaped death. Ten more minutes passed in silence before Wächter felt justified in assuming the enemy aircraft must have gone away. Either she had not been carrying depth charges, or she had used them up on some other unfortunate boat. However, there could be no escaping the fact that they had been seen, and their position was even then being broadcast to all enemy ships and aircraft in the vicinity. Wächter decided to quit the area before they came searching for him.

Remaining submerged, he headed north at the best speed his motors would give him, not surfacing until after dark that night. When they did come up, it was onto a glassy calm sea and under a cloak of thick drizzle. The conditions appeared ideal for operating on the surface unseen but, when the diesels kicked in, *U-223*'s propeller churned up a glaring white froth of phosphorescence that must have been visible from the air despite the drizzle. Wächter disengaged one engine and crept away to the west, his wake still dangerously evident.

By noon on the 30th, *U-223* was thirty miles north of Algiers, where Wächter decided to lay in wait for a passing convoy. He waited in vain. No ships of any sort were seen by day or night, although the loom of the lights of Algiers, clearly visible at night, indicated that the port was busy.

Wächter gave up his vigil after twenty-four hours and moved further to the west, and at noon on 2 December was close inshore off Cape Tenez, very near the position where, two months earlier, he had torpedoed the *Stanmore*. Hopes were raised when a signal from Toulon advised that a large Allied convoy was due to pass Cape Tenez soon, but all that came in sight was a westbound hospital ship, British or American, which was not a legitimate target. During the course of that afternoon Wächter discovered that he had problems on board in the way of a serious leak in the stern gland of the starboard propeller shaft. Tightening the gland only resulted in the shaft overheating, and it was necessary to disengage the starboard engine. On the surface that evening, the sound of heavy gunfire could be heard coming from the direction of Oran, which seemed to be under attack from the air, possibly accounting for the dearth of shipping.

As Karl Wächter listened to the rumble of gunfire coming from Oran, 800 miles to the east, in the Italian Adriatic port of Bari, one of the most bizarre episodes of the war was about to be enacted.

Bari, one of the major discharging ports for the supply convoys Wächter was lying in wait for, was working to full capacity that night, with as many as thirty Allied merchant ships being unloaded under the glare of floodlights. This was a practice fraught with great risks in such a fiercely contested war zone, but was dictated by dire need. The British 8th Army was advancing up the trunk of Italy so fast that it was in danger of running out of supplies. In order to remedy the situation, the military authorities in Bari had thrown caution to the winds, and were about to pay the price for their folly.

At exactly 19.35 that night, a massed formation of 105 Junkers 88 Bombers, led by *Oberleutnant* Teuber, roared in from seaward flying at 150 feet. The German pilots could hardly believe their eyes at what they saw. Teuber later said:

> We had been told at the briefing that the Allies at Bari were not blacking out the harbour at night because of the large number of ships to be unloaded, but I was sceptical of the statement until, as I approached the city from the Adriatic Sea, I saw the lights with my own eyes. I saw the dock cranes moving back and forth between the piers and the ships, a light on top of each crane. There was a beam of light at the lighthouse on the seaward side of one of the jetties, many lights along the dock bordering on the city, scattered lights along Molo Foraneo and Molo Pizzoli. Further north, on Molo San Cataldo, where the main petroleum line was located, there were more lights. Accustomed to wartime blackouts, Bari harbour looked like Berlin's Unter den Linden on a New Year's eve as I roared in from the sea at 200 mph . . .

The port of Bari was taken completely by surprise, and although the merchant ships were quick to man their guns and throw up a heavy barrage into the night sky, the German bombers reaped a rich harvest. The first ship to be hit was the Norwegian-manned, British-flag *Laps Kruse*. Bracketed by a stick of bombs, she capsized and sank, taking her crew of twenty-three with her. Close by, the US Liberty *Samuel Tilden* took a bomb straight down her funnel, which then exploded and wrecked her engine-room. Her cargo of drums of gasoline and cases of ammunition caught fire and she began to blow herself apart as her crew jumped overboard.

For the circling Ju88s it was like shooting fish in a barrel. Direct hits were scored on four more American ships, the *John L. Motley*, *Joseph Wheeler*, *John Bascom* and *John Harvey*, each of which was loaded with ammunition. All four caught fire and blew up, the *John Motley* and *John Harvey* simultaneously, the blast from their combined explosion severely damaging another nearby US ship, the *Lyman Abbott*. The British ship *Fort Athabaska* was also hit and on fire, the flames eventually reaching the two captured German 1,000lb rocket bombs she had in her holds, which exploded and ripped her apart, killing forty-four of her fifty-six crew as they tried in vain to fight the fires.

The air raid on Bari was short and brutal, lasting only twenty minutes, during which the Ju88s exacted a frightening toll. *Oberleutnant* Teuber reported it as a sight he would never forget. Flames were reaching upwards as high as a hundred feet in some spots. But it was the blasts that occurred periodically that made the night reminiscent of a giant fireworks display. Red, yellow, green – every colour that he had ever seen – was visible as the ammunition ships exploded and, even at a distance of several miles out over the sea, the *Oberleutnant* could feel the violence of the blasts as they rocked his Ju88.

Twelve ships were sunk at their moorings, of which the *Teesbank*, *Fort Athabaska*, *Devon Coast* and *Laps Kruse* were British, the *John L. Motley*, *John Bascom*, *John Harvey*, *Joseph Wheeler* and *Samuel Tilden* American, and the *Barletta*, *Cassola* and *Frasinone* uninvolved Italians, who happened to be in port at the wrong time. Six other ships, namely the *Brittany Coast* (British), *Christa* (British), *Fort Lajoie* (British), *Lymon Abbott* (American), *Vest* (Norwegian) and *Odysseus* (Dutch) were so badly damaged that they never sailed again.

It had been a good night for the Ju88s, and a disastrous one for the Allies – how disastrous was yet to be revealed. It was only after the German planes had flown away, and people were still dying, that it became known that the American ship *John Harvey* was carrying ninety tons of mustard gas. When she blew up, all her crew were killed, so there was no one to warn of the cloud of deadly poisonous gas spreading its silent death over Bari. No exact casualty figures are available for the Bari raid, but it is thought that at least 1,000 Allied servicemen, merchant seamen and Italian civilians died that night, many of them from the effects of mustard gas. Not unexpectedly, for many years after the war, most official reports omitted to mention this, the only use of poison gas by either side in the Second World War.

While Bari burned, Karl Wächter continued to keep his vigil off Cape Tenez. He remained on watch for another forty-eight hours, much of the time below the surface, for there was a great deal of coming and going of aircraft overhead. At night, the guns ashore rumbled constantly, and at times planes were seen caught in the beams of searchlights. The Ju88s were at work here, too.

Wächter's patience was at last rewarded on the night of 4 December. His War Diary reads:

4.12.43

2120	CH8513	Weak destroyer hydrophone effect bearing 100 degrees. Wandering to 120 degrees and becoming stronger.
2215		Surfaced. Course 120 degrees. Fairly good visibility.
		Horizon astern very light. Nothing seen all round.
2235		Smoke cloud sighted with dark shapes beneath. Possibly two vessels. They are too slow for escorts..
2241		Fire T5 at largest shadow under smoke cloud as she presents the best target.
		Alarm (Boat dived)
	CH8513	Loud detonation after 12 minutes 45 seconds. Boat rocked by shock wave then all is quiet. No further hydrophone effect heard, only sinking noises lasting one minute.
		Again quiet. Then hydrophone effect bearing 160 degrees. This vessel is fast and propeller has whistling noise.
2253		Hydrophone effect between 190 and 200 degrees. Destroyer moving quickly away.
2340		No more hydrophone effect. I am not sure if I scored a hit. Hopefully B-Dienst will have something to say about it.

Assuming he must have been detected, Wächter moved out to sea, but returned again early on the 5th and resumed patrolling within sight of Cape Tenez. Over the next six days, as the U-boat ploughed her monotonous furrow back and fore in the calm sea, the visibility varied from good to very poor, and was often spoiled at night by brilliant sheet lightning. The phosphorescence on the sea was again heavy, making movement on the surface at night a dangerous game, but Wächter persisted in his quest for a worthwhile target. His diligence was finally rewarded a little before noon on the 11th, when his hydrophones picked up the propeller beat of a steamer close in to the coast. The War Diary reads:

11.12.43

1235	I hug the coast and at last I sight the steamer. It is a small one, 2-300 tons. Bearing 190 degrees, course 300 degrees. As I am heading into the sun she is not very easily seen.
1259	The hydrophone effect is poor, but she appears to be doing 260 revs. Possibly a destroyer. The horizon to seaward is clear of ships.
1300 CH8512	A destroyer bearing 250 degrees. He turns and comes towards me at full speed. I can see the colours of his funnel. He comes quite close and must have detected me. Suddenly he starts using his Asdic. I turn towards him and fire No.5 tube set for 1500 metres.
	I go deep. Loud detonation heard after 71 seconds.
	Noises of ship breaking up and sinking heard throughout the boat.
1305	I can hear another escort and steamers bearing 270 degrees and coming nearer.
1306	They pass directly over the boat. The destroyer has stopped. They must be picking up survivors.
1319	Three steamers passing overhead. Must be small convoy.

162

	It is annoying that I did not see them earlier. The second destroyer is moving away. Faint asdic.
1320	I steer course 270 degrees. I have developed a serious leak on the starboard side. In the past hour and a half have taken in two tons of water. It would have been just too bad if they had dropped depth charges.
1400	Course 000 degrees
1600 CH8514	All attempts to stop the leak have failed. I must return to base.

Unable to stem the leak which was in the starboard stern gland again, Wächter set course for Toulon, arriving back at the port on the morning of 17 December. *U-223* had been continuously at sea for twenty-six days, in which Karl Wächter claimed to have sunk two destroyers. There is no record of any Allied ship being attacked in the position given on 4 December, when he claimed his first victim, so he must have been mistaken, even though he reported hearing a loud detonation and sinking noises after firing his T5. As to the second claim, this is more realistic. Close to the shore off Algiers on the 11th *U-223* had fallen in with the east-bound convoy KMS 34, and her torpedo scored a hit on the British River-class frigate *Cuckmere*. Contrary to Wächter's claim, however, *Cuckmere* did not sink. She was badly damaged and reached port under tow, but was subsequently declared a total loss.

The re-occurrence of *U-223*'s leak, claimed by Wächter to be a result of poor dockyard work, prevented him from doing further damage to KMS 34, but where he left off, Gerd Kelbling in *U-593* took over.

Kelbling and *U-593* had travelled a long road together. She was Kelbling's first and only command, which he took over when she came out of the Blohm & Voss yard at Hamburg in October 1941. Sixteen successful war patrols followed, during which Kelbling sank fourteen Allied ships of 51,243 tons. Now he was about to cross swords again with an old adversary. Their association went back to the morning of 27 March 1942.

U-593 was at periscope depth in the Bay of Biscay and heading in for St Nazaire at the end of her first war patrol. At about 07.00, estimating that he was near the pre-arranged rendezvous position, Kelbling scanned the horizon through his periscope. Right ahead, and some two and a half miles off, he saw the low outline of what appeared to be a small warship. She was heading his way, and he assumed she must be his escort – right on time. Kelbling blew tanks and came to the surface, then firing the recognition signal five white stars. To his great surprise and consternation, instead of acknowledging his signal, the warship charged at him, her bow-wave foaming as she worked up to full speed. Realizing he was about to be rammed, be it by friend or foe, Kelbling crash dived.

By some stroke of bad luck, *U-593* had made an involuntary rendezvous with the attack force of Operation Chariot, a British expedition to destroy the gates of St Nazaire's huge dry dock, the only one in the area capable of accommodating the 41,000-ton German battleship *Tirpitz*, then believed to be at sea in the Atlantic. The British force consisted of the old ex-US Navy destroyer HMS *Campbeltown*, her bows packed with explosives, whose task it was to ram and blow open the dry dock gates, escorted by the destroyers *Atherstone* and *Tynedale*, who were also carrying the Commando landing party, and a flotilla of small craft comprising sixteen MLs, one MGB and one MTB.

U-593's attacker was the Hunt-class destroyer *Tynedale*, 1,087 tons, 27 knots and armed with four 4-inch guns. *Tynedale*'s commander knew it was essential that the proposed raid remain secret, and he had no hesitation in attacking the U-boat, straddling her with depth charges set to shallow as Kelbling struggled to take her down. The exploding charges blew *U-593* back to the surface, but very fortunately for Kelbling and his crew, they surfaced too close to the destroyer for her to train her 4-inch guns. But before she gained the shelter of the depths again, *U-593* was heavily strafed by the *Tynedale*'s 20-mm cannon and machine guns.

Tynedale and *Atherstone* hunted the U-boat for the next two hours, determined not to allow her to come to the surface to alert St Nazaire of the presence of a large force of British ships. It is probable they would have sunk her had it not been for the fact that *Tynedale*'s Asdic was not working. By some clever manoeuvring, Kelbling was able to evade his pursuers, and that afternoon, when the coast was clear, he surfaced and radioed St Nazaire, reporting three British destroyers in the area. As he had not seen the eighteen smaller warships, he did not report them, leading the German Naval Staff to conclude that the destroyers were on a minelaying expedition. Operation Chariot was successfully carried out, *Campbeltown* ramming and blowing up the gates of St Nazaire's giant dry dock, thereby denying it to the German Navy for the rest of the war.

Twenty-one months on, while *U-223* was making good her escape to the north after sinking HMS *Cuckmere*, *U-593* was cruising the convoy route near Djidjelli, twenty-five miles east of Bougie. Gerd Kelbling, now the proud wearer of the coveted Ritterkreuz, had been alerted to the approach of KMS 34 and was prudently spending the night on the surface recharging batteries. At 06.30 on the 12th, he went to periscope depth, and almost immediately his hydrophones picked up the sound of fast-revving propellers. This was the vanguard of KMS 34's escort, and by sheer coincidence it proved to be the same British destroyer, HMS *Tynedale*, that had so nearly put paid to *U-593* off St Nazaire in the previous March.

Completely unaware that he was about to exact revenge for his earlier humiliation, Kelbling, his No. 2 tube loaded with a T5 acoustic torpedo, spent the next forty minutes stalking the destroyer at periscope depth. It must have been that *Tynedale*'s Asdic was still not working, for she seemed completely oblivious to the danger she was in.

At precisely 07.10, with the sun just lifting above the horizon, Kelbling fired his No. 2 tube, and the T5, homing in on *Tynedale*'s propeller, blew the destroyer's stern off. She sank in a matter of minutes.

Under the cover of the confusion caused by *Tynedale*'s sinking, Kelbling made good his escape to the west. Leigh-Light equipped Wellingtons of 458 Squadron, flying out of Bone, took off in pursuit of the attacker, and when the Admiralty received news of the second British escort vessel torpedoed off the Algerian coast in twenty-four hours, they called in a hunter-killer group. This was an Anglo/American force consisting of the British Hunt-class destroyers *Calpe* and *Holcombe* and the US Navy destroyers *Benson*, *Niblack* and *Wainwright*.

Having put some fifteen miles between himself and the scene of the *Tynedale*'s sinking, Kelbling lay stopped and submerged to await developments. Around 14.00, propeller noises were again picked up, and half an hour later, HMS *Holcombe* was looming large in his sights. At 14.45, he fired a T5, and *Holcombe* followed *Tynedale* to the bottom.

The uproar caused by the sinking of the second British Hunt-class destroyer in less than eight hours was loud enough to be heard all over the Mediterranean. Kelbling would have had the opportunity to celebrate his success, had not his attack on HMS *Holcombe* been witnessed by a passing British aircraft. The hunt for *U-593* now began in earnest. Radar-equipped Wellingtons were called in to fly search patterns overhead, and the remaining destroyers of the hunter-killer group working in pairs combed the surface and beneath. Retribution was the order of the day.

The hunt went on without interruption for ten hours, and was beginning to resemble the proverbial search for a needle in a haystack when, just after midnight on 12–13th, *U-593* was sighted on the surface by a Wellington of 36 Squadron. The Wellington was diving to the attack before Kelbling had time to flood his tanks, and he was forced to use his guns to fight off the plane. The U-boat's formidable anti-aircraft firepower, a total of six 20mm cannon, carried the day, the Wellington being hit twice as it swooped to attack. Partially out of control, the aircraft failed to deliver her depth bombs, but her rear gunner opened fire and knocked *U-593*'s guns out of action. Kelbling dived and crept away, but his position was now known with some certainty.

Within the hour, two more Wellingtons were overhead and sweeping the seas around with their powerful Leigh Lights. They were soon joined by the hunter-killer group's destroyers with their Asdics and sonars probing the depths. They had a worthy opponent; Gerd Kelbling was a wily fox who had survived count-less such hunts during his two years in command, and this one proved to be no exception. Sinking deep and maintaining silent routine, he deftly evaded his pursuers, and even spent some time on the surface re-charging his batteries during the night.

Gerd Kelbling's luck finally ran out on the afternoon of 13

December, when USS *Wainwright* made contact with her sonar. *Wainwright* and *Calpe*, working as a team, then carried out a series of brutally accurate depth charge attacks, each destroyer directing the other as she ran in to attack.

It was *Calpe*'s second 10-charge pattern, set deep, that caused the critical damage. *U-593*'s inlet valve was smashed, water poured into the boat, and with his compressed air almost exhausted, Kelbling had no alternative but to surface. Scuttling charges were set, the control room instruments smashed, and the main ballast tanks blown for the last time.

The attacking destroyers were taken by surprise when *U-593* shot to the surface in a welter of white water. *Calpe* was too close and unable to depress her main armament sufficiently, but opened fire with her pom-poms, while *Wainwright*, further away, joined in with her 5-inch, 38 calibre guns. In the confusion, both ships' opening rounds went wide, and when it was seen that the U-boat's crew were abandoning ship in a rush, a ceasefire was called.

The commander of USS *Wainwright*, scenting an opportunity to capture the abandoned U-boat, launched his pinnace with a boarding party. His ambitions were thwarted by Gerd Kelbling, who with his engineer and another man was still inside the submarine. When the American pinnace approached, the Germans opened the torpedo hatch, then jumped over the side and swam clear. *Wainright*'s boarding party could only lay back on their oars and watch as *U-593* went down bow-first, her scuttling charges exploding as she slipped beneath the waves for the last time. Kelbling and his crew of fifty were picked up by boats from the destroyers.

The Mediterranean U-boat flotilla was further depleted some hours after *U-593* went down when Horst Deckert's *U-73* launched an attack on Convoy GUS 24 near Oran. Deckert hit and damaged the American Liberty ship *John S. Copley*, but was then set upon by a hunter-killer group composed of the three American destroyers *Edison*, *Trippe* and *Woolsey* which had raced to the scene from Mers el-Kebir. *Woolsey* was first to get a sonar contact, and attacked with well-aimed depth charges which cracked *U-73*'s pressure hull. The boat began to flood and Deckert surfaced, only to meet a hail of fire from the American destroyers which riddled the boat and killed sixteen men. It was all over then. Deckert set the charges and scuttled the boat before the Americans could board. Deckert and the thirty-three surviving members of his crew, two of whom were wounded, were picked up by *Woolsey* and *Edison*.

The numbers of the 29th U-boat Flotilla were slowly being whittled away by these losses. Paul Siegmann brought *U-230* through the Gibraltar blockade to join them, but it now seemed that the days of Karl-Jurgen Wächter's flotilla were numbered.

Chapter Twelve

The End of the Road

After a refit that ran into more than just a quick overhaul, *U-223* returned to sea on 18 January 1944. Karl-Jurgen Wächter, having moved on to higher things, was no longer in command, his place being taken by twenty-two-year-old *Oberleutnant* Peter Gerlach. This appointment to command a Type VIIC on a war patrol in the enemy-dominated waters of the Mediterranean at such an early age was a sure indication of the parlous state of manning in the U-boat arm. Lithuanian-born Gerlach's only previous experience of command was a seven-week spell with the 22nd Training Flotilla in the Baltic, where under the experienced eye of one of Dönitz's North Atlantic aces *Korvettenkapitän* Wilhelm Ambrosius he had commanded the 'school' boat *U-37*. Young Gerlach's mettle was about to be tested to destruction.

Peter Gerlach's troubles began twenty-four hours after sailing from Toulon, when he discovered that one of his exhaust valves was leaking. The boat was taking some water, but the leak was not yet serious enough to warrant turning back. Any doubts Gerlach may have had were put aside when, on the afternoon of the 20th, *U-223* then being to the north-east of Minorca, he received a signal from Toulon instructing him to join forces with *U-230* and head for the west coast of Italy, where a build-up of Allied landing craft had been detected.

B-Dienst's suspicions were well founded. At that time the Gulf of Gaeta, a large bay thirty miles north of Naples, was crowded with tank landing ships, infantry landing ships, and all the various accompanying craft of an invasion force. Operation Shingle was about to begin. For some time the Allied armies advancing on Rome from the south had been held up by stiff

German resistance in the mountainous region of Cassino, and with the Italian winter closing in, urgent action was needed. The object of Shingle was to land a large force behind the German lines and make a dash for Rome, 75 miles to the north, where the enemy's defences were known to be weak.

Allied troops, consisting of the 3rd United States Division and the British 1st Division, began landing on the beaches of Anzio, thirty miles behind the German lines, at 02.00 on 22 January. The invasion force was under the overall command of the American Lieutenant General J. P. Lucas, who had played a major part in the Salerno landings early in September.

The Anzio landings caught the Germans completely by surprise, and there was little in the way of resistance as the Allied troops poured ashore. By midnight on the 2nd, 36,000 men and some 3,000 vehicles had landed with a minimum of casualties.

The capture of the Italian capital should have been an early *fait accompli* if the Allied troops, which included British Commandos and US Rangers, had taken advantage of the element of surprise and had immediately pushed inland. As it was, the whole enterprise came near to failure through the refusal of General Lucas to get the men off the beaches until all equipment, supplies, vehicles and tanks were ashore. By the 29th, the beachhead and its immediate surroundings were bulging with four divisions of fighting men, 12,000 vehicles and 350 tanks. And whereas when the landings commenced only two battalions of second-rate German troops barred the way to Rome, eight divisions of Field Marshal Kesselring's crack men had been moved in while Lucas prevaricated. The breakthrough was eventually made, but it cost the Allies a total of 6,923 dead, injured and missing.

While Allied troops were fighting their way inland from the Anzio beaches, Peter Gerlach had begun his contribution to the German cause in the Mediterranean. In the early hours of the 25th, *U-223* was in the Tyrrhenian Sea sixty miles east-north-east of Cape Carbonara, on the south coast of Sardinia. Gerlach was running submerged when he had his first contact with the enemy. His War Diary reads:

0300   Hydrophone effect bearing 095 degrees at 11
              miles.

	Sounds like a steamer. Moves ahead and to the right.
	Getting louder.
0316	Surfaced. Nothing in sight. Course 120 degrees.
0338	Shadow seen 3 degrees to starboard. Possibly corvette steering 260 degrees.
0340	Action Stations!
0353 CJ8519	Fired No.2 tube. T5.
N'ly 5, Sea 3	Enemy moving right, bearing 129 degrees. Speed 10 knots
5/10 cloud	Set depth at 4 metres.
Moderate visibility	Heavy double detonation after 12 minutes 10 seconds.
	Enemy disappears. I go after him but see nothing.
0421	Dived. I follow the same course as the corvette, but no hydrophone heard.
0430	New hydrophone effect bearing 060 degrees. Turbines.
	Enemy speed 14 knots.
	Steer course 040 degrees. As the effect is of turbines this cannot be a corvette. Target on zig-zag course around mean of 230 degrees.
0545	Hydrophone effect fades.
	Nothing seen or heard of corvette above or below surface.

Gerlach was of the opinion that his T5 had run true and found its target, but much as he would have liked to confirm this, the turbine engines heard suggested the presence of an enemy destroyer, and he decided it would be safer to leave the area. Despite the lack of confirmation, he later claimed to have sunk a corvette, but no Allied ship was reported missing.

U-223, now in company with Paul Siegmann's *U-230*, arrived off the Anzio beaches on the afternoon of the 26th with orders to attack enemy shipping, particularly the landing craft running a non-stop shuttle service between Naples and the beachhead with the vast quantity of equipment required by General Lucas before he was prepared to move inland. By this time, Gerlach was facing a hard decision, for he now had four leaking exhaust valves, and there was a great deal of water in the after part of the boat. His head told him he should return to Toulon, but this was his first war patrol, and the sea off the coast was thick with enemy ships, big and small. His fellow commander, Paul Siegmann was claiming to have already sunk two destroyers, and Gerlach wished to emulate his success. So long as *U-223* floated, he intended to take the fight to the enemy, even though the area was crawling with destroyers and corvettes, and aircraft were patrolling overhead.

Around noon on the 27th, having so far escaped detection, *U-223* was fifteen miles off the coast near Capo d'Anzio. Gerlach brought her to periscope depth, intending to move closer in to the landing area, but found his periscope lenses fogged up. It was like trying to peer through a thick mist, a mist that the periscope heater failed to clear. He contemplated surfacing to look around, but the hydrophones warned him of a great deal of shipping activity above, with the fast-revving propellers of warships predominating. He was in the thick of the enemy and powerless to attack.

It was after three o'clock on the morning of the 28th before Gerlach, with a pressing need to recharge batteries and air the boat, felt it safe to surface. Within two minutes of breaking the surface, *U-223* was in action.

0326	Destroyer suddenly appears and crosses my bow.
0327	Action Stations!
	Destroyer bearing 210 degrees. I turn to get in her wake.
0410	Fired No.2 tube. T5.
	Enemy bearing 180 degrees. Speed 10 knots.

	Torpedo set for 4 metres. Aimed for amidships.
0412	Dived.
	Hydrophone effect to port. Moving quickly astern.
	More hydrophone effect on port quarter.
	Loud detonation after 15 minutes 40 seconds. Then nothing further heard.
	No Asdic from destroyer. In spite of long run of torpedo I believe I hit target. Cannot even detect disturbed water in her wake. She must have sunk.

Once again, Peter Gerlach's optimism was running ahead of him. No destroyer, or other ship was reported to have been torpedoed at the time and place.

Gerlach spent another twenty-four hours submerged, listening to the beat of Allied propellers as ships hurried to and fro above his head. That the enemy destroyers did not seem to be using their Asdics was an indication of their confidence in their control of these waters. It was even possible for Gerlach to surface in the small hours of the 29th and remain on the surface for nearly two hours while he recharged his batteries, at the same time dashing off a brief radio message to Toulon reporting his progress. Then, in the afternoon, he suddenly found himself in a position to strike a blow for the German troops fighting ashore.

1615	Faint hydrophone effect between 230 and 300 degrees.
	Appears to be destroyer.
	Went to periscope depth.
	Eight landing craft in line astern steering 140 degrees. If I had come up earlier I could have sunk them all.
1630	Action Stations!
1634 CJ5912	Fire T 5 at rear landing craft.

NNE 2, Sea 3-4	Bearing 104 degrees. Speed 11 knots.
4/10 cloud	Torpedo set to 4 metres.
Good visibility	Loud detonation after 13 minutes 40 seconds. Sinking noises. Very brief.
	I remain at periscope depth. After detonation the last landing craft disappears in a big eruption of water and does not appear again. Six of the craft make wide alteration of course and make off at full speed.
	The other craft stops and is presumably picking up survivors.
	I watch her through the periscope for a few minutes and then restart my engines and go after the other six.

Inevitably, Gerlach's action brought the enemy destroyers racing to the attack, and for the next twenty-four hours *U-223* became the hunted. But Gerlach, for all that he lacked experience, was a tenacious fighter. Another opportunity to inflict damage presented itself on the afternoon of the 30th, when he found a convoy of sixteen tank landing ships crossing the wires of his periscope. Not unexpectedly, these prime targets well were escorted.

1647	Periscope depth.
1650	Action Stations!
	Convoy of tank landing ships in double line and steering 150 degrees.
	Destroyer on starboard bow bearing 100 degrees.
	The sea is like a mirror, so she must have seen me.
	She turns directly towards me, but does not come any closer, then turns away. No hydrophone effect. She may have stopped. I hold my fire.

The destroyer is using signal lamp and looking around I see two more destroyers, bearing 300 and 340 degrees.

Both come closer, but they are not heading towards me.

The destroyer bearing 100 degrees is too far away for a torpedo. I should be able to hit the landing craft.

1703 CJ5912	Fire Nos. 1,3 and 4 tubes at landing craft,
NNW 1, Sea 0	which appears to be around 3000 tons BRT.
Overcast	Detonation after 5 minutes 22 seconds.
Good visibility	5 minutes 27 seconds
to the south	5 minutes 37 seconds

A further unidentified detonation after 5 minutes 45 seconds. This does not sound like a depth charge. Perhaps from one of the landing craft.

Two disappear from sight. I cannot confirm that they have been hit as there are too many enemy ships about, but having fired fan of three from 150 metres, a third craft should have been hit.

Despite having, in his opinion, sunk three tank landing ships, the destroyers appeared to take no notice of *U-223* and Gerlach, emboldened by his easy success, decided to tempt them within range. He raised his periscope to its full height, which in the mirror-like sea must have been clearly visible for some miles. The effect was immediate and dramatic, a two-funnelled destroyer which he identified as a British V & W- class, heeling over under full helm and coming at him with her bow-wave creaming. He stayed at periscope depth long enough to aim a T5 in the general direction of the destroyer, and then dived deep. He heard his torpedo explode after three minutes and forty-five seconds, the explosion being almost inaudible above the crash of depth charges falling around *U-223*.

Gerlach lingered off the Anzio beachhead in company with Paul Siegmann in *U-230* until their torpedoes ran out on 3 February, having caused a good deal of disruption amongst Allied shipping. Siegmann claimed two destroyers sunk, while Peter Gerlach laid claim to one destroyer, one corvette, one tank landing ship and one anti-aircraft landing craft sunk, with a second tank landing ship possibly sunk. The two U-boats may have made a thorough nuisance of themselves off Anzio, but records since released do not credit them with any Allied ships sunk.

U-223 arrived back in Toulon on 12 February, down by the stern and with a substantial amount of water in her after part from the persistent leaks which had been worsened by the heavy depth charging she had been subjected to. More than a month would pass before she was in a fit state to go to sea again. She sailed from Toulon on 16 March with Peter Gerlach, older and wiser since his baptism of fire, still in command. Gerlach's orders were to harass Allied shipping north of Sicily. Thanks to the hesitation of General Lucas, British and American troops were still boxed in around Anzio, and no further in their advance to Rome, but increased shipping activity in the Tyrrhenian Sea indicated that the Allies were building up to a determined push north. Hundreds of ships and landing craft were running a frequent service between Palermo and Naples, crammed with troops and equipment, and offering a multitude of targets for the U-boats. But the risks were greater than ever, for enemy hunter-killer groups were out in force continuously sweeping the sea lanes for marauding U-boats. *U-223* met up with one when she was twenty miles to the north of Palermo half an hour before dawn on 29 March.

Led by Captain Harold Armstrong, DSO, DSC & Bar, in HMS *Laforey*, three British destroyers were on an anti-submarine sweep, steaming in line abreast on a north-easterly course out of Palermo with one and a half miles between each ship. HMS *Ulster*, commanded by Lieutenant Commander William Donald, DSC, was to starboard of *Laforey*, with HMS *Tumult*, under the command of Lieutenant Commander Norman Lanyon to port. The weather was fine, with a light north-easterly wind and a slight sea, and the three ships were steaming at a leisurely 14 knots, their Asdics sweeping the sea beneath them, and their crews at pre-dawn action stations. It was most unfortunate for Peter Gerlach that the destroyers were manned by men whose skills at U-boat hunting had been honed in the North Atlantic, and beyond, over five years of bitter fighting. Their leader, Captain Harold Armstrong, was one of the most distinguished and experienced destroyer captains in the Royal Navy, his battle honours being won in the Norwegian campaign of 1940, in the *Bismarck* chase, and in the defence of the Russian convoys. This was a formidable opponent for a young U-boat commander on his second war patrol.

Gerlach, who with the approach of daylight had submerged only a few minutes earlier, was at periscope depth and scanning lazily around the horizon when he saw the destroyers approaching from astern. They were then no more than three darker shadows against the gloom of the receding night, but even at their reduced speed the phosphorescent glow of their bow-waves was visible and unmistakeable. Not waiting to confirm his assessment, Gerlach took *U-223* deep.

Ulster was first to make contact, her Asdic operators reporting an echo bearing 070 degrees at 1,700 yards. Lieutenant Commander Donald immediately altered onto the bearing and reduced speed to 7 knots. When the echo was classified as 'submarine', he informed *Laforey* by signal lamp.

While *Ulster* held the contact, *Laforey* and *Tumult* homed in on the bearing with their Asdics. Captain Armstrong was at first inclined to regard the contact as doubtful, possibly just a shoal of fish, of which there were plenty in these warm waters. However, he ordered *Ulster* to attack while *Laforey* and *Tumult* stood by, *Laforey* acting as directing ship, with *Tumult* providing a protective screen for the other two. It was a copybook tactic that this experienced group had used many times before, in practice drills and in earnest.

Lieutenant Commander Donald was only too eager to oblige. Taking *Ulster* up to 18 knots, he ran in and dropped a pattern of ten depth charges, five set to 350 feet and five at 550 feet. The sea in the destroyer's wake erupted in a thundering convulsion of white water as the 300lb canisters of Torpex exploded in rolling succession.

Seven hundred feet below, *U-223*, lay stopped and on silent routine. She was near her maximum recommended diving depth of 250 metres, her hull under twenty times surface pressure, and the ominous creaks and occasional tiny spurts of water from strained rivets were a warning. She bucked and rolled as the shock waves punched at her, but apart from a few broken gauge glasses and bruised ribs suffered by the unwary, the boat and its occupants were unharmed. When the boat came back on an even keel, Gerlach went ahead on the electric motors and crept away at 2 knots, making a bold alteration to port. The cat and mouse game had begun.

Gerlach would have been well advised to stay where he was, for Armstrong was experienced in the ways of cornered U-boats, the sudden movement confirming for him that the target was no shoal of fish. He signalled *Ulster* to carry on attacking under his direction, which Donald did with enthusiasm. Time and time again, *Ulster* ran in over the moving target, now held in the beams of the other ships' Asdics, dropping patterns of ten charges as before. At 09.00, Armstrong ordered *Tumult* to join in the attack, and the quiet of the Mediterranean morning was shattered by the constant boom of exploding depth charges, and the once-placid sea became a seething maelstrom.

Beneath the waves, *U-223* twisted and turned like a startled eel. Gerlach, although he had little experience of the horrors of depth charging, remained calm, and used every trick in the training manual. Held by *Laforey*'s insistently pinging Asdic, which was clearly audible in the boat, almost like a pointing finger, *U-223* was fighting for her life. Gerlach's only real hope of survival now was to shake off his attackers and escape to the north, and in desperation he fired a *Pillenwerfer*, an air-bubble decoy. The ruse worked momentarily, and *Laforey*'s operators lost their target, but as *U-223* tried to creep away, the destroyer's beam began to bounce off her hull again.

Ulster and *Tumult* had by this time used a total of ninety-six depth charges in their effort to destroy their unseen foe, but without apparent result. *Ulster* made one more run, and then, with no more charges left, was reduced to acting as a spectator to the unfolding drama, her only useful contribution being her Asdic transmissions.

Ashore, in the office of the Commander of the Allied Naval Base in the Sicilian port of Palermo, the hunt for *U-223* was being followed with great interest. One observer was Lieutenant George Martin, DSC, commanding officer of the small Blankney-class destroyer HMS *Wilton*. When news came through from *Laforey* that *Ulster* had exhausted her depth charges, Martin, whose ship had been stood down for the day, volunteered to take her out to replace *Ulster*. His request was granted, and by 11.15, with some of her crew still on shore leave, *Wilton* had cleared the moles of Palermo harbour and was heading out to sea. Within minutes, Martin had worked her up to 25 knots, and just before noon the cluster of three British destroyers was sighted ahead. Half an hour later, *Wilton* took *Ulster*'s place on *Laforey*'s starboard beam, and Lieutenant Commander Donald was racing for Palermo to refill his depth charge racks.

Soon after she was in position, HMS *Wilton*'s Asdic operator reported a contact bearing 026 degrees at 1,750 yards, moving right at about 1½ knots. *U-223* was in her sights. On instructions from Captain Armstrong to 'attack with an extra deep pattern', Martin took up the challenge eagerly, increasing speed to 15 knots for his run in over the target, which was by then bearing 022 degrees at 2,000 yards, and drawing slowly to the left. *Wilton* dropped a ten-charge pattern, five set at 500 feet and five at 750 feet.

U-223 had now been submerged and under continuous attack for over seven hours, and conditions on board were rapidly deteriorating. At the best of times, the Type VIIC was purely a war machine, and not designed with the comfort of its crew in mind. Much of the pressure hull was taken up with machinery, torpedoes and provisions, leaving the crew of fifty men precious little room to move around. Under attack by depth charges, with the watertight doors between compartments closed, in the dim glow of the emergency lighting, and with all the devils of Hell hammering on the outside, the hull became a steel coffin waiting for the undertaker to arrive. It was this way with *U-223*. Peter Gerlach, wedged in the control room that he had not left for seven hours, tried desperately to anticipate the fall of the British water bombs, altering first to port, then to starboard, but the boat's forward speed was so slow that his efforts were largely wasted.

He went deeper. The depth gauge registered 242 metres, and the creaks and groans coming from the tortured hull as the tremendous outside pressure strove to crush it flat were frightening. The men were reluctant to speak, whispering as though they were already in the presence of death, and when they moved it was slowly and hesitantly.

Wilton's first attack produced no detectable results, and with Armstrong's permission, Martin now tried two 'creeping' attacks, which involved running over the target at 8 knots and firing charges from the forward throwers at the same time dropping others from the stern racks. In this way Martin was able to use his own Asdic to home in. The results were again disappointing. No wreckage, no oil came to the surface, not even a bubble of air. Then to add to Martin's frustration, he discovered his steering was not answering correctly, most probably damaged by one of his charges bursting prematurely and very shallow.

Realizing that this chase could go on well into the night, thereby giving his wily opponent the chance to surface and escape at full speed under the cover of darkness, Armstrong, albeit reluctantly, radioed for reinforcements. The response was immediate, two more British destroyers, *Blencathra* and *Hambledon* sailing from Naples. A few hours later, the American Benson-class destroyers *Ericsson* and *Kearny*, accompanied by the three high-speed submarine chasers PC 556, 558 and 626, were dispatched from Palermo.

Meanwhile, *Laforey*, *Tumult* and *Wilton* continued to hound *U-223*, taking turn and turn about at tracking and attacking. By late afternoon, all three destroyers were running low on depth charges and the remaining hours of daylight were slipping away. It was with some relief, therefore, that at 1600 Armstrong saw *Blencathra* and *Hambledon* coming over the horizon. By the time *Blencathra*, commanded by Lieutenant Richard Howard, and *Hambledon*, commanded by Lieutenant Louis Toone, had taken up their stations both *Laforey* and *Wilton* were out of depth charges. *Wilton* was sent to Augusta to replenish her racks, but Armstrong, being the senior officer on the spot, remained with *Laforey* to direct the hunt. When the US Navy ships joined an hour and a half later, he was satisfied that, whatever transpired during the night, the enemy would not get away.

180

By the time darkness closed in, *U-223* had been the subject of twenty-two attacks by the British destroyers, three of which had completely exhausted their stocks of depth charges, and all without any appreciable result. The U-boat was still there deep below them, twisting and turning, but showing no signs of being a defeated foe. After dark, Armstrong considered it unwise to make any further attacks for fear of losing contact with the enemy, deciding to stalk her until daylight before resuming depth charging. He formed his four destroyers into line abreast, *Hambledon* on the port wing, then *Blencathra*, *Laforey*, and *Tumult* to starboard. All ships had working Asdics, so there seemed little possibility that they would lose track of the U-boat. In the event of that unlikely happening, *Ericsson* and *Kearny*, now under Armstrong's command, were ordered to conduct a box search centred on the British destroyers and between three and four miles off. The PCs were to patrol outside the box in order to cut off any avenue of escape which might be open to the U-boat, should she surface.

In spite of this impressive and apparently impenetrable screen, Peter Gerlach succeeded in giving his pursuers the slip during the night. A frantic search ensued, but another hour passed before *U-223* was again caught in the probing beams of the Asdics and held there. She now appeared to be on an easterly course, closely tracked by four of the British destroyers steaming in line abreast and on slow speed. There was no way out for *U-223*, her demise being only a matter of time.

Around 01.00 on the 30th, events happened in a rush. The Asdic operators in the various ships, by now very tired men, suddenly reported the target had turned and was doubling back on her course through the line of destroyers. Lieutenant Commander Lanyon, in HMS *Tumult*, wrote in his report:

> From 0015 until 0400 *Laforey* was switching her searchlight on for short periods in the direction of the contact. At about 0100 a thin wisp of smoke was seen rising and shortly afterwards the hull of the U-boat appeared.

Finally, after twenty-five hours under water, most of the time at a depth nearing 800 feet, constantly hunted by Asdic, and being on the receiving end of over 300 depth charges, *U-223* had come to the surface. It was a decision over which her commander, Peter Gerlach had very little choice. The air in the boat stank, being almost all stale carbon dioxide after passing through the lungs of fifty men over such a long period, the boat's batteries were nearly flat, with barely enough power left to produce half a knot, and the bilges were overflowing from the numerous leaks in the hull. But what decided Gerlach to surface more than anything else was the fact that his men were completely exhausted and demoralized. It was better that they took their chances on the surface than to die a lingering death beneath the waves.

When *U-223* broke the surface, the reaction by her hunters was immediate and fierce, aptly described by Lieutenant Louis Toone, commanding HMS *Hambledon*:

Rapid salvoes were fired throughout using short range spotting procedure. The first salvo was in line but over, the second found the target. Further hits were observed and close range weapons engaged the target. After 24 rounds of starshell there was a delay in supply resulting in a temporary lack of illumination during which time the submarine started to turn 180 degrees away in a tight turn and resumed a northerly course.

Fire was checked at 0110 until the submarine had steadied on its new course, when a new inclination was passed. At 0112 a direct hit on the conning tower produced a red glow and smoke. About this time a single explosion was heard. This was presumed to be from the submarine and no flash was observed. A minute later one hit was observed which produced smoke and a hit aft produced a shower of sparks. Submarine then appeared out of control and altered course to the southward and momentarily stopped (confirmed by the absence of HE).

U-223 was caught in a torrent of fire from all four destroyers, which were using every gun that could be brought to bear, main armament and light weapons. Gerlach had one more move left, and this he took, presenting his stern to the enemy and going full ahead on both diesels. As he ran, he played his last remaining trump card, firing a T5 from his stern tube at his attackers. The torpedo sped through the water searching for propeller noise. It was unfortunate for HMS *Laforey* – although not surprising, for she had led from the start – that she was nearest to the fleeing U-boat. Gerlach's torpedo struck just abaft the destroyer's funnel with devastating results, as described by *Laforey*'s first lieutenant Lieutenant T.W. Stocker:

> The U-boat made a recognition signal consisting of 4 or 5 red Very lights fired simultaneously. No notice was taken of this attempt at bluff. The third burst of pom-pom fire appeared to hit as also did the fourth or fifth round of 4.7".
>
> 'Simultaneously there was a large explosion in *Laforey* and I was thrown against the side of the bridge and almost immediately blown up into the air, coming down on B gun deck. The ship had by then a considerable list to port and was still rolling over. I dived into the sea expecting the ship to roll on top of me, but when I had swum clear and I looked around, the forward half of the ship had disappeared and the remainder had a 45 degree trim fore and aft and a 45 degrees list to port. It slowly altered to a vertical position with about 60' of the stern showing. The ship finally disappeared about 2 minutes later.'

It appears that in the confusion of the fight only *Blencathra* witnessed the sinking of *Laforey*, and she was first to move in to pick up survivors. Her commander, Lieutenant Richard Howard reported:

> Of the living survivors picked up, eight were suffering from injuries. All were in a greatly shocked condition even though some had been only half an hour in the water at a temperature of 57° F.
>
> Artificial respiration was carried out on five apparently drowned persons, unfortunately with no result. Four were by Schafer's method for ¾ of an hour and one by the rocking method for three hours. Novex oxygen apparatus was used on two cases. The actual cause of drowning could not be ascertained and external examination revealed nothing.
>
> Every survivor was immediately taken to a warm place, stripped, dried and wrapped in warm blankets. It is interesting to note that even so, it was at least 3-4 hours before any of them ceased to feel cold.
>
> Of the injured, the fatal case appeared to be caused by explosives, two of the serious cases by damage when entering the water and the third by the effect of depth charge explosions.

Although once the alarm was raised by *Blencathra* all ships joined in the search for survivors from *Laforey*, only sixty-nine of the destroyer's crew of 258 were rescued alive. Captain Harold Armstrong was not among them.

For *U-223*, the fact that *Blencathra* was the only witness to the torpedoing of *Laforey* proved to be the final nail in her coffin. Had the other British destroyers been aware of *Laforey*'s predicament, they would almost certainly have been diverted from the chase. As it was, they continued their attack on the U-boat. Gerlach had by this time concluded that their position was hopeless, and in order to save as many of his crew as possible, he ordered them to abandon ship, first sending his engineer, twenty-year-old Ernst Sheid, below to set the scuttling charges. Sheid and the others jumped over the side while the boat was still going ahead at full speed. Peter Gerlach, whose last words to Sheid were that he 'was no good without his boat', stayed on board, and was never seen again.

Twenty-seven of *U-223*'s crew of fifty were rescued by *Blencathra*, *Hambledon* and *Tumult*. Of those lost, a few had been killed by gunfire but, ironically, the majority were probably killed by the propellers of their own boat which, still going ahead at full speed, doubled back and ran through them as they struggled in the water.

And so, on 30 March 1944, ended the short career of *U-223*. She was gone, broken apart by her own charges, spiralling down into the dark depths of the blue Tyrrhenian Sea, taking Peter Gerlach with her.

Chapter Thirteen

The End of a Dream

Had *U-223* been fitted with a schnorkel, both Peter Gerlach and his boat might have lived to fight another day. The schnorkel, originally a Dutch invention, the plans of which were captured by the Germans when they overran Holland in 1940, was essentially a 9-inch diameter tube with a non-return valve at the top, which could be raised above the surface when a submarine was at periscope depth. This provided sufficient air for the diesel engines to be run underwater without creating a vacuum in the pressure hull. Batteries could then be recharged without surfacing, and there would always be a circulation of fresh air. In theory, a U-boat so equipped would become a true submarine, rather than a submersible, able to remain underwater indefinitely. There were, however, some serious drawbacks to the schnorkel. It was liable to break off at speeds in excess of 7 knots, and the diesel exhaust smoke from a submerged U-boat was easily spotted from the air. It was also found that the noise of the diesels running underwater rendered the hydrophones useless. These may have been the reasons why the German Navy ignored the schnorkel for much of the war. It was not until May 1944 that it was widely fitted in operational Type VIIC boats, and only then as a last-ditch measure to help turn the tide of the war at sea. By then it was plainly evident that the fortunes of the U-boat were on the wane. In that month, they sank only five Allied merchant ships totalling 27,297 tons, and this for the loss of twenty-two of their own number. This was a far cry from the heady days of early 1942, when up to 150 Allied ships were going down every month, while only two or three U-boats were lost.

On land, Nemesis was knocking at Germany's door. At dawn on 6 June 1944, a huge Allied fleet of 5000 ships appeared off the beaches of Normandy, and the long-planned Operation Overlord began. The German generals, perhaps rendered complacent by so many easy victories in the West in past years, were taken completely unawares. While this may have been predictable, with so many Allied ships at sea in the confined waters of the English Channel – in all some 7,000 ships and landing craft were involved – that Dönitz's U-boats were unable to inflict massive losses is almost beyond belief. At that time, it is on record that 168 U-boats were operational, and of these at least forty were at sea in the Western Approaches or the Bay of Biscay, and ready to oppose the invasion. For reasons best known to Grand Admiral Dönitz, these boats did not receive orders to intervene until twelve hours after the first Allied troops came ashore in Europe. Even then, only fourteen boats went into action against the enemy, and six of these were sunk in the Bay and Western Channel long before they came near the invasion area. Of the others, most were damaged and forced to return to port. Not one Allied ship was sunk by a U-boat.

Karl-Jurgen Wächter went back to sea in November 1944, in command of a brand new Type XXI, *U-2503*. The Type XXI was the ultimate underwater weapon on which Dönitz was by then pinning his hopes to win the war at sea. At a meeting in Stettin in January of that year, he had said:

The enemy has succeeded in gaining the advantage in submarine defence. The day will come when I shall offer Churchill a first-rate submarine war. The submarine weapon has not been broken by the setbacks of 1943. On the contrary, it has become stronger. In 1944, which will be a successful but a hard year, we shall smash Britain's supply with a new submarine weapon.

Undoubtedly, the Type XXI was a vast improvement on the Type VIIC, with which the U-boat men had fought most of the war, and had it come a year earlier, it might well have changed the course of history. With a displacement of 1,621 tons, the Type

XXI was ten metres longer and two metres wider in the beam than the Type VIIC, and had a rubber outerskin designed to reflect radar and Asdic. Its own radar was a much improved model, and it was equipped with the Balkon hydrophone which could detect ships at a range of fifty miles. Two 4,000 horse power diesels gave it a speed of 15.6 knots on the surface and 16.8 knots submerged, with a range of 15,000 miles at 10 knots cruising speed. It could dive in eighteen seconds, as compared with thirty seconds for the VIIC, and using the schnorkel it could, in theory at least, stay underwater permanently. The acoustic torpedo was standard, and with a hydraulic torpedo loader all six tubes could be reloaded in twelve minutes. This was a great advance on the manhandling of torpedoes in the VIIC, where it usually took anything up to twenty minutes to reload one tube. For defence against attacking aircraft, considered the greatest danger at this stage of the war, two 37mm and two twin 20mm AA guns were fitted on deck. And, not least as far as its crew was concerned, the Type XXI offered much more in the way of comfort. There was more room to move around, a ventilation plant to purify the air, and a refrigerator to keep the food fresh.

Dönitz's optimistic opinion of the capabilities of the Type XXI was ill-founded, for the time was long past when any new weapon could have saved Germany from the forces of retribution. As 1944 drew to a close, British and American troops were poised to cross the Rhine, and in the east Russian armies had crossed the East Prussian border and were pushing towards Berlin.

Karl-Jurgen Wächter took command of *U-2503* on 12 November 1944 in Hamburg, where she was attached to the 31st Training Flotilla. In the spring of 1945, with British troops advancing north towards Hamburg, Wächter was ordered to take his boat through the North Sea Canal to Kiel to join the 11th Flotilla. Here, the punishing work of bringing *U-2503* and her crew to a pitch of operational efficiency began at once.

Although the U-boats had by now lost their convenient bases in the Bay of Biscay, and faced an increasingly dominant enemy at sea, and to any clear thinking German the war on land was lost, Dönitz still believed he might tip the scales with his new weapon. And there were some grounds for his belief. By the end of April 1945, more than 100 Type XXI boats, including *U-2503* were in training and almost ready to go to war. Dönitz intended to move them to new bases in Norway, and from there mount a renewed attack on Allied shipping in the Atlantic. The boats would have a longer voyage to reach the operational area, but the potential threat they would then pose to the sea lanes was enormous. This had not escaped the attention of the Allies, and the RAF was given the task of nipping Dönitz's plan in the bud. Mosquitoes and Beaufighters of Coastal Command based in Holland began to patrol in force over the Skaggerak and Kattegat, their primary objective to stop the Type XXIs reaching their Norwegian bases.

U-2503 sailed from Kiel on 3 May, bound for Bergen. It was Karl-Jurgen Wächter's intention to remain on the surface whilst among the islands of the Kattegat, relying on his anti-aircraft armament to protect him from sudden attack from the air. This proved to be taking a risk too far. Late that afternoon, while *U-2503* was north of the Danish island of Fyn, she was sighted by patrolling Beaufighters of the North Coates Strike Wing, 236 Squadron, RAF. Five of the thirteen fighter-bombers, led by Wing Commander E.P. Hutton, attacked immediately with rockets and cannon fire. Wächter's AA gunners fought back, but they were quickly overwhelmed by the concentrated firepower of the British aircraft. One rocket went straight down the U-boat's conning tower hatch, and exploded in the control room. Karl-Jurgen Wächter was killed instantly.

On fire, and with fourteen men, including her commander dead, *U-2503* still fought on, and managed to escape her attackers, but she was so badly damaged that her surviving crew had little alternative but to run her ashore on the Danish coast and abandon her.

U-2503 ended her brief career without having had the opportunity to demonstrate how deadly Grand Admiral Dönitz's new weapon was. The same applied to many others of her class, caught by marauding British aircraft which completely dominated the skies over the North Sea and Baltic. Only one Type XXI, *Korvettenkapitän* Adalbert Schnee's *U-2511*, ever went to sea on an offensive patrol, and she sank nothing. The long awaited super U-boat had arrived too late.

On 5 May 1945, Karl Dönitz, who with Hitler dead in his

Berlin bunker was the new German Fuehrer, agreed to surrender his armed forces to the victorious British and Americans, and that included all his beloved U-boats. His last message to the men of the U-boat arm read:

> My U-boat men, six years of war lie behind you. You have fought like lions. An overwhelming material superiority had driven us into a tight corner from which it is no longer possible to continue the war. Unbeaten and unblemished, you lay down your arms after a heroic fight without parallel. We proudly remember our fallen comrades who gave their lives for Fuehrer and Fatherland. Comrades, preserve that spirit in which you have fought so long and so gallantly for the sake of the future of the Fatherland. Long live Germany.

> Your Grand Admiral

When the ceasefire was declared, the Admiralty broadcast instructions for all U-boats to surface, report their positions, and then make for specified British ports to surrender. This was the ultimate humiliation for the proud U-boat men, and many commanders refused to surrender. A few fought on, Heinrich Schroeteler in *U-1023* sinking the Norwegian fleet minesweeper *NYMS 382* in the English Channel on 7 May, and Emil Klusmeier's *U-2336* sinking the British steamer *Avondale Park* and the Norwegian-flag *Sneland* in the North Sea on the same day. But these were the last desperate actions of a beaten force, and finally drew the line under the U-boat war once and for all. Dönitz had refused to give the order to scuttle the boats, but now the code word *Regenbogen*, scuttle all boats, was passed by word of mouth and radio amongst those U-boats still in German ports. Soon, the crash of demolition charges was reverberating around the North Sea and Baltic. A total of 221 boats were scuttled by their crews; another 156 surrendered to the Allies. It was an ignominious end to Karl Dönitz's dream, but even so, he went to his grave thirty-five years later still convinced that, given sufficient U-boats, he could have won the war for Germany. He might well have been right.

Bibliography

Beaver, Paul, *U-boats in the Atlantic*, Patrick Stephens, 1979

Bekker, Cajus, *The German Navy 1939–1945*, Hamlyn, 1974

Bennett, Ralph, *Ultra and Mediterranean Strategy 1941–1945*, Hamish Hamilton, 1989

Blair, Clay, *Hitler's U-boat War – The Hunted 1942–1945*, Weidenfeld & Nicolson, 1999

Bucheim, Lothar-Günther, *U-boat War*, Collins, 1978

Churchill, Winston, *The Second World War Vols IV to VI*, Cassell, 1951

Course, Captain A. G., *The Deep Sea Tramp*, Hollis & Carter, 1960

Franks, Norman L. R., *Dark Sky, Deep Water*, Grub Street, 1997

Franks, Norman & Eric Zimmerman, *U-boat Versus Aircraft*, Grub Street, 1988

Haldane, R. A., *The Hidden War*, Robert Hale, 1978

HMSO, *British Vessels Lost at Sea 1939–45*, HMSO, 1984

—— *The Battle of the Atlantic*, HMSO, 1946

—— *The U-boat War in the Atlantic – MOD (Navy)*, HMSO, 1989

Hoyt, Edwin P., *U-boats*, Magraw-Hill, 1987

Jones, Geoffrey, *Defeat of the Wolf Packs*, William Kimber, 1986

Kemp, Paul, *U-boats Destroyed – German Submarine Losses in the World Wars*, Arms & Armour, 1997

Lamb, James B., *The Corvette Navy*, Macmillan of Canada, 1977

Macintyre, Captain Donald, *U-boat Killer*, Weidenfeld & Nicolson, 1956

Martienssen, Anthony, *Hitler and his Admirals*, Secker & Warburg, 1948

Mason, David, *U-boats, the Secret Menace*, Macdonald, 1968

Middlebrook, Martin, *Convoy – The Battle for Convoys SC122 and HX229*, Allan Lane, 1976

Padfield, Peter, *Dönitz – The Last Führer*, Cassell, 1993

Rohwer, Jürgen, *Axis Submarine Successes 1939–1945*, Patrick Stephens, 1983

Roskill, Captain S. W., *The War at Sea*, HMSO, 1954

Showell, Jak P. Mallmann, *Enigma U-boats – Breaking the Code*, Ian Allan, 2000

—— *U-boats Under the Swastika*, Ian Allan, 1973

Slader, John, *The Fourth Service – Merchantmen at War*, Robert Hale, 1994

Tennent, Alan J., *British & Commonwealth Merchant Ship Losses to Axis Submarines 1939–1945*, Sutton Publishing, 2001

Terraine, John, *Business in Great Waters*, Leo Cooper, 1989

Werner, Herbert A., *Iron Coffins*, Cassell, 1999

Williams, Andrew, *The Battle of the Atlantic*, BBC Worldwide, 2002

Wynn, Kenneth, *U-boat Operations of the Second World War Vols 1 & 2*, Chatham Publishing, 1997/1998

The author also acknowledges information received from The Public Record Office, Kew, the National Archives Washington, and www.u-boat.net

Index

193

194

Toward, 45, 46, 48, 53, 56;
Treworlas, 4; Turcurina, 77; Vanja,
2–4, 8, 9, 11, 13; Vannik, 47, 48;
Vojvoda Putnik, 76; Walter Q.
Gresham, 88, 89; War Forest, 112;
Wentworth, 104; West Madaket,
104; West Maximus, 104; West
Portal, 50; William C. Gorgas, 77–9;
William Eustis, 85; Winkler, 69–71,
91; Zaanland, 84; Zagloba, 52;
Zamalek, 80, 86; Zeus, 61; Zouave,
88

Ships Naval

Abelia HMS, 45, 49; Aberdeen HMS,
81; Aconit HMS, 77–9; Active
HMS, 156; Anemone HMS, 81, 85,
87, 88; Atherstone HMS, 164;
Babbitt USS, 51–3; Belknap USS, 77;
Benson USS, 166; Beverley HMS, 45,
48, 50, 80; Bismarck, 177; Biter
HMS, 109, 120, 121; Blencathra
HMS, 180, 181, 183, 184; Bogue
USS, 77, 79; Broadway HMS, 109,
121; Burza HMS, 66, 67, 77;
Buttercup HMS, 80; Calpe HMS,
166, 167; Campanula HMS, 45, 109;
Campbell USS, 62, 65, 67, 71;
Campbeltown HMS, 164, 165;
Campobello HMS, 80, 82, 83; Card
USS, 113; Chambly HMCS, 109,
121, 129, 132; Charon HMS, 150,
151; Chilliwack HMCS, 62, 67;
Clematis HMS, 109; Comanche USS,
24, 25, 40, 42; Cuckmere HMS, 163,
165; Dauphin HMCS, 62, 65, 66;
Dianthus HMS, 62, 70, 71; Douglas
HMS, 156; Drumheller HMCS, 109,
121, 124, 129; Duncan HMS, 96–8,
101; Ericson USS, 180, 181; Edison
USS, 167, 168; Escanaba USS, 24,
25, 34, 36, 39–43; Escapade HMS,
77, 128, 129; Filla HMS, 150;
Fleetwood HMS, 156; Garland
HMS, 77; Gatineau HMCS, 129;
Gentian HMS, 109, 113; George M.
Bibb USS, 45, 48, 52, 56; Godetia
HMS, 2–4, 7, 80, 83, 88; Greer USS,
75; Haarlam HMS, 140; Hambledon
HMS, 180–2, 184; Harvester HMS,
77–9; Hastings HMS, 81; Havelock
HMS, 2–8, 10–13, 80; Heather
HMS, 109; Hesperus HMS, 109–11,
114, 115, 117–20, 126; Highlander

HMS, 89; Holcombe HMS, 166;
Hyacinth HMS, 140; Icarus HMS,
129; Imperialist HMS, 156;
Impulsive HMS, 101; Ingham USS,
51, 56, 89; Itchen HMS, 129, 131,
132; Jed HMS, 106; Kamloops
HMCS, 129; Kearny USS, 180, 181;
Keppel HMS, 128, 130–2, 136;
Landguard HMS, 81; Laforey HMS,
176, 177, 179–84; Lagan HMS, 109,
121, 129, 130, 132; Lavender HMS,
80; LCT 2335, 55; Lobelia HMS,
45, 49, 52, 54, 56, 128; Loch Osaig
HMS, 156; Loosestrife HMS, 96,
101; Lulworth HMS, 81; Manhassett
USS, 102; Mansfield
HMS, 80, 85; Mayola HMS, 81;
Migonette HMS, 45; Montgomery
HMS, 73; Morden HMCS, 109, 121,
129, 132; Narcissus HMS, 77, 79,
128, 131; Niblack USS, 166;
Northern Foam HMS, 128, 132, 134,
135; Northern Gem HMS, 96, 99,
101, 105; Northern Spray HMS, 96,
101, 102, 104; NYMS 382, 189;
Obdurate HMS, 109, 121; Offa
HMS, 98, 101; Opportune HMS,
109, 121, 125; Orchis HMS, 77, 79,
128; Oribi HMS, 98, 100–2;
Osmond-Ingram USS, 77; Panther
HMS, 101; Pathfinder HMS, 109,
121; PC 556, 180; PC 558, 180; PC
626, 180; Pelican HMS, 106; Penn
HMS, 13, 101; Pennywort HMS, 81,
84–6, 88; Pimpernel HMS, 2, 3, 7, 8,
80; Pink HMS, 96, 101; Primrose
HMS, 109, 121; Polyanthus HMS,
129–32; Puckeridge HMS, 140;
Quiberon HMAS, 13 ; Reconule
HMS, 77, 128; Roselys HMS, 77,
128, 131; Rosthern HMCS, 62, 73;
Rother HMS, 106; St. Croix HMCS,
129, 131, 132; St. Francis HMCS,
129; Sackville HMCS, 129; Salvestor
HMS, 151, 152; Salvina HMT, 151;
Saxifrage HMS, 2, 3, 6, 8–12, 80;
Sennen HMS, 106; Schenck USS, 51;
Snowflake HMS, 96, 98, 101, 102;
Spencer USS, 62, 64, 75; Spey HMS,
106; Sunflower HMS, 96, 98, 101,
110; Swale HMS, 80; Sweetbriar
HMS, 109; Tampa USS, 24, 25, 40,
42; Tay HMS, 96, 101; Tirpitz, 164;

196